KU-465-308

PENGUIN MODERN CLASSICS

The Divided Self

R.D. Laing, one of the best-known psychiatrists of modern times, was born in Glasgow in 1927. His writings range from books on social theory to verse, as well as numerous articles and reviews in scientific journals and the popular press. His many publications include *The Divided Self*, *Self and Others*, *Interpersonal Perception*, *The Politics of Experience*, *The Bird of Paradise* and *Madness and Folly*. R. D. Laing died in 1989.

Anthony David graduated in medicine from Glasgow University in 1980. After training in neurology he switched to psychiatry at the Maudsley & Bethlem Hospitals. He is currently Professor of Cognitive Neuropsychiatry at the Institute of Psychiatry, King's College, London. He has edited several books including *The Self in Neuroscience and Psychiatry* (2003) with T. Kircher, and *Insight and Psychosis* (2nd ed., 2004) with X. Amador, and is author of over 350 publications in peer-reviewed medical and scientific journals.

R.D. LAING

The Divided Self

An Existential Study in Sanity and Madness
With an Introduction by Anthony David

PENGUIN BOOKS

PENGUIN CLASSICS

Published by the Penguin Group
Penguin Books Ltd, 80 Strand, London WC2R 0RL, England
Penguin Group (USA) Inc., 375 Hudson Street, New York, New York 10014, USA
Penguin Group (Canada), 90 Eglinton Avenue East, Suite 700, Toronto, Ontario, Canada M4P 2Y3
(a division of Pearson Penguin Canada Inc.)
Penguin Ireland, 25 St Stephen's Green, Dublin 2, Ireland (a division of Penguin Books Ltd)
Penguin Group (Australia), 250 Camberwell Road, Camberwell, Victoria 3124, Australia
(a division of Pearson Australia Group Pty Ltd)
Penguin Books India Pvt Ltd, 11 Community Centre, Panchsheel Park, New Delhi – 110 017, India
Penguin Group (NZ), 67 Apollo Drive, Rosedale, North Shore 0632, New Zealand
(a division of Pearson New Zealand Ltd)
Penguin Books (South Africa) (Pty) Ltd, 24 Sturdee Avenue, Rosebank, Johannesburg 2196, South Africa

Penguin Books Ltd, Registered Offices: 80 Strand, London WC2R 0RL, England

www.penguin.com

First published by Tavistock Publications Ltd 1960
Published in Penguin Classics 2010

006

Copyright © Tavistock Publications Ltd, 1960
Preface copyright © R. D. Laing, 1965
Copyright © R. D. Laing, 1969
Introduction copyright © Anthony David, 2010
All rights reserved

The moral right of the author and the introducer has been asserted

Printed in England by Clays Ltd, St Ives plc

Except in the United States of America, this book is sold subject
to the condition that it shall not, by way of trade or otherwise, be lent,
re-sold, hired out, or otherwise circulated without the publisher's
prior consent in any form of binding or cover other than that in
which it is published and without a similar condition including this
condition being imposed on the subsequent purchaser

978-0-141-18937-6

www.greenpenguin.co.uk

MIX
Paper from
responsible sources
FSC   FSC® C018179
www.fsc.org

Penguin Books is committed to a sustainable
future for our business, our readers and our planet.
This book is made from Forest Stewardship
Council™ certified paper.

Introduction

The Divided Self (*DS*) by Ronald David Laing was first published in 1959/1960, subtitled 'An Existential Study in Sanity and Madness'. It is divided into three parts: the first establishes the theoretical basis for the book with a technical description of what Laing called the 'existential-phenomenological foundations for a science of persons', followed by an application of this foundation to psychosis. Part Two contains further theoretical development on the idea of the self and 'false self system' with illustrations from literature (e.g., Kafka, Kierkegaard) as well as clinical cases, while Part Three sees the application of these ideas to Laing's own more detailed case descriptions and published case histories. If anyone had said at the time that they thought the foregoing had the makings of a best-seller, a 'must-read' text for any would-be counter-culture guru, an inspirational work for future sociologists, psychologists and dramatists – well, you would have said they were mad.

This is of course not the whole story. *DS* was the first of several books and the beginning of an intellectual and personal trajectory for the author. Subsequent work was more controversial. In *Sanity, Madness and the Family* (1964), R.D. Laing took a more openly defiant stance against the psychiatric establishment, and in *The Politics of Experience and The Bird of Paradise* (1967), he extended his critical thinking to wider aspects of health and society, to personal discovery and spirituality; this was after all the swinging sixties. He covered a wider territory both intellectually and physically, engaging with prophets – real and false – being fêted and at times reviled. None of this, it turned out, was compatible with the continued sober (in both senses) reflection on psychiatric research and the comfortable certainties of regular working and family life.

When we return to *DS* after half a century, we do so through the lens of subsequent work and events. We have some distinct advantages, including a thorough biography by his son Adrian (*R. D. Laing: A Life*, 2006), and some autobiographical sketches, including those published as *Wisdom, Madness and Folly* (1985). I particularly value a thoughtful reconsideration at, as it turns out, roughly the halfway point between publication and this special edition, by Andrew Smith in the *British Journal of Psychiatry* in 1982. We may be aided (distracted?) by the reams of comments and analyses by scholars, journalists and creative writers, as well as published interviews, a corpus of work far exceeding the man's own not inconsiderable output. We also have, as additional material, reactions to his untimely death in 1989 at the age of sixty-one. Not that any of these sources can be described as 'objective' – a word to which Laing had an almost Pavlovian-rage response and to which he returned again and again in his writings. Laing located many of the problems of humanity as being a consequence of one person – they could be a mother or father, a therapist, a psychiatrist, a politician, etc., – viewing another as an object rather than a human being.

One of the most famous sections of *DS* occurs early on when he quotes verbatim from *Lectures on Clinical Psychiatry* (1905) by Emil Kraepelin, whose description of 'dementia praecox' became the template for the modern-day diagnosis of schizophrenia. The signs and symptoms of disease are coolly elicited by Professor Kraepelin. The young patient's utterances, dismissed as not containing *'a single piece of useful information'*, are then forensically recast by Laing as nothing less than the desperate and vivid attempts of a tormented individual to be heard (pp.29–31). In the subsequent paragraphs he writes that it is simply impossible to be objective in the manner deemed desirable of a psychiatrist, without deforming the supposed object of contemplation into a dehumanized 'thing', a process which, if not the cause of the problem (psychosis or other forms of alienation) in the first place, at least perpetuates it.

Despite the sense of such admonishments raining down from the hereafter, I think it is possible to be objective, but in a good way, when reconsidering *DS*; that is to say avoiding obvious prejudices – positive or negative – and taking a stance that sees the work and its author in a historical context. In doing so I cannot help but reveal that, as a practising psychiatrist, working in the bastion of British psychiatry, the Maudsley-Institute of Psychiatry, in London, I remain true to my training and my profession. I am no Laingian.

Book reviews at the time provide a contemporaneous judgement unbiased by later opinion. These show that, within the psychoanalytic establishment (which was 'housing' Laing at the time), there was a touch of 'damning with faint praise', an impression that this book was a restatement in existentialist terms of truths already well known and accepted. Certainly the idea of a 'false self' had been articulated by D. W. Winnicott, one of Laing's supervisors at the Tavistock Clinic where the writing of *DS* took place. But these reviewers and their intellectual leaders were themselves to become victims of the rise of scientific psychiatry with its emphasis on genetics and brain chemistry and demand for verifiable data. Psychoanalysis has become marginalized, a minor player within current psychiatric practice, while its influence on wider cultural discourse remains potent. Its practitioners nowadays seldom venture into the realms of schizophrenia.

Mainstream psychiatry was indifferent to *DS* when the book first appeared. Spokesmen from that mainstream were to engage with Laing combatively over ensuing decades with vitriol pouring out from both sides, but that was mostly provoked by later broadsides against psychiatry by Laing. The term 'antipsychiatry' was coined by Laing's one-time colleague David Cooper in 1967 and was a catch-all term for a number of loosely connected radical ideas and individuals. Laing was haunted by this term, which he often tried to repudiate. The Laing of *DS* is a reformer, a critic from the inside. His later thinking and that of the antipsychiatry 'movement' was that it was unreformable, pathogenic by definition and possibly downright evil. In parallel, the person with schizophrenia in *DS*, 'must remain incomprehensible to us. As long as we are sane and he is insane…' But, Laing suggests, we must struggle to recognize the person's distinctiveness as well as their 'loneliness and despair' (p. 39). By *Sanity, Madness and the Family* (1964), he asserts, the experience and behaviour of schizophrenics is much more socially intelligible than has come to be supposed by most psychiatrists', and by 1967, it is a voyage of discovery and transcendence; it is the world that is insane. All the thinkers identified with antipsychiatry outside Laing's immediate orbit, such as American psychiatrist Thomas Szasz (*c.* 1961) and French philosopher Michel Foucault (*c.* 1961–7), published their major works attacking psychiatry after *DS*. Indeed, on reflection, the links between them are tenuous.

Before coming to that elusive 'objective' view about *DS*, some background. Ronnie Laing was born in 1927 to a lower-middle-class family in Glasgow. He was a studious boy, talented musically and in sports, but drawn to philosophy and literature. He has explained his choice to study medicine ironically as a means of learning the 'facts of life'. His first job after qualifying in 1951 was on a neurosurgical unit where he dealt with many seriously ill and incurable patients and saw the dramatic effects that brain damage could have on behaviour. Towards the end of that year he was called up for national service and worked as an army psychiatrist. There he gained experience in a range of psychiatric conditions, from psychosis to conversion disorders ('hysteria'). He found he enjoyed 'hanging out' with certain patients in the padded cell. After serving the required two years he returned to Glasgow to the Royal Mental Hospital in Gartnaval. There he worked on the wards filled with long-term patients most of whom were diagnosed as having chronic schizophrenia. The care at the time provided safety and security and the basic necessities but interaction with patients was perfunctory and thought to be pointless. It was here that Laing started to gain confidence that he could in fact make contact with 'withdrawn' patients. Interestingly, powerful and effective antipsychotic drugs had just been discovered and were beginning to be used more widely at this time, replacing the more invasive and drastic treatments (coma therapy; leucotomy), which were ineffective. Also, the field of social psychiatry was beginning to develop which was to detail the adverse consequences of such care, which came to be known as 'institutionalization'.

It was at Gartnavel that Laing described a novel approach (sanctioned by the hospital superintendent) to managing patients on a long-stay ward. The approach was less custodial, based mainly on ensuring continuity of care from a few nurses who were 'allowed' to interact with the patients. Apparently this led to dramatic if temporary improvements. This work, published in the *Lancet* in 1955, could be seen as a striking early example of one of several experimental therapies which psychiatry was developing, although the consistency and quality of Laing's actual input with some of these patients has been challenged. Laing's next post was in the academic department at Glasgow University based in the large Southern General Hospital. There he was responsible for what were then termed 'ambulatory schizophrenics' – less disabled outpatients. Throughout this time he was accumulating experience and 'clinical material' (how he would have hated that expression) that would be used in *DS*. In 1956, after completing these posts, Laing moved to London to train in psychoanalysis at the Tavistock Clinic. Although an obvious place to go for any aspiring analyst wishing to pursue the detailed and leisurely exploration of the psyche, it was not somewhere where patients with the most severe and 'neurological-looking' condition, schizophrenia were treated. The manuscript for *DS* was completed in 1957 when the author was just thirty, an important milestone in R. D. Laing's mind. It was circulated among several supervisors and mentors at the Tavistock and was no doubt honed in the process, prior to publication.

Despite later fame and acclaim those who shared Laing's original concerns and aspirations have returned again and again to *DS*. It is this work that has endured. Perhaps the later books are just too radical for us, still, or maybe they are just not as good. One of Laing's adversaries was the young Anthony Clare. In *Psychiatry in Dissent* (1976), Clare rebuts point by point many of the claims of antipsychiatrists, and while he takes on Laing for blaming families for their children's ills he leaves the *DS* relatively untouched. Twenty years later, in an introduction to a radio interview with Laing as part of the *In the Psychiatrist's Chair* series, Clare wrote,

We are still too close to R. D. Laing's death to be able fully to assess the ultimate worth and impact of his views. His was a powerful voice in the movement to demystify mental illness and he undoubtedly contributed to the process whereby psychiatry moved out of the large, isolated, grim mental hospitals into acute units attached to general hospitals and into the community … He influenced a whole generation of young men and women in their choice of psychiatry as a career.

Indeed a number of leading psychiatrists from around the world have put on the record their debt to Laing, and especially *DS*.

So what is the appeal of D*S*? All of us in the mental health professions feel to some extent impelled to try to understand the understandable – to reach out across Karl Jaspers' 'abyss', to the person distressed, cut off and isolated in their psychotic world of fear, bizarreness and desolation. Laing's compulsion to do so was irresistible. *DS* shows him almost in the actual process of discovering his special talent for this making contact: his empathic gift. We see him struggle with how far he should go. Should he cast his anchor and leap 'to the other side' or would this be a one-way journey? Could the notion of 'Us and Them' be abolished by a personal act of will or was this a vain indulgence? *After DS* he thought he had the answers; today we are not so sure.

The legacy of *DS* lives on in the hearts and minds of those still struggling with these very questions. Academic psychology has started to undermine the 'Us and Them' divide by showing that psychotic experiences, hallucinations and strange beliefs, are surprisingly common and may be on a continuum with clinical disorders. Current research has shown that one effective way of reducing the psychotic patient's sense of alienation is to offer him or her 'normalizing rationales' for paranoid beliefs and ways for breaking them down, effectively 'neutralizing' them, into testable chunks (see Bentall, 2005). This is not strictly Laingian since it tries to bolster patients' 'objectivity' in the face of strange experiences but this is done collaboratively with the therapist, not by the therapist on their behalf.

As for psychiatric care – it is certainly more effective and, we would all hope, more humane than fifty years ago. As noted, such progress would have occurred without Laing but he contributed to a general climate of opinion which made it inevitable. Scientific advances to understanding brain and mind have continued apace in the neurosciences in a way which would have dismayed Laing but might just have brought out the critical best in him. Abuses and lapses in standards still occur and mental illness remains stigmatized, poorly tolerated and misunderstood by many. We need to draw on our 'inner-Laing' from time to time and exclaim, 'No, this is not right.'

Laing as a therapist is absent from *DS* as he is from most subsequent writings although survives in the therapeutic communities of Kingsley Hall and it successors. In a thinly disguised lampoon of this, published by Clancy Segal as the novel *Zone of the Interior* (1976), the chief psychiatrist was a Scotsman called 'Willie Last'. Today's answer to the implied question is an emphatic 'yes'.

Ronnie Laing proved that a sensibility to poetry, art and philosophy was not only not incompatible with psychiatric practice but also a positive boon. He showed all intelligent people willing to listen a method for challenging received wisdom – whether it emanates from the patriarchs of psychiatry or psychoanalysis or any intellectual authority figures. It comprises careful reading and scholarship combined with the trick of paring away interpretive structures so that musty dogma can be viewed afresh, rounded off with that most rare ingredient: the courage to speak the truth.

Anthony David

References

Clare, A.W., *Psychiatry in Dissent* (London: Tavistock, 1976)

Bentall, R. P., 'An Appraisal in the Light of Recent Research', in *R. D. Laing: Contemporary Perspectives* (ed. Salman Raschid) (London: Free Association Books, 2005)

Laing, A., *R. D. Laing: A Life* (Gloucester: Sutton Publishing, 2006)

Laing, R. D. (*The Divided Self.* London: Tavistock, 1960)

—, *The Politics of Experience and The Bird of Paradise* (Harmondsworth: Penguin Books, 1967)

—, *Wisdom, Madness and Folly* (London: Macmillan, 1985)

Laing, R. D. & Esterson, A., *Sanity, Madness and the Family.* (London: Tavistock, 1964)

Segal, C., *Zone of the Interior* (New York: Thomas Cromwell, 1976)

Smith, A. C., 'Books Reconsidered: R. D. Laing: *The Divided Self* , British Journal of Psychiatry, 140 (1982), 637–42

To my mother and father

Contents

Preface to the Original Edition

This is the first of a series of studies in existential psychology and psychiatry, in which it is proposed to present original contributions to this field by a number of authors.

The present book is a study of schizoid and schizophrenic persons; its basic purpose is to make madness, and the process of going mad, comprehensible. Readers will judge variously the success or failure of this aim. I would ask, however, that the book should not be judged in terms of what it does not attempt to do. Specifically, no attempt is made to present a comprehensive theory of schizophrenia. No attempt is made to explore constitutional and organic aspects. No attempt is made to describe my own relationship with these patients, or my own method of therapy.

A further purpose is to give in plain English an account, in *existential* terms, of some forms of madness. In this I believe it to be the first of its kind. Most readers will find a few terms strangely used in the first few chapters. I have, however, given careful thought to any such usage, and have not employed it unless I felt compelled by the sense to do so.

Here again, a brief statement about what I have not tried to do may avoid misunderstanding. The reader versed in existential and phenomenological literature will quickly see that this study is not a direct application of any established existential philosophy. There are important points of divergence from the work of Kierkegaard, Jaspers, Heidegger, Sartre, Binswanger, and Tillich, for instance.

To discuss points of convergence and divergence in any detail would have taken me away from the immediate task. Such a discussion belongs to another place. It is to the existential tradition, however, that I acknowledge my main intellectual indebtedness.

I wish to express here my gratitude to the patients and their parents about whom I have written in the following pages. All of those to whom I have referred at any length have given their willing consent to this publication. Names, places, and all identifying details have been changed, but the reader can be assured that he is not reading fiction.

I wish to register my gratitude to Dr Angus MacNiven and Professor T. Ferguson Rodger for the facilities they provided for the clinical basis for this study and the encouragement they gave me.

The clinical work upon which these studies are based was all completed before 1956, that is, before I became an assistant physician at the Tavistock Clinic, when Dr J. D. Sutherland generously made secretarial help available in the preparation of the final manuscript. Since the book was completed in 1957 it has been read by many people, and I have received much encouragement and helpful criticism from more individuals than I can conveniently list. I would like to thank particularly Dr Karl Abenheimer, Mrs Marion Milner, Professor T. Ferguson Rodger, Professor J. Romano, Dr Charles Rycroft, Dr J. Schorstein, Dr J. D. Sutherland, and Dr D. W. Winnicott for their constructive 'reactions' to the MS.

R. D. LAING

Preface to the Pelican Edition

284

One cannot say everything at once. I wrote this book when I was twenty-eight. I wanted to convey above all that it was far more possible than is generally supposed to understand people diagnosed as psychotic. Although this entailed understanding the social context, especially the power situation within the family, today I feel that, even in focusing upon and attempting to delineate a certain type of schizoid existence, I was already partially falling into the trap I was seeking to avoid. I am still writing in this book too much about Them, and too little of Us.

Freud insisted that our civilization is a repressive one. There is a conflict between the demands of conformity and the demands of our instinctive energies, explicitly sexual. Freud could see no easy resolution of this antagonism, and he came to believe that in our time the possibility of simple natural love between human beings had already been abolished.

Our civilization represses not only 'the instincts', not only sexuality, but any form of transcendence. Among one-dimensional men,* it is not surprising that someone with an insistent experience of other dimensions, that he cannot entirely deny or forget, will run the risk either of being destroyed by the others, or of betraying what he knows.

In the context of our present pervasive madness that we call normality, sanity, freedom, all our frames of reference are ambiguous and equivocal.

A man who prefers to be dead rather than Red is normal. A man

* *See* recently, Herbert Marcuse, *One-Dimensional Man*, Beacon Press, 1964.

who says he has lost his soul is mad. A man who says that men are machines may be a great scientist. A man who says he *is* a machine is 'depersonalized' in psychiatric jargon. A man who says that Negroes are an inferior race may be widely respected. A man who says his whiteness is a form of cancer is certifiable.

A little girl of seventeen in a mental hospital told me she was terrified because the Atom Bomb was inside her. That is a delusion. The statesmen of the world who boast and threaten that they have Doomsday weapons are far more dangerous, and far more estranged from 'reality' than many of the people on whom the label 'psychotic' is affixed.

Psychiatry could be, and some psychiatrists are, on the side of transcendence, of genuine freedom, and of true human growth. But psychiatry can so easily be a technique of brainwashing, of inducing behaviour that is adjusted, by (preferably) non-injurious torture. In the best places, where straitjackets are abolished, doors are unlocked, leucotomies largely forgone, these can be replaced by more subtle lobotomies and tranquillizers that place the bars of Bedlam and the locked doors *inside* the patient. Thus I would wish to emphasize that our 'normal' 'adjusted' state is too often the abdication of ecstasy, the betrayal of our true potentialities, that many of us are only too successful in acquiring a false self to adapt to false realities.

But let it stand. This was the work of an old young man. If I am older, I am now also younger.

London   September 1964

Acknowledgements

Thanks are due to the author and to Grune & Stratton for permission to quote from *Meaning and Content of Sexual Perversions*, by Medard Boss; to George Allen & Unwin in respect of *The Phenomenology of Mind*, by Hegel, translated by J. B. Baillie; to Baillière, Tindall & Cox in respect of *Lectures on Clinical Psychiatry*, by E. Kraepelin; to The Hogarth Press and the Institute of Psycho-Analysis in respect of *Beyond the Pleasure Principle*, by Sigmund Freud, from *The Complete Psychological Works of Sigmund Freud*, Vol. XVIII; to Rider & Co., London, in respect of *The Analysis of Dreams*, by Medard Boss, and *The Psychology of Imagination*, by Jean-Paul Sartre; and to Martin Secker & Warburg in respect of *The Opposing Self*, by Lionel Trilling.

The author wishes to thank Dr M. L. Hayward and Dr J. E. Taylor for their kind permission to quote at some length in Chapter 10 from their paper 'A Schizophrenic Patient Describes the Action of Intensive Psychotherapy', which appeared in the *Psychiatric Quarterly*, 30, 211–66.

Je donne une œuvre subjective ici, œuvre cependant qui tend de toutes ses forces vers l'objectivité.

E. MINKOWSKI

Part 1

The existential-phenomenological
foundations for a science of persons

The term schizoid refers to an individual the totality of whose experience is split in two main ways: in the first place, there is a rent in his relation with his world and, in the second, there is a disruption of his relation with himself. Such a person is not able to experience himself 'together with' others or 'at home in' the world, but, on the contrary, he experiences himself in despairing aloneness and isolation; moreover, he does not experience himself as a complete person but rather as 'split' in various ways, perhaps as a mind more or less tenuously linked to a body, as two or more selves, and so on.

This book attempts an existential-phenomenological account of some schizoid and schizophrenic persons. Before beginning this account, however, it is necessary to compare this approach to that of formal clinical psychiatry and psychopathology.

Existential phenomenology attempts to characterize the nature of a person's experience of his world and himself. It is not so much an attempt to describe particular objects of his experience as to set all particular experiences within the context of his whole being-in-his-world. The mad things said and done by the schizophrenic will remain essentially a closed book if one does not understand their existential context. In describing one way of going mad, I shall try to show that there is a comprehensible transition from the sane schizoid way of being-in-the-world to a psychotic way of being-in-the-world. Although retaining the terms *schizoid* and *schizophrenic* for the sane and psychotic positions respectively, I shall not, of course, be using these terms in their usual clinical psychiatric frame of reference, but phenomenologically and existentially.

The clinical focus is narrowed down to cover only some of the ways there are of being schizoid or of going schizophrenic from a schizoid starting-point. However, the account of the issues lived out by the individuals studied in the following pages is intended to demonstrate that these issues cannot be grasped through the methods of clinical psychiatry and psychopathology as they stand today but, on the contrary, require the existential-phenomeno-logical method to demonstrate their true human relevance and significance.

In this volume I have gone as directly as possible to the patients themselves and kept to a minimum the discussion of the historical, theoretical, and practical issues raised particularly *vis-à-vis* psychiatry and psycho-analysis. The particular form of human tragedy we are faced with here has never been presented with suffi-cient clarity and distinctness. I felt, therefore, that the sheer descriptive task had to come before all other considerations. This chapter is thus designed to give only the briefest statement of the basic orientation of this book necessary to avoid the most disas-trous misunderstandings. It faces in two directions: on the one hand, it is directed to psychiatrists who are very familiar with the type of 'case' but may be unused to seeing the 'case' *qua person* as described here; on the other hand, it is addressed to those who are familiar with or sympathetic to such persons but who have not encountered them as 'clinical material'. It is inevitable that it will be somewhat unsatisfactory to both.

As a psychiatrist, I run into a major difficulty at the outset: how can I go straight to the patients if the psychiatric words at my dis-posal keep the patient at a distance from me? How can one demon-strate the general human relevance and significance of the patient's condition if the words one has to use are specifically designed to isolate and circumscribe the meaning of the patient's life to a par-ticular clinical entity? Dissatisfaction with psychiatric and psycho-analytic words is fairly widespread, not least among those who most employ them. It is widely felt that these words of psychiatry and psycho-analysis somehow fail to express what one 'really means'. But it is a form of self-deception to suppose that one can say one thing and think another.

It will be convenient, therefore, to start by looking at some of the words in use. The thought *is* the language, as Wittgenstein has put it. A technical vocabulary is merely a language within a language. A consideration of this technical vocabulary will be at the same time an attempt to discover the reality which the words disclose or conceal.

The most serious objection to the technical vocabulary currently used to describe psychiatric patients is that it consists of words which split man up verbally in a way which is analogous to the existential splits we have to describe here. But we cannot give an adequate account of the existential splits unless we can begin from the concept of a unitary whole, and no such concept exists, nor can any such concept be expressed within the current language system of psychiatry or psycho-analysis.

The words of the current technical vocabulary either refer to man in isolation from the other and the world, that is, as an entity not *essentially* 'in relation to' the other and in a world, or they refer to falsely substantialized aspects of this isolated entity. Such words are: mind and body, psyche and soma, psychological and physical, personality, the self, the organism. All these terms are abstracta. Instead of the original bond of *I* and *You*, we take a single man in isolation and conceptualize his various aspects into 'the ego', 'the superego', and 'the id'. The other becomes either an internal or external object or a fusion of both. How can we speak in any way adequately of the relationship between me and you in terms of the interaction of one mental apparatus with another? How, even, can one say what it means to hide something from oneself or to deceive oneself in terms of barriers between one part of a mental apparatus and another? This difficulty faces not only classical Freudian metapsychology but equally any theory that begins with man or a part of man abstracted from his relation with the other in his world. We all know from our personal experience that we can be ourselves only in and through our world and there is a sense in which 'our' world will die with us although 'the' world will go on without us. Only existential thought has attempted to match the original experience of oneself in relationship to others in one's world by a term that adequately reflects this totality. Thus, existentially, the concretum is seen as a man's *existence*, his *being-in-the-world*. Unless we begin with the concept of man in relation to other men and from the beginning 'in' a world, and unless we realize that man does not exist without 'his' world nor can his world exist without him, we are condemned to start our study of schizoid and schizophrenic people with a verbal and conceptual splitting that matches the split up of the totality of the schizoid being-in-the-world. Moreover, the secondary verbal and conceptual task of reintegrating the various bits and pieces will parallel the despairing efforts of the schizophrenic to put his disintegrated self and world together again. In short, we have an already shattered Humpty Dumpty who cannot be put together again by any number of hyphenated or compound words: psycho-physical, psycho-somatic, psycho-biological, psycho-pathological, psycho-social, etc., etc.

If this is so, it may be that a look at how such schizoid theory originates would be highly relevant to the understanding of schizoid experience. In the following section, I shall use a phenomenological method to try to answer this question.

Man's *being* (I shall use 'being' subsequently to denote simply *all that a man is*) can be seen from different points of view and one or other aspect can be made the focus of study. In particular, man can be seen as person or thing. Now, even the same thing, seen from different points of view, gives rise to two entirely different descriptions, and the descriptions give rise to two entirely different theories, and the theories result in two entirely different sets of action. The initial way we see a thing determines all our subsequent dealings with it. Let us consider an equivocal or ambiguous figure:

In this figure, there is one thing on the paper which can be seen as a vase or as two faces turned towards each other. There are not two things on the paper: there is one thing there, but, depending on how it strikes us, we can see two different objects. The relation of the parts to the whole in the one object is quite different from the relation of the parts to the whole in the other. If we describe one of the faces seen we would describe, from top to bottom, a forehead, a nose, an upper lip, a mouth, a chin, and a neck. Although we have described the same line, which, if seen differently, can be the one side of a vase, we have not described the side of a vase but the outline of a face.

Now, if you are sitting opposite me, I can see you as another person like myself; without *you* changing or doing anything differently, I can now see you as a complex physical-chemical system, perhaps with its own idiosyncrasies but chemical none the less for that; seen in this way, you are no longer a person but an organism. Expressed in the language of existential phenomenology, the other, as seen as a person or as seen as an organism, is the object of different intentional acts. There is no dualism in the sense of the co-existence of two different essences or substances there in the object, psyche and soma; there are two different experiential Gestalts: person and organism.

One's *relationship* to an organism is different from one's relation to a person. One's description of the other as organism is as different from one's description of the other as person as the description of side of vase is from profile of face; similarly, one's theory of the other as organism is remote from any theory of the other as person. One acts towards an organism differently from the way one acts towards a person. The science of persons is the study of human beings that begins from a relationship with the other as person and proceeds to an account of the other still as person.

For example, if one is listening to another person talking, one may either (*a*) be studying verbal behaviour in terms of neural processes and the whole apparatus of vocalizing, or (*b*) be trying to understand what he is saying. In the latter case, an explanation of verbal behaviour in terms of the general nexus of organic changes that must necessarily be going on as a *conditio sine qua non* of his verbalization, is no contribution to a possible understanding of what the individual is saying. Conversely, an understanding of what the individual is saying does not contribute to a knowledge of how his brain cells are metabolizing oxygen. That is, an understanding of what he is saying is no substitute for an explanation of the relevant organismic processes, and vice versa. Again, there is no question here or anywhere of a mind-body dualism. The two accounts, in this case personal and organismic, taken up in respect to speech or any other observable human activity, are each the outcome of one's initial intentional act; each intentional act leads in its own direction and yields its own results. One chooses the point of view or intentional act within the overall context of what one is 'after' with the other. Man as seen as an organism or man as seen as a person discloses different aspects of the human reality to the investigator. Both are quite possible methodologically but one must be alert to the possible occasion for confusion.

The other as person is seen by me as responsible, as capable of choice, in short, as a self-acting agent. Seen as an organism, all that goes on in that organism can be conceptualized at any level of complexity – atomic, molecular, cellular, systemic, or organismic. Whereas behaviour seen as personal is seen in terms of that person's experience and of his intentions, behaviour seen organismically can only be seen as the contraction or relaxation of certain muscles, etc. Instead of the experience of sequence, one is concerned with a sequence of processes. In man seen as an organism, therefore, there is no place for his desires, fears, hope or despair as such. The ultimates of our explanations are not his intentions to his world but quanta of energy in an energy system.

Seen as an organism, man cannot be anything else but a complex of things, of *its*, and the processes that ultimately comprise an organism are *it*-processes. There is a common illusion that one somehow increases one's understanding of a person if one can translate a personal understanding of him into the impersonal terms of a sequence or system of *it*-processes. Even in the absence of theoretical justifications, there remains a tendency to translate our personal experience of the other as a person into an account of him that is depersonalized. We do this in some measure whether we use a machine analogy or a biological analogy in our 'explanation'. It should be noted that I am not here objecting to the use of mechanical or biological analogies as such, nor indeed to the intentional act of seeing man as a complex machine or as an animal. My thesis is limited to the contention that the theory of man as person loses its way if it falls into an account of man as a machine or man as an organismic system of it-processes. The converse is also true (see Brierley, 1951).

It seems extraordinary that whereas the physical and biological sciences of it-processes have generally won the day against tendencies to personalize the world of things or to read human intentions into the animal world, an authentic science of persons has hardly got started by reason of the inveterate tendency to depersonalize or reify persons.

In the following pages, we shall be concerned specifically with people who experience themselves as automata, as robots, as bits of machinery, or even as animals. Such persons are rightly regarded as crazy. Yet why do we not regard a theory that seeks to transmute persons into automata or animals as equally crazy? The experience of oneself and others as persons is primary and self-validating. It exists prior to the scientific or philosophical difficulties about how such experience is possible or how it is to be explained.

Indeed, it is difficult to explain the persistence in all our thinking of elements of what MacMurray has called the 'biological analogy': 'We should expect,' writes MacMurray (1957), 'that the emergence of a scientific psychology would be paralleled by a transition from an organic to a personal . . . conception of unity' (p. 37), that we should be able to *think* of the individual man as well as to experience him neither as a thing nor as an organism but as a person and that we should have a way of expressing that form of unity which is specifically personal. The task in the following pages is, therefore, the formidable one of trying to give an account of a quite specifically personal form of depersonalization and disintegration at a time when the discovery of 'the logical form through which the unity of the personal can be coherently conceived' (ibid.) is still a task for the future.

There are, of course, many descriptions of depersonalization and splitting in psychopathology. However, no psychopathological theory is entirely able to surmount the distortion of the person imposed by its own premisses even though it may seek to deny these very premisses. A psychopathology worthy of its name must presuppose a 'psyche' (mental apparatus or endopsychic structure). It must presuppose that the objectification, with or without reification imposed by thinking in terms of a fictional 'thing' or system, is an adequate conceptual correlate of the other as a person in action with others. Moreover, it must presuppose that its conceptual model has a way of functioning analogous to the way that an organism functions in health and a way of functioning analogous to an organism's way of functioning when physically diseased. However pregnant with partial analogies such comparisons are, psychopathology by the very nature of its basic approach precludes the possibility of understanding a patient's disorganization as a failure to achieve a specifically personal form of unity. It is like trying to make ice by boiling water. The very existence of psychopathology perpetuates the very dualism that most psychopathologists wish to avoid and that is clearly false. Yet this dualism cannot be avoided within the psychopathological frame of references except by falling into a monism that reduces one term to the other, and is simply another twist to a spiral of falsity.

It may be maintained that one cannot be scientific without retaining one's 'objectivity'. A genuine science of personal existence must attempt to be as unbiased as possible. Physics and the other sciences of things must accord the science of persons the right to be unbiased in a way that is true to its own field of study. If it is held that to be unbiased one should be 'objective' in the sense of depersonalizing the person who is the 'object' of our study, any temptation to do this under the impression that one is thereby being scientific must be rigorously resisted. Depersonalization in a theory that is intended to be a theory of persons is as false as schizoid depersonalization of others and is no less ultimately an intentional act. Although conducted in the name of science, such reification yields false 'knowledge'. It is just as pathetic a fallacy as the false personalization of things.

It is unfortunate that personal and subjective are words so abused as to have no power to convey any genuine act of seeing the other as person (if we mean this we have to revert to 'objective'), but imply immediately that one is merging one's own feelings and attitudes into one's study of the other in such a way as to distort our perception of him. In contrast to the reputable 'objective' or 'scientific', we have the disreputable 'subjective', 'intuitive', or, worst of all, 'mystical'. It is interesting, for example, that one frequently encounters 'merely' before subjective, whereas it is almost inconceivable to speak of anyone being 'merely' objective.

The greatest psychopathologist has been Freud. Freud was a hero. He descended to the 'Underworld' and met there stark terrors. He carried with him his theory as a Medusa's head which turned these terrors to stone. We who follow Freud have the benefit of the knowledge he brought back with him and conveyed to us. He survived. We must see if we now can survive without using a theory that is in some measure an instrument of defence.

THE RELATIONSHIP TO THE PATIENT AS PERSON
OR AS THING

In existential phenomenology the existence in question may be one's own or that of the other. When the other is a patient, existential phenomenology becomes the attempt to reconstruct the patient's way of being himself in his world, although, in the therapeutic relationship, the focus may be on the patient's way of being-with-me.

Patients present themselves to a psychiatrist with complaints that may be anywhere in the range between the most apparently localized difficulty ('I have a reluctance for jumping from a plane '), to the most diffuse difficulty possible ('I can't say why I've come really. I suppose it is just me that's not right'). However, no matter how circumscribed or diffuse the initial complaint may be, one knows that the patient is bringing into the treatment situation, whether intentionally or unintentionally, his existence, his whole being-in-his-world. One knows also that every aspect of his being is related in some way to every other aspect, although the manner in which these aspects are articulated may be by no means clear. It is the task of existential phenomenology to articulate what the other's 'world' is and his way of being in it. Right at the start, my own idea of the scope or extension of a man's being may not coincide with his, nor for that matter with that of other psychiatrists. I, for instance, regard any particular man as finite, as one who has had a beginning and who will have an end. He has been born, and he is going to die. In the meantime, he has a body that roots him to this time and this place. These statements I believe to be applicable to each and every particular man. I do not expect to re-verify them each time I meet another person. Indeed, they cannot be proved or falsified. I have had a patient whose notion of the horizons of his own being extended beyond birth and death: 'in fact' and not just 'in imagination' he said he was not essentially bound to one time and one place. I did not regard him as psychotic, nor could I prove him wrong, even if I cared to. Nevertheless, it is of considerable practical importance that one should be able to see that the concept and/or experience that a man may have of his being may be very different from one's own concept or experience of his being. In these cases, one has to be able to orientate oneself as a person in the other's scheme of things rather than only to see the other as an object in one's own world, i.e. within the total system of one's own reference. One must be able to effect this reorientation without prejudging who is right and who is wrong. The ability to do this is an absolute and obvious prerequisite in working with psychotics.

There is another aspect of man's being which is the crucial one in psychotherapy as contrasted with other treatments. This is that each and every man is at the same time separate from his fellows and related to them. Such separateness and relatedness are mutually necessary postulates. Personal relatedness can exist only between beings who are separate but who are not isolates. We are not isolates and we are not parts of the same physical body. Here we have the paradox, the potentially tragic paradox, that our relatedness to others is an essential aspect of our *being*, as is our separateness, but any particular person is not a necessary part of our being.

Psychotherapy is an activity in which that aspect of the patient's being, his relatedness to others, is used for therapeutic ends. The therapist acts on the principle that, since relatedness is potentially present in everyone, then he may not be wasting his time in sitting for hours with a silent catatonic who gives every evidence that he does not recognize his existence.

The existential-phenomenological
foundations for the understanding
of psychosis

There is a further characteristic of the current psychiatric jargon.
It speaks of psychosis as a social or biological *failure* of adjustment,
or *mal*-adaptation of a particularly radical kind, of *loss* of contact
with reality, of *lack* of insight. As van den Berg (1955) has said,
this jargon is a veritable 'vocabulary of denigration'. The denigration is not moralistic, at least in a nineteenth-century sense; in
fact, in many ways this language is the outcome of efforts to
avoid thinking in terms of freedom, choice, responsibility. But it
implies a certain standard way of being human to which the
psychotic cannot measure up. I do not, in fact, object to all the
implications in this 'vocabulary of denigration'. Indeed, I feel we
should be more frank about the judgements we implicitly make
when we call someone psychotic. When I certify someone insane,
I am not equivocating when I write that he is of unsound mind,
may be dangerous to himself and others, and requires care and
attention in a mental hospital. However, at the same time, I am
also aware that, in my opinion, there are other people who are
regarded as sane, whose minds are as radically unsound, who may
be equally or more dangerous to themselves and others and
whom society does not regard as psychotic and fit persons to be
in a madhouse. I am aware that the man who is said to be deluded
may be in his delusion telling me the truth, and this in no equivocal
or metaphorical sense, but quite literally, and that the cracked
mind of the schizophrenic may *let in* light which does not enter the
intact minds of many sane people whose minds are closed.
Ezekiel, in Jaspers's opinion, was a schizophrenic.

I must confess here to a certain personal difficulty I have in being a psychiatrist, which lies behind a great deal of this book. This is that except in the case of chronic schizophrenics I have difficulty in actually discovering the 'signs and symptoms' of psychosis in persons I am myself interviewing. I used to think that this was some deficiency on my part, that I was not clever enough to get at hallucinations and delusions and so on. If I compared my experience with psychotics with the accounts given of psychosis in the standard textbooks, I found that the authors were not giving a description of the way these people behaved with me. Maybe they were right and I was wrong. Then I thought that maybe they were wrong. But this is just as untenable. The following seems to be a statement of fact:

The standard texts contain the descriptions of the behaviour of people in a behavioural field that includes the psychiatrist. The behaviour of the patient is to some extent a function of the behaviour of the psychiatrist in the same behavioural field. The standard psychiatric patient is a function of the standard psychiatrist, and of the standard mental hospital. The figured base, as it were, which underscores all Bleuler's great description of schizophrenics is his remark that when all is said and done they were stranger to him than the birds in his garden.

Bleuler, we know, approached his patients as a non-psychiatric clinician would approach a clinical case, with respect, courtesy, consideration, and scientific curiosity. The patient, however, is diseased in a medical sense, and it is a matter of diagnosing his condition, by observing the signs of his disease. This approach is regarded as so self-evidently justifiable by so many psychiatrists that they may find it difficult to know what I am getting at. There are now, of course, many other schools of thought, but this is still the most extensive one in this country. It certainly is the approach that is taken for granted by non-medical people. I am speaking here all the time of psychotic patients (i.e. as most people immediately say to themselves, *not* you or me). Psychiatrists still hang on to it in practice even though they pay lip-service to incompatible views, outlook, and manner. Now, there is so much that is good and worth while in this, so much also that is *safe* in it, that anyone has a right to examine most closely any view that a clinical professional attitude of this kind may not be all that is required, or may even be misplaced in certain circumstances. The difficulty consists not simply in noticing evidence of the patient's feelings as they reveal themselves in his behaviour. The good medical clinician will allow for the fact that if his patient is anxious, his blood pressure may be somewhat higher than usual, his pulse may be rather faster than normal, and so on. The crux of the matter is that when one examines 'a heart', or even the whole man as an organism, one is not interested in the nature of one's own personal feelings about him; whatever these may be are irrelevant, discounted. One maintains a more or less standard professional outlook and manner.

That the classical clinical psychiatric attitude has not changed in principle since Kraepelin can be seen by comparing the following with the similar attitude of any recent British textbook of psychiatry (e.g. Mayer-Gross, Slater and Roth).

Here is Kraepelin's (1905) account to a lecture-room of his students of a patient showing the signs of catatonic excitement:

The patient I will show you today has almost to be carried into the rooms, as he walks in a straddling fashion on the outside of his feet. On coming in, he throws off his slippers, sings a hymn loudly, and then cries twice (in English), 'My father, my real father!' He is eighteen years old, and a pupil of the Oberrealschule (higher-grade modern-side school), tall, and rather strongly built, but with a pale complexion, on which there is very often a transient flush. The patient sits with his eyes shut, and pays no attention to his surroundings. He does not look up even when he is spoken to, but he answers beginning in a low voice, and gradually screaming louder and louder. When asked where he is, he says, 'You want to know that too? I tell you who is being measured and is measured and shall be measured. I know all that, and could tell you, but I do not want to.' When asked his name, he screams, 'What is your name? What does he shut? He shuts his eyes. What does he hear? He does not understand; he understands not. How? Who? Where? When? What does he mean? When I tell him to look he does not look properly. You there, just look! What is it? What is the matter? Attend; he attends not. I say, what is it, then? Why do you give me no answer? Are you getting impudent again? How can you be so impudent? I'm coming! I'll show you! You don't whore for me. You mustn't be smart either; you're an impudent, lousy fellow, such an impudent, lousy fellow I've never met with. Is he beginning again? You understand nothing at all, nothing at all; nothing at all does he understand. If you follow now, he won't follow, will not follow. Are you getting still more impudent? Are you getting impudent still more? How they attend, they do attend,' and so on. At the end, he scolds in quite inarticulate sounds.

Kraepelin notes here among other things the patient's 'inaccessibility':

Although he undoubtedly understood all the questions, *he has not given us a single piece of useful information.* His talk was . . . *only a series of disconnected sentences having no relation whatever to the general situation* (1905, pp. 79–80, italics my own).

Now there is no question that this patient is showing the 'signs' of catatonic excitement. The construction we put on this behaviour will, however, depend on the relationship we establish with the patient, and we are indebted to Kraepelin's vivid description which enables the patient to come, it seems, alive to us across fifty years and through his pages as though he were before us. What does this patient seem to be doing? Surely he is carrying on a dialogue between his own parodied version of Kraepelin, and his own defiant rebelling self. 'You want to know that too? I tell you who is being measured and is measured and shall be measured. I know all that, and I could tell you, but I do not want to.' This seems to be plain enough talk. Presumably he deeply resents this form of interrogation which is being carried out before a lecture-room of students. He probably does not see what it has to do with the things that must be deeply distressing him. But these things would not be 'useful information' to Kraepelin except as further 'signs' of a 'disease'.

Kraepelin asks him his name. The patient replies by an exasperated outburst in which he is now saying what he feels is the attitude implicit in Kraepelin's approach to him: What is your name? What does he shut? He shuts his eyes. . . . Why do you give me no answer? Are you getting impudent again? You don't whore for me? (i.e. he feels that Kraepelin is objecting because he is not prepared to prostitute himself before the whole classroom of students), and so on . . . such an impudent, shameless, miserable, lousy fellow I've never met with . . . etc.

Now it seems clear that this patient's behaviour can be seen in at least two ways, analogous to the ways of seeing vase or face. One may see his behaviour as 'signs' of a 'disease'; one may see his behaviour as expressive of his existence. The existential-pheno-menological construction is an inference about the way the other is feeling and acting. What is the boy's experience of Kraepelin? He seems to be tormented and desperate. What is he 'about' in speaking and acting in this way? He is objecting to being measured and tested. He wants to be heard.

INTERPRETATION AS A FUNCTION OF THE RELATIONSHIP WITH THE PATIENT

The clinical psychiatrist, wishing to be more 'scientific' or 'objective', may propose to confine himself to the 'objectively' observable behaviour of the patient before him. The simplest reply to this is that it is impossible. To see 'signs' of 'disease' is not to see neutrally. Nor is it neutral to see a smile as contractions of the circumoral muscles (Merleau-Ponty, 1953). We cannot help but see the person in one way or other and place our constructions or interpretations on 'his' behaviour, as soon as we are in a rela-tionship with him. This is so, even in the negative instance where we are drawn up or baffled by an absence of reciprocity on the part of the patient, where we feel there is *no one there* who is res-ponding to our approaches. This is very near the heart of our problem.

The difficulties facing us here are somewhat analogous to the difficulties facing the expositor of hieroglyphics, an analogy Freud was fond of drawing; they are, if anything, greater. The theory of the interpretation or deciphering of hieroglyphics and other ancient texts has been carried further forward and made more explicit by Dilthey in the last century than the theory of the interpretation of psychotic 'hieroglyphic' speech and actions. It may help to clarify our position if we compare our problem with that of the historian as expounded by Dilthey.* In both cases, the essential task is one of interpretation.

* The immediate source for the Dilthey quotations in the following pas-sage is Bultmann's 'The problem of hermeneutics' (*Essays*, 1955, pp. 234–61).

Ancient documents can be subjected to a formal analysis in terms of structure and style, linguistic traits, and characteristic idiosyncrasies of syntax, etc. Clinical psychiatry attempts an analogous formal analysis of the patient's speech and behaviour. This formalism, historical or clinical, is clearly very limited in scope. Beyond this formal analysis, it may be possible to shed light on the text through a knowledge of the nexus of socio-historical conditions from which it arose. Similarly, we usually wish to extend as far as we can our formal and static analysis of isolated clinical 'signs' to an understanding of their place in the person's life history. This involves the introduction of dynamic-genetic hypotheses. However, historical information, *per se*, about ancient texts or about patients, will help us to understand them better only if we can bring to bear what is often called sympathy, or, more intensively, *em*pathy.

When Dilthey, therefore, 'characterizes *the relationship between the author and the expositor* as the conditioning factor for the possibility of the comprehension of the text, he has, in fact, laid bare the presupposition of all interpretation which has comprehension as its basis' (Bultmann, op. cit.).

We explain [writes Dilthey] by means of purely intellectual processes, but we understand by means of the cooperation of all the powers of the mind in comprehension. In understanding we start from the connection of the given, living whole, in order to make the past comprehensible in terms of it.

Now, our view of the other depends on our willingness to enlist all the powers of every aspect of ourselves in the act of comprehension. It seems also that we require to orientate ourselves to this person in such a way as to leave open to us the *possibility* of understanding him. The art of understanding those aspects of an individual's being which we can observe, as expressive of his mode of being-in-the-world, requires us to relate his actions to *his* way of experiencing the situation he is in with us. Similarly it is in terms of his present that we have to understand his past, and not exclusively the other way round. This again is true even in the negative instances when it may be apparent through his behaviour that he is denying the existence of any situation he may be in with us, for instance, when we feel ourselves treated as though we did not exist, or as existing only in terms of the patient's own wishes or anxieties. It is not a question here of affixing predetermined meanings to this behaviour in a rigid way. If we look at his actions as 'signs' of a 'disease', we are already imposing our categories of thought on to the patient, in a manner analogous to the way we may regard him as treating us; and we shall be doing the same if we imagine that we can 'explain' his present as a mechanical resultant of an immutable 'past'.

If one is adopting such an attitude towards a patient, it is hardly possible at the same time to understand what he may be trying to communicate to us. To consider again the instance of listening to someone speaking, if I am sitting opposite you and speaking to you, you may be trying (i) to assess any abnormalities in my speech, or (ii) to explain what I am saying in terms of how you are imagining my brain cells to be metabolizing oxygen, or (iii) to discover why, in terms of past history and socio-economic background, I should be saying these things at this time. Not one of the answers that you may or may not be able to supply to these questions will in itself supply you with a simple understanding of what I am getting at.

It is just possible to have a thorough knowledge of what has been discovered about the hereditary or familial incidence of manic-depressive psychosis or schizophrenia, to have a facility in recognizing schizoid 'ego distortion' and schizophrenic ego defects, plus the various 'disorders' of thought, memory, perceptions, etc., to know, in fact, just about everything that can be known about the psychopathology of schizophrenia or of schizophrenia as a disease without being able to understand one single schizophrenic. Such data are all ways of *not* understanding him. To look and to listen to a patient and to see 'signs' of schizophrenia (as a 'disease') and to look and to listen to him simply as a human being are to see and to hear in as radically different ways as when one sees, first the vase, then the faces in the ambiguous picture.

Of course, as Dilthey says, the expositor of a text has a right to presume that despite the passage of time, and the wide divergence of world view between him and the ancient author, he stands in a not entirely different context of living experience from the original writer. He exists, in the world, like the other, as a permanent object in time and place, with others like himself. *It is just this presupposition that one cannot make with the psychotic.* In this respect, there may be a greater difficulty in understanding the psychotic in whose presence we are here and now, than there is in understanding the writer of a hieroglyphic dead for thousands of years. Yet the distinction is not an essential one. The psychotic, after all, as Harry Stack Sullivan has said, is more than anything else 'simply human'. The personalities of doctor and psychotic, no less than the personalities of expositor and author, do not stand opposed to each other as two external facts that do not meet and cannot be compared. Like the expositor, the therapist must have the plasticity to transpose himself into another strange and even alien view of the world. In this act, he draws on his own psychotic possibilities, without forgoing his sanity. Only thus can he arrive at an understanding of the patient's *existential position*.

I think it is clear that by 'understanding' I do not mean a purely intellectual process. For understanding one might say love. But no word has been more prostituted. What is necessary, though not enough, is a capacity to know how the patient is experiencing himself and the world, including oneself. If one cannot understand him, one is hardly in a position to begin to 'love' him in any effective way. We are commanded to love our neighbour. One cannot, however, love this particular neighbour for himself without knowing who he is. One can only love his abstract humanity. One cannot love a conglomeration of 'signs of schizophrenia'. No one *has* schizophrenia, like having a cold. The patient has not 'got' schizophrenia. He is schizophrenic. The schizophrenic has to be known without being destroyed. He will have to discover that this is possible. The therapist's hate as well as his love is, therefore, in the highest degree relevant. What the schizophrenic is to us determines very considerably what we are to him, and hence his actions. Many of the textbook 'signs' of schizophrenia vary from hospital to hospital and seem largely a function of nursing. Some psychiatrists observe certain schizo-phrenic 'signs' much less than others.*

* There is now an extensive literature to support this view. See, for example, 'In the Mental Hospital' (articles from *The Lancet*, 1955–6).

I think, therefore, that the following statement by Frieda Fromm-Reichmann is indeed true, however disturbing it is:

... psychiatrists can take it for granted now that in principle a workable doctor-patient relationship can be established with the schizophrenic patient. If and when this seems impossible, it is due to the doctor's personality difficulties, not to the patient's psychopathology (1952, p. 91).

Of course, as with Kraepelin's catatonic young man, the individual reacts and feels towards oneself only partially in terms of the person one takes oneself to be and partially in terms of his phantasy of what one is. One tries to make the patient see that his way of acting towards oneself implies a phantasy of one kind or another, which, most likely, he does not fully recognize (of which he is unconscious), but which, nevertheless, is a necessary postulate if one is to make any sense of this way of conducting himself.

When two sane persons are together one expects that *A* will recognize *B* to be more or less the person *B* takes himself to be, and vice versa. That is, for my part, I expect that my own definition of myself should, by and large, be endorsed by the other person, assuming that I am not deliberately impersonating someone else, being hypocritical, lying, and so on.* Within the context of mutual sanity there is, however, quite a wide margin for conflict, error, misconception, in short, for a disjunction of one kind or another between the person one is in one's own eyes (one's being-for-oneself) and the person one is in the eyes of the other (one's being-for-the-other), and, conversely, between who or what he is for me and who or what he is for himself; finally, between what one imagines to be his picture of oneself and his attitude and intentions towards oneself, and the picture, attitude, and intentions he has in actuality towards oneself, and vice versa.

That is to say, when two sane persons meet, there appears to be a reciprocal recognition of each other's identity. In this mutual recognition there are the following basic elements:

(a) I recognize the other to be the person he takes himself to be.
(b) He recognizes me to be the person I take myself to be.

* There is the story of the patient in a lie-detector who was asked if he was Napoleon. He replied, 'No'. The lie-detector recorded that he was lying.

Each has his own autonomous sense of identity and his own definition of who and what he is. You are expected to be able to recognize me. That is, I am accustomed to expect that the person you take me to be, and the identity that I reckon myself to have, will coincide by and large: let us say simply 'by and large', since there is obviously room for considerable discrepancies.

However, if there are discrepancies of a sufficiently radical kind remaining after attempts to align them have failed, there is no alternative but that one of us must be insane. I have no difficulty in regarding another person as psychotic, if for instance:

he says he is Napoleon, whereas I say he is not;

or if he says I am Napoleon, whereas I say I am not;

or if he thinks that I wish to seduce him, whereas I think that I have given him no grounds in actuality for supposing that such is my intention;

or if he thinks that I am afraid he will murder me, whereas I am not afraid of this, and have given him no reason to think that I am.

I suggest, therefore, that *sanity or psychosis is tested by the degree of conjunction or disjunction between two persons where the one is sane by common consent*.

The critical test of whether or not a patient is psychotic is a lack of congruity, an incongruity, a clash, between him and me.

The 'psychotic' is the name we have for the other person in a disjunctive relationship of a particular kind. It is only because of this interpersonal disjunction that we start to examine his urine, and look for anomalies in the graphs of the electrical activity of his brain.

It is worth while at this point to probe a little farther into what is the nature of the barrier or disjunction between the sane and the psychotic.

If, for instance, a man tells us he is 'an unreal man', and if he is not lying, or joking, or equivocating in some subtle way, there is no doubt that he will be regarded as deluded. But, existentially, what does this delusion mean? Indeed, he is not joking or pretending. On the contrary, he goes on to say that he has been pretending for years to have been a real person but can maintain the deception no longer.

His whole life has been torn between his desire to reveal himself and his desire to conceal himself. We all share this problem with him and we have all arrived at a more or less satisfactory solution. We have our secrets and our needs to confess. We may remember how, in childhood, adults at first were able to look right through us, and into us, and what an accomplishment it was when we, in fear and trembling, could tell our first lie, and make, for ourselves, the discovery that we are irredeemably alone in certain respects, and know that within the territory of ourselves there can be only our footprints. There are some people, however, who never fully real-ize themselves in this position. This genuine privacy is the basis of genuine relationship; but the person whom we call 'schizoid' feels both more exposed, more vulnerable to others than we do, and more isolated. Thus a schizophrenic may say that he is made of glass, of such transparency and fragility that a look directed at him splinters him to bits and penetrates straight through him. We may suppose that precisely as such he experiences himself.

We shall suggest that it was on the basis of this exquisite vulnerability that the unreal man became so adept at self-concealment. He learnt to cry when he was amused, and to smile when he was sad. He frowned his approval, and applauded his displeasure. 'All that you can see is not me,' he says to himself. But only in and through all that we do see can he be anyone (in reality). If these actions are not his real self, he is irreal; wholly symbolical and equivocal; a purely virtual, potential, imaginary person, a 'mythical' man; nothing 'really'. If, then, he once stops pretending to be what he is not, and steps out as the person he has come to be, he emerges as Christ, or as a ghost, but not as a man: by existing with no body, he is no-body.

A 'truth' about his 'existential position' is lived out. What is 'existentially' true is lived as 'really' true.

Undoubtedly, most people take to be 'really' true only what has to do with grammar and the natural world. A man says he is dead but he *is* alive. But his 'truth' is that he is dead. He expresses it perhaps in the only way common (i.e. the communal) sense allows him. He means that he is 'really' and quite 'literally' dead, not merely symbolically or 'in a sense' or 'as it were', and is seriously bent on communicating his truth. The price, however, to be paid for transvaluating the communal truth in this manner is to 'be' mad, for the only *real* death *we* recognize is biological death.

The schizophrenic is desperate, is simply without hope. I have never known a schizophrenic who could say he was loved, as a man, by God the Father or by the Mother of God or by another man. He either *is* God, or the Devil, or in hell, estranged from God. When someone says he is an unreal man or that he is dead, in all seriousness, expressing in radical terms the stark truth of his existence as he experiences it, that is – insanity.

What is required of us? Understand him? The kernel of the schizophrenic's experience of himself must remain incomprehensible to us. As long as we are sane and he is insane, it will remain so. But comprehension as an effort to reach and grasp him, while remaining within our own world and judging him by our own categories whereby he inevitably falls short, is not what the schizophrenic either wants or requires. We have to recognize all the time his distinctiveness and differentness, his separateness and loneliness and despair.*

* Schizophrenia cannot be understood without understanding despair. See especially Kierkegaard, *The sickness unto death*, 1954; Binswanger, 'The case of Ellen West' 1944–5; Leslie Farber, 'The therapeutic despair', 1958.

We can now state more precisely the nature of our clinical inquiry. A man may have a sense of his presence in the world as a real, alive, whole, and, in a temporal sense, a continuous person. As such, he can live out into the world and meet others: a world and others experienced as equally real, alive, whole, and continuous.

Such a basically *ontologically** secure person will encounter all the hazards of life, social, ethical, spiritual, biological, from a centrally firm sense of his own and other people's reality and identity. It is often difficult for a person with such a sense of his integral selfhood and personal identity, of the permanency of things, of the reliability of natural processes, of the substantiality of natural processes, of the substantiality of others, to transpose himself into the world of an individual whose experiences may be utterly lacking in any unquestionable self-validating certainties.

This study is concerned with the issues involved where there is the partial or almost complete absence of the assurances derived from an existential position of what I shall call *primary ontological security*: with anxieties and dangers that I shall suggest arise *only* in terms of *primary ontological insecurity*; and with the consequent attempts to deal with such anxieties and dangers.

The literary critic, Lionel Trilling (1955), points up the contrast that I wish to make between a *basic existential position of ontological security* and one of *ontological insecurity* very clearly

---

* Despite the philosophical use of 'ontology' (by Heidegger, Sartre, Tillich, especially), I have used the term in its present empirical sense because it appears to be the best adverbial or adjectival derivative of 'being'.

in comparing the worlds of Shakespeare and Keats on the one hand, and of Kafka on the other:

... for Keats the awareness of evil exists side by side with a very strong sense of personal identity and is for that reason the less immediately apparent. To some contemporary readers, it will seem for the same reason the less intense. In the same way it may seem to a contemporary reader that, if we compare Shakespeare and Kafka, leaving aside the degree of genius each has, and considering both only as expositors of man's suffering and cosmic alienation, it is Kafka who makes the more intense and complete exposition. And, indeed, the judgement may be correct, exactly because for Kafka the sense of evil is not contradicted by the sense of personal identity. Shakespeare's world, quite as much as Kafka's, is that prison cell which Pascal says the world is, from which daily the inmates are led forth to die; Shakespeare no less than Kafka forces upon us the cruel irrationality of the conditions of human life, the tale told by an idiot, the puerile gods who torture us not for punishment but for sport; and no less than Kafka, Shakespeare is revolted by the fetor of the prison of this world, nothing is more characteristic of him than his imagery of disgust. But in Shakespeare's cell the company is so much better than in Kafka's, the captains and kings and lovers and clowns of Shakespeare are alive and complete before they die. In Kafka, long before the sentence is executed, even long before the malign legal process is even instituted, something terrible has been done to the accused. We all know what that is – he has been stripped of all that is becoming to a man except his abstract humanity, which, like his skeleton, never is quite becoming to a man. He is without parents, home, wife, child, commitment, or appetite; he has no connexion with power, beauty, love, wit, courage, loyalty, or fame, and the pride that may be taken in these. So that we may say that Kafka's knowledge of evil exists without the contradictory knowledge of the self in its health and validity, that Shakespeare's knowledge of evil exists with that contradiction in its fullest possible force (pp. 38–9).

We find, as Trilling points out, that Shakespeare does depict characters who evidently experience themselves as real and alive and complete however riddled by doubts or torn by conflicts they may be. With Kafka this is not so. Indeed, the effort to communicate what being alive is like in the absence of such assurances seems to characterize the work of a number of writers and artists of our time. Life, without feeling alive.

With Samuel Beckett, for instance, one enters a world in which there is no contradictory sense of the self in its 'health and validity' to mitigate the despair, terror, and boredom of existence. In such a way, the two tramps who wait for Godot are condemned to live:

ESTRAGON: We always find something, eh, Didi, to give us the impression that we exist?

VLADIMIR (*impatiently*): Yes, yes, we're magicians. But let us persevere in what we have resolved, before we forget.

In painting, Francis Bacon, among others, seems to be dealing with similar issues. Generally, it is evident that what we shall discuss here clinically is but a small sample of something in which human nature is deeply implicated and to which we can contribute only a very partial understanding.

To begin at the beginning:

Biological birth is a definitive act whereby the infant organism is precipitated into the world. There it is, a new baby, a new biological entity, already with its own ways, real and alive, from *our* point of view. But what of the baby's point of view? Under usual circumstances, the physical birth of a new living organism into the world inaugurates rapidly ongoing processes whereby within an amazingly short time the infant *feels* real and alive and has a *sense* of being an entity, with continuity in time and a location in space. In short, physical birth and biological aliveness are followed by the baby becoming existentially born as real and alive. Usually this development is taken for granted and affords the certainty upon which all other certainties depend. This is to say, not only do adults see children to be real biologically viable entities but they experience themselves as whole persons who are real and alive, and conjunctively experience other human beings as real and alive. These are self-validating data of experience.

The individual, then, may experience his own being as real, alive, whole; as differentiated from the rest of the world in ordinary circumstances so clearly that his identity and autonomy are never in question; as a continuum in time; as having an inner consistency, substantiality, genuineness, and worth; as spatially co-extensive with the body; and, usually, as having begun in or around birth and liable to extinction with death. He thus has a firm core of ontological security.

This, however, may not be the case. The individual in the ordinary circumstances of living may feel more unreal than real; in a literal sense, more dead than alive; precariously differentiated from the rest of the world, so that his identity and autonomy are always in question. He may lack the experience of his own temporal continuity. He may not possess an over-riding sense of personal consistency or cohesiveness. He may feel more insubstantial than substantial, and unable to assume that the stuff he is made of is genuine, good, valuable. And he may feel his self as partially divorced from his body.

It is, of course, inevitable that an individual whose experience of himself is of this order can no more live in a 'secure' world than he can be secure 'in himself'. The whole 'physiognomy' of his world will be correspondingly different from that of the individual whose sense of self is securely established in its health and validity. Relatedness to other persons will be seen to have a radically different significance and function. To anticipate, we can say that in the individual whose own being is secure in this primary experiential sense, relatedness with others is potentially gratifying; whereas the ontologically insecure person is preoccupied with preserving rather than gratifying himself: the ordinary circumstances of living threaten his *low threshold* of security.*

If a position of primary ontological security has been reached, the ordinary circumstances of life do not afford a perpetual threat to one's own existence. If such a basis for living has not been reached, the ordinary circumstances of everyday life constitute a continual and deadly threat.

Only if this is realized is it possible to understand how certain psychoses can develop.

If the individual cannot take the realness, aliveness, autonomy, and identity of himself and others for granted, then he has to become absorbed in contriving ways of trying to be real, of keeping himself or others alive, of preserving his identity, in efforts, as he

---

* This formulation is very similar to those of H. S. Sullivan, Hill, F. Fromm-Reichmann, and Arieti in particular. Federn, although expressing himself very differently, seems to have advanced a closely allied view.

will often put it, to prevent himself losing his self. What are to most people everyday happenings, which are hardly noticed because they have no special significance, may become deeply significant in so far as they either contribute to the sustenance of the individual's being or threaten him with non-being. Such an individual, for whom the elements of the world are coming to have, or have come to have, a different hierarchy of significance from that of the ordinary person, is beginning, as we say, to 'live in a world of his own', or has already come to do so. It is not true to say, however, without careful qualification, that he is losing 'contact with' reality, and withdrawing into himself. External events no longer affect him in the same way as they do others: it is not that they affect him less; on the contrary, frequently they affect him more. It is frequently not the case that he is becoming 'indifferent' and 'withdrawn'. It may, however, be that the world of his experience comes to be one he can no longer share with other people.

But before these developments are explored, it will be valuable to characterize under three headings three forms of anxiety encountered by the ontologically insecure person: engulfment, implosion, petrification.

1. Engulfment.

An argument occurred between two patients in the course of a session in an analytic group. Suddenly, one of the protagonists broke off the argument to say, 'I can't go on. You are arguing in order to have the pleasure of triumphing over me. At best you win an argument. At worst you lose an argument. *I am arguing in order to preserve my existence.*'

This patient was a young man who I would say was sane, but, as he stated, his activity in the argument, as in the rest of his life, was not designed to gain gratification but to 'preserve his existence'. Now, one might say that if he did, in fact, really imagine that the loss of an argument would jeopardize his existence, then he was 'grossly out of touch with reality' and was virtually psychotic. But this is simply to beg the question without making any contribution towards understanding the patient. It is, however, important to know that if you were to subject this patient to a type of psychiatric interrogation recommended in many psychiatric textbooks, within ten minutes his behaviour and speech would be revealing 'signs' of psychosis. It is quite easy to evoke such 'signs' from such a person whose threshold of basic security is so low that practically any relationship with another person, however tenuous or however apparently 'harmless', threatens to over-whelm him.

A firm sense of one's own autonomous identity is required in order that one may be related as one human being to another. Otherwise, any and every relationship threatens the individual with loss of identity. One form this takes can be called engulfment. In this the individual dreads relatedness as such, with anyone or anything or, indeed, even with himself, because his uncertainty about the stability of his autonomy lays him open to the dread lest in any relationship he will lose his autonomy and identity. Engulf-ment is not simply envisaged as something that is liable to happen willy-nilly despite the individual's most active efforts to avoid it. The individual experiences himself as a man who is only saving himself from drowning by the most constant, strenuous, desperate activity. Engulfment is felt as a risk in being understood (thus grasped, comprehended), in being loved, or even simply in being seen. To be hated may be feared for other reasons, but to be hated as such is often less disturbing than to be destroyed, as it is felt, through being engulfed by love.

The main manoeuvre used to preserve identity under pressure from the dread of engulfment is isolation. Thus, instead of the polarities of separateness and relatedness based on individual autonomy, there is the antithesis between complete loss of being by absorption into the other person (engulfment), and complete aloneness (isolation). There is no safe third possibility of a dialec-tical relationship between two persons, both sure of their own ground and, on this very basis, able to 'lose themselves' in each other. Such merging of being can occur in an 'authentic' way only when the individuals are sure of themselves. If a man hates himself, he may wish to lose himself in the other: then being engulfed by the other is an escape from himself. In the present case it is an ever-present possibility to be dreaded. It will be shown later, however, that what at one 'moment' is most dreaded and strenuously avoided can change to what is most sought.

This anxiety accounts for one form of a so-called 'negative therapeutic reaction' to apparently correct interpretation in psychotherapy. To be understood correctly is to be engulfed, to be enclosed, swallowed up, drowned, eaten up, smothered, stifled in or by another person's supposed all-embracing comprehension. It is lonely and painful to be always misunderstood, but there is at least from this point of view a measure of safety in isolation.

The other's love is therefore feared more than his hatred, or rather all love is sensed as a version of hatred. By being loved one is placed under an unsolicited obligation. In therapy with such a person, the last thing there is any point in is to pretend to more 'love' or 'concern' than one has. The more the therapist's own necessarily very complex motives for trying to 'help' a person of this kind genuinely converge on a concern for him which is prepared to 'let him be' and is not *in fact* engulfing or merely indifference, the more hope there will be in the horizon.

There are many images used to describe related ways in which identity is threatened, which may be mentioned here, as closely related to the dread of engulfment, e.g. being buried, being drowned, being caught and dragged down into quicksand. The image of fire recurs repeatedly. Fire may be the uncertain flickering of the individual's own inner aliveness. It may be a destructive alien power which will devastate him. Some psychotics say in the acute phase that they are on fire, that their bodies are being burned up. A patient describes himself as cold and dry. Yet he dreads any warmth or wet. He will be engulfed by the fire or the water, and either way be destroyed.

2. Implosion

This is the strongest word I can find for the extreme form of what Winnicott terms the *impingement* of reality. Impingement does not convey, however, the full terror of the experience of the world as liable at any moment to crash in and obliterate all identity as a gas will rush in and obliterate a vacuum. The individual feels that, like the vacuum, he is empty. But this emptiness is him. Although in other ways he longs for the emptiness to be filled, he dreads the possibility of this happening because he has come to feel that all he can be is the awful nothingness of just this very vacuum. Any 'contact' with reality is then in itself experienced as a dreadful threat because reality, as experienced from this position, is necessarily *implosive* and thus, as was relatedness in engulfment, *in itself* a threat to what identity the individual is able to suppose himself to have.

Reality, as such, threatening engulfment or implosion, is the persecutor.

In fact, we are all only two or three degrees Fahrenheit from experiences of this order. Even a slight fever, and the whole world can begin to take on a persecutory, impinging aspect.

3. *Petrification and depersonalization*

In using the term 'petrification', one can exploit a number of the meanings embedded in this word:

1. A particular form of terror, whereby one is petrified, i.e. turned to stone.
2. The dread of this happening: the dread, that is, of the possibility of turning, or being turned, from a live person into a dead thing, into a stone, into a robot, an automaton, without personal autonomy of action, an *it* without subjectivity.
3. The 'magical' act whereby one may attempt to turn someone else into stone, by 'petrifying' him; and, by extension, the act whereby one negates the other person's autonomy, ignores his feelings, regards him as a thing, kills the life in him. In this sense one may perhaps better say that one depersonalizes him, or reifies him. One treats him not as a person, as a free agent, but as an it.

Depersonalization is a technique that is universally used as a means of dealing with the other when he becomes too tiresome or disturbing. One no longer allows oneself to be responsive to his feelings and may be prepared to regard him and treat him as though he had no feelings. The people in focus here both tend to feel themselves as more or less depersonalized and tend to depersonalize others; they are constantly afraid of being depersonalized by others. The act of turning him into a thing is, *for him*, actually petrifying. In the face of being treated as an 'it', his own subjectivity drains away from him like blood from the face. Basically he requires constant confirmation from others of his own existence as a person.

A partial depersonalization of others is extensively practised in everyday life and is regarded as normal if not highly desirable. Most relationships are based on some partial depersonalizing tendency in so far as one treats the other not in terms of any awareness of who or what he might be in himself but as virtually an android robot playing a role or part in a large machine in which one too may be acting yet another part.

It is usual to cherish if not the reality, at least the illusion that there is a limited sphere of living free from this dehumanization. Yet it may be in just this sphere that the greater risk is felt, and the ontologically insecure person experiences this risk in highly potentiated form.

The risk consists in this: if one experiences the other as a free agent, one is open to the possibility of experiencing oneself as an *object* of his experience and thereby of feeling one's own subjectivity drained away. One is threatened with the possibility of becoming no more than a thing in the world of the other, without any life for oneself, without any being for oneself. In terms of such anxiety, the very act of experiencing the other as a person is felt as virtually suicidal. Sartre discusses this experience brilliantly in Part 3 of *Being and Nothingness*.

The issue is in principle straightforward. One may find oneself enlivened and the sense of one's own being enhanced by the other, or one may experience the other as deadening and impoverishing. A person may have come to anticipate that any possible relationship with another will have the latter consequences. Any other is then a threat to his 'self' (his capacity to act autonomously) not by reason of anything he or she may do or not do specifically, but by reason of his or her very existence.

Some of the above points are illustrated in the life of James, a chemist, aged twenty-eight.

The complaint he made all along was that he could not become a 'person'. He had 'no self'. 'I am only a response to other people, I have no identity of my own.' (We shall have occasion to describe in detail later the sense of not being one's true self, of living a false self [Chapters 5, 6].) He felt he was becoming more and more 'a mythical person'. He felt he had no weight, no substance of his own. 'I am only a cork floating on the ocean.'

This man was very concerned about not having become a person: he reproached his mother for this failure. 'I was merely her emblem. She never recognized my identity.' In contrast to his own belittlement of and uncertainty about himself, he was always on the brink of being overawed and crushed by the formidable reality that other people contained. In contrast to his own light weight, uncertainty, and insubstantiality, *they* were solid, decisive, emphatic, and substantial. He felt that in every way that mattered others were more 'large scale' than he was.

At the same time, in practice he was not easily overawed. He used two chief manoeuvres to preserve security. One was an outward compliance with the other (Chapter 7). The second was an inner intellectual Medusa's head he turned on the other. Both manoeuvres taken together safeguarded his own subjectivity which he had never to betray openly and which thus could never find direct and immediate expression for itself. Being secret, it was safe. Both techniques together were designed to avoid the dangers of being engulfed or depersonalized.

With his outer behaviour he forestalled the danger to which he was perpetually subject, namely that of becoming someone else's *thing*, by pretending to be no more than a cork. (After all, what safer thing to be in an ocean?) At the same time, however, he turned the other person into a thing in his own eyes, thus magically nullifying any danger to himself by secretly totally disarming the enemy. By destroying, in his own eyes, the other person as a person, he robbed the other of his power to crush him. By depleting him of his personal aliveness, that is, by seeing him as a piece of machinery rather than as a human being, he undercut the risk to himself of this aliveness either swamping him, imploding into his own emptiness, or turning him into a mere appendage.

This man was married to a very lively and vivacious woman, highly spirited, with a forceful personality and a mind of her own. He maintained a paradoxical relationship with her in which, in one sense, he was entirely alone and isolated and, in another sense, he was almost a parasite. He dreamt, for instance, that he was a clam stuck to his wife's body.

Just because he could dream thus, he had the more need to keep her at bay by contriving to see her as no more than a machine. He described her laughter, her anger, her sadness, with 'clinical' precision, even going so far as to refer to her as 'it', a practice that was rather chilling in its effect. 'It then started to laugh.' She was an 'it' because everything she did was a predictable, determined response. He would, for instance, tell her (it) an ordinary funny joke and when she (it) laughed this indicated her (its) entirely 'conditioned', robot-like nature, which he saw indeed in much the same terms as certain psychiatric theories would use to account for all human actions.

I was at first agreeably surprised by his apparent ability to reject and disagree with what I said as well as to agree with me. This seemed to indicate that he had more of a mind of his own than he perhaps realized and that he was not too frightened to display some measure of autonomy. However, it became evident that his apparent capacity to act as an autonomous person with me was due to his secret manoeuvre of regarding me not as a live human being, a person in my own right with my own selfhood, but as a sort of robot interpreting device to which he fed input and which after a quick commutation came out with a verbal message to him. With this secret outlook on me as a thing he could appear to be a 'person'. What he could not sustain was a person-to-person relationship, experienced as such.

Dreams in which one or other of the above forms of dread is expressed are common in such persons. These dreams are not variations on the fears of being eaten which occur in ontologically secure persons. To be eaten does not necessarily mean to lose one's identity. Jonah was very much himself even within the belly of the whale. Few nightmares go so far as to call up anxieties about actual loss of identity, usually because most people, even in their dreams, still meet whatever dangers are to be encountered as persons who may perhaps be attacked or mutilated but whose basic existential core is not itself in jeopardy. In the classical nightmare the dreamer wakes up in terror. But this terror is not the dread of losing the 'self'. Thus a patient dreams of a fat pig which sits on his chest and threatens to suffocate him. He wakes in terror. At worst, in this nightmare, he is threatened with suffocation, but not with the dissolution of his very being.

The defensive method of turning the threatening mother- or breast-figure into a *thing* occurs in patients' dreams. One patient dreamt recurrently of a small black triangle which originated in a corner of his room and grew larger and larger until it seemed about to engulf him – whereupon he always awoke in great terror. This was a psychotic young man who stayed with my family for several months, and whom I was thus able to get to know rather well. There was only one situation as far as I could judge in which he could let himself 'go' without anxiety at not recovering himself again, and that was in listening to jazz.

The fact that even in a dream the breast-figure has to be so depersonalized is a measure of its potential danger to the self, presumably on the basis of its frightening original personalizations and the failure of *a normal process of depersonalization*.

Medard Boss (1957a) gives examples of several dreams heralding psychosis. In one, the dreamer is engulfed by fire:

A woman of hardly thirty years dreamt, at a time when she still felt completely healthy, that she was afire in the stables. Around her, the fire, an ever larger crust of lava was forming. Half from the outside and half from the inside her own body she could see how the fire was slowly becoming choked by this crust. Suddenly she was entirely outside this fire and, as if possessed, she beat the fire with a club to break the crust and to let some air in. But the dreamer soon got tired and slowly she (the fire) became extinguished. Four days after this dream she began to suffer from acute schizophrenia. In the details of the dream the dreamer had exactly predicted the special course of her psychosis. She became rigid at first and, in effect, encysted. Six weeks afterwards she defended herself once more with all her might against the choking of her life's fire, until finally she became completely extinguished both spiritually and mentally. Now, for some years, she has been like a burnt-out crater (p. 162).

In another example, petrification of others occurs, anticipating the dreamer's own petrification:

. . . a girl of twenty-five years dreamt that she had cooked dinner for her family of five. She had just served it and she now called her parents and her brothers and sister to dinner. Nobody replied. Only her voice returned as if it were an echo from a deep cave. She found the sudden emptiness of the house uncanny. She rushed upstairs to look for her family. In the first bedroom, she could see her two sisters sitting on two beds. In spite of her impatient calls they remained in an unnaturally rigid position and did not even answer her. She went up to her sisters and wanted to shake them. Suddenly she noticed that they were stone statues. She escaped in horror and rushed into her mother's room. Her mother too had turned into stone and was sitting inertly in her arm chair staring into the air with glazed eyes. The dreamer escaped into the room of her father. He stood in the middle of it. In her despair she rushed up to him and, desiring his protection, she threw her arms round his neck. But he too was made of stone and, to her utter horror, he turned into sand when she embraced him. She awoke in absolute terror, and was so stunned by the dream experience that she could not move for some minutes. This same horrible dream was dreamt by the patient on four successive occasions within a few days. At that time she was apparently the picture of mental and physical health. Her parents used to call her the sunshine of the whole family. Ten days after the fourth repetition of the dream, the patient was taken ill with an acute form of schizophrenia displaying severe catatonic symptoms. She fell into a state which was remarkably similar to the physical petrification of her family that she had dreamt about. She was now overpowered in waking life by behaviour patterns that in her dreams she had merely observed in other persons (pp. 162–3).

It seems to be a general law that at some point those very dangers most dreaded can themselves be encompassed to forestall their actual occurrence. Thus, to forgo one's autonomy becomes the means of secretly safeguarding it; to play possum, to feign death, becomes a means of preserving one's aliveness (see Oberndorf, 1950). To turn oneself into a stone becomes a way of not being turned into a stone by someone else. 'Be thou hard,' exhorts Nietzsche. In a sense that Nietzsche did not, I believe, himself intend, to be stony hard and thus far dead forestalls the danger of being turned into a dead thing by another person. Thoroughly to understand oneself (engulf oneself) is a defence against the risk involved in being sucked into the whirlpool of another person's way to comprehending oneself. To consume oneself by one's own love prevents the possibility of being consumed by another.

It seems also that the preferred method of attack on the other is

The Divided Self

based on the same principle as the attack felt to be implicit in the other's relationship to oneself. Thus, the man who is frightened of his own subjectivity being swamped, impinged upon, or congealed by the other is frequently to be found attempting to swamp, to impinge upon, or to kill the other person's subjectivity. The process involves a vicious circle. The more one attempts to preserve one's autonomy and identity by nullifying the specific human individuality of the other, the more it is felt to be necessary to continue to do so, because with each denial of the other person's ontological status, one's own ontological security is decreased, the threat to the self from the other is potentiated and hence has to be even more desperately negated.

In this lesion in the sense of personal autonomy there is both a failure to sustain the sense of oneself as a person with the other, and a failure to sustain it alone. There is a failure to sustain a sense of one's own being without the presence of other people. It is a failure *to be* by oneself, a failure to exist alone. As James put it, 'Other people supply me with my existence.' This appears to be in direct contradiction to the aforementioned dread that other people will deprive him of his existence. But contradictory or absurd as it may be, these two attitudes existed in him side by side, and are indeed entirely characteristic of this type of person.

The capacity to experience oneself as autonomous means that one has really come to realize that one is a separate person from everyone else. No matter how deeply I am committed in joy or suffering to someone else, he is not me, and I am not him. However lonely or sad one may be, one can exist alone. The fact that the other person in his own actuality is not me, is set against the equally real fact that my attachment to him is a part of me. If he dies or goes away, he has gone, but my attachment to him persists. But in the last resort I cannot die another person's death for him, nor can he die my death. For that matter, as Sartre comments on this thought of Heidegger's, he cannot love for me or make my decisions, and I likewise cannot do this for him. In short, he cannot be me, and I cannot be him.

If the individual does not feel himself to be autonomous this means that he can experience neither his separateness from, nor his relatedness to, the other in the usual way. A lack of sense of autonomy implies that one feels one's being to be bound up in the other, or that the other is bound up in oneself, in a sense that transgresses the actual possibilities within the structure of human relatedness. It means that a feeling that one is in a position of ontological dependency on the other (i.e. dependent on the other for one's very being), is substituted for a sense of relatedness and attachment to him based on genuine mutuality. Utter detachment and isolation are regarded as the only alternative to a clam- or vampire-like attachment in which the other person's life-blood is necessary for one's own survival, and yet is a threat to one's survival. Therefore, the polarity is between complete isolation or complete merging of identity rather than between separateness and relatedness. The individual oscillates perpetually, between the two extremes, each equally unfeasible. He comes to live rather like those mechanical toys which have a positive tropism that impels them towards a stimulus until they reach a specific point, whereupon a built-in negative tropism directs them away until the positive tropism takes over again, this oscillation being repeated *ad infinitum*.

Other people were necessary for his existence, said James. Another patient, in the same basic dilemma, behaved in the following way: he maintained himself in isolated detachment from the world for months, living alone in a single room, existing frugally on a few savings, day-dreaming. But in doing this, he began to feel he was dying inside; he was becoming more and more empty, and observed 'a progressive impoverishment of my life mode'. A great deal of his pride and self-esteem was implicated in thus existing on his own, but as his state of depersonalization progressed he would emerge into social life for a brief foray in order to get a 'dose' of other people, but 'not an overdose'. He was like an alcoholic who goes on sudden drinking orgies between dry spells, except that in his case his addiction, of which he was as frightened and ashamed as any repentant alcoholic or drug-addict, was to other people. Within a short while, he would come to feel that he was in danger of being caught up or trapped in the circle he had entered and he would withdraw again into his own isolation in a confusion of frightened hopelessness, suspicion, and shame.

Some of the points discussed above are illustrated in the following two cases:

Case 1. Anxiety at feeling alone. Mrs R.'s presenting difficulty was a dread of being in the street (agoraphobia). On closer inspection, it became clear that her anxiety arose when she began to feel on her own in the street or elsewhere. She could *be* on her own, as long as she did not feel that she was really alone.

Briefly, her story was as follows: she was an only and a lonely child. There was no open neglect or hostility in her family. She felt, however, that her parents were always too engrossed in each other for either of them ever to take notice of her. She grew up wanting to fill this hole in her life but never succeeded in becoming self-sufficient, or absorbed in her own world. Her longing was always to be important and significant *to someone else*. There always had to be someone else. Preferably she wanted to be loved and admired, but, if not, then to be hated was much to be preferred to being unnoticed. She wanted to be *significant* to someone else in whatever capacity, in contrast to her abiding memory of herself as a child that she did not really matter to her parents, that they neither loved nor hated, admired nor were ashamed of her very much.

In consequence, she tried looking at herself in her mirror but never managed to convince herself that she was *somebody*. She never got over being frightened if there was no one there.

She grew into a very attractive girl and was married at seventeen to the first man who really noticed this. Characteristically, it seemed to her, her parents had not noticed that any turmoil had been going on in their daughter until she announced that she was engaged. She was triumphant and self-confident under the warmth of her husband's attentions. But he was an army officer and was shortly posted abroad. She was not able to go with him. At this separation she experienced severe panic.

We should note that her reaction to her husband's absence was not depression or sadness in which she pined or yearned for him. It was panic (as I would suggest) because of the dissolution of something in her, which owed its existence to the presence of her husband and his continued attentions. She was a flower that withered in the absence of one day's rain. However, help came to her through a sudden illness of her mother. She received an urgent plea for help from her father, asking her to come to nurse her mother. For the next year, during her mother's illness, she had never been, as she put it, so much herself. She was the pivot of the household. There was not a trace of panic until after her mother's death when the prospect of leaving the place where she had at last come to mean so much, to join her husband, was very much in her mind. Her experience of the last year had made her feel for the first time that she was now her parents' child. Against this, being her husband's wife was now somehow superfluous.

Again, one notes the absence of grief at her mother's death. At this time she began to reckon up the chances of her being alone in the world. Her mother had died; then there would be her father; possibly her husband: 'beyond that – nothing'. This did not depress her, it frightened her.

She then joined her husband abroad and led a gay life for a few years. She craved for all the attention he could give her but this became less and less. She was restless and unsatisfied. Their marriage broke up and she returned to live in a flat in London with her father. While continuing to stay with her father she became the mistress and model of a sculptor. In this way she had lived for several years before I saw her when she was twenty-eight.

This is the way she talked of the street: 'In the street people come and go about their business. You seldom meet anyone who recognizes you; even if they do, it is just a nod and they pass on or at most you have a few minutes' chat. Nobody knows who you are. Everyone's engrossed in themselves. No one cares about you.' She gave examples of people fainting and everyone's casualness about it. 'No one gives a damn.' It was in this setting and with these considerations in mind that she felt anxiety.

This anxiety was at being in the street alone or rather at feeling on her own. If she went out with or met someone who really knew her, she felt no anxiety.

In her father's flat she was often alone but there it was different. There she never felt *really* on her own. She made his breakfast. Tidying up the beds, washing up, was protracted as long as possible. The middle of the day was a drag. But she didn't mind too much. 'Everything was familiar.' There was her father's chair and his pipe rack. There was a picture of her mother on the wall looking down on her. It was as though all these familiar objects somehow illumined the house with the presence of the people who possessed and used them or had done so as a part of their lives. Thus, although she was by herself at home, she was always able to have someone with her in a magical way. But this magic was dispelled in the noise and anonymity of the busy street.

An insensitive application of what is often supposed to be the classical psycho-analytic theory of hysteria to this patient might attempt to show this woman as unconsciously libidinally bound to her father; with, consequently, unconscious guilt and unconscious need and/or fear of punishment. Her failure to develop lasting libidinal relationships away from her father would seem to support the first view, along with her decision to live with him, to take her mother's place, as it were, and the fact that she spent most of her day, as a woman of twenty-eight, actually thinking about him. Her devotion to her mother in her last illness would be partly the consequences of unconscious guilt at her unconscious ambivalence to her mother; and her anxiety at her mother's death would be anxiety at her unconscious wish for her mother's death coming true. And so on.*

However, the central or pivotal issue in this patient's life is not to be discovered in her 'unconscious'; it is lying quite open for her to see, as well as for us (although this is not to say that there are not many things about herself that this patient does not realize).

The pivotal point around which all her life is centred is her *lack of ontological autonomy*. If she is not in the actual presence of another person who knows her, or if she cannot succeed in evoking this person's presence in his absence, her sense of her own identity drains away from her. Her panic is at the fading away of her being. She is like Tinker Bell. In order to exist she needs someone else to believe in her existence. How necessary that her lover should be a sculptor and that she should be his model! How inevitable, given this basic premiss of her existence, that when her existence was not

* For extremely valuable psycho-analytic contributions to apparently 'hysterical' symptom-formation, see Segal (1954).

recognized she should be suffused with anxiety. For her, *esse* is *percipi*; to be seen, that is, not as an anonymous passer-by or casual acquaintance. It was just that form of seeing which *petrified* her. If she was seen *as* an anonymity, *as* no one who especially mattered or as a *thing*, then she *was* no one in particular. She was as she was seen to be. If there was no one to see her, at the moment, she had to try to conjure up someone (father, mother, husband, lover, at different times in her life) to whom she felt she mattered, for whom she was a *person*, and to imagine herself in his or her presence. If this person on whom her being depended went away or died, it was not a matter for grief, it was a matter for panic.

One cannot transpose her central problem into 'the unconscious'. If one discovers that she has an unconscious phantasy of being a prostitute, this does not explain her anxiety about streetwalking, or her preoccupation with women who fall in the street and are not helped to get on their feet again. The unconscious phantasy is, on the contrary, to be explained by and understood in terms of the central issue implicating her self-being, her being-for-herself. Her fear of being alone is not a 'defence' against incestuous libidinal phantasies or masturbation. She had incestuous phantasies. *These phantasies were a defence against the dread of being alone*, as was her whole 'fixation' on being a daughter. They were a means of overcoming her anxiety at being by herself. The unconscious phantasies of this patient would have an entirely different meaning if her basic existential position were such that she had a starting-point in herself that she could leave behind, as it were in pursuit of gratification. As it was, *her sexual life and phantasies were efforts, not primarily to gain gratification, but to seek first ontological security*. In love-making an illusion of this security was achieved, and on the basis of this illusion gratification was possible.

It would be a profound mistake to call this woman narcissistic in any proper application of the term. She was unable to fall in love with her own reflection. It would be a mistake to translate her problem into phases of psychosexual development, oral, anal, genital. She grasped at sexuality as at a straw as soon as she was 'of age'. She was not frigid. Orgasm could be physically gratifying if she was temporarily secure in the prior ontological sense. In intercourse with someone who loved her (and she was capable of believing in being loved by another), she achieved perhaps her best moments. But they were short-lived. She could not be alone or let her lover be alone with her.

Her need to be taken notice of might facilitate the application of a further cliché to her, that she was an exhibitionist. Once more, such a term is only valid if it is understood existentially. Thus, and this will be discussed in greater detail subsequently, she 'showed herself off' while never 'giving herself away'. That is, she ex-hibited herself while always holding herself in (in-hibited). She was, therefore, always alone and lonely although superficially her difficulty was not in being together with other people; her difficulty was *least in evidence* when she was most together with another person. But it is clear that her realization of the autonomous existence of other people was really quite as tenuous as her belief in her own autonomy. If they were not there, they ceased to exist for her. Orgasm was a means of possessing herself, by holding in her arms the man who possessed her. But she could not be herself, by herself, and so could not really be herself at all.

Case 2. A most curious phenomenon of the personality, one which has been observed for centuries, but which has not yet received its full explanation, is that in which the individual seems to be the vehicle of a personality that is not his own. Someone else's personality seems to 'possess' him and to be finding expression through his words and actions, whereas the individual's own personality is temporarily 'lost' or 'gone'. This happens with all degrees of malignancy. There seem to be all degrees of the same basic process from the simple, benign observation that so-and-so 'takes after his father', or 'that's her mother's temper coming out in her', to the extreme distress of the person who finds himself under a compulsion to take on the characteristics of a personality he may hate and/or feel to be entirely alien to his own.

This phenomenon is one of the most important in occasioning disruption in the sense of one's own identity when it occurs unwanted and compulsively. The dread of this occurring is one factor in the fear of engulfment and implosion. The individual may be afraid to like anyone, for he finds that he is under a compulsion to become like anyone he likes. As I shall seek to show later, this is one motive for schizophrenic withdrawal.

The way in which the individual's self and personality is profoundly modified even to the point of threatened loss of his or her own identity and sense of reality by engulfment by such an alien sub-identity, is illustrated in the following case:

Mrs D., a woman of forty, presented the initial complaint of vague but intense fear. She said she was frightened of everything, 'even of the sky'. She complained of an abiding sense of dissatisfaction, of unaccountable accesses of anger towards her husband, in particular of a 'lack of a sense of responsibility'. Her fear was 'as though somebody was trying to rise up inside and was trying to get out of me'. She was very afraid that she was like her mother, whom she hated. What she called 'unreliability' was a feeling of bafflement and bewilderment which she related to the fact that nothing she did had ever seemed to please her parents. If she did one thing and was told it was wrong, she would do another thing and would find that they still said that that was wrong. She was unable to discover, as she put it, 'what they wanted me to be'. She reproached her parents for this above all, that they hadn't given her any way of knowing who or what she really was or had to become. She could be neither bad nor good with any 'reliability' because her parents were, or she felt they were, completely unpredictable and unreliable in their expression of love or hatred, approval or disapproval. In retrospect, she concluded that they hated her; but at the time, she said, she was too baffled by them and too anxious to discover what she was expected to be to have been able to hate them, let alone love them. She now said that she was looking for 'comfort'. She was looking for a line from me that would give her an indication of the path she was to follow. She found my non-directive attitude particularly hard to tolerate since it seemed to her to be so clearly a repetition of her father's attitude: 'Ask no questions and you'll be told no lies.' For a spell, she became subject to compulsive thinking, in which she was under a necessity to ask such questions as, 'What is this for?' or 'Why is this?', and to provide herself with the answers. She interpreted this to herself as her effort to get comfort from her own thoughts since she could derive comfort from no one. She began to be intensely depressed and to make numerous complaints about her feelings, saying how childish they were. She spoke a great deal about how sorry she was for herself.

Now it seemed to me that 'she' was not really sorry for her own true self. She sounded to me much more like a querulous mother complaining about a difficult child. Her mother, indeed, seemed to be 'coming out of her' all the time, complaining about 'her' childishness. Not only was this so as regards the complaints which 'she' was making about herself, but in other respects as well. For instance, like her mother, she kept screaming at her husband and child; like her mother,* she hated everyone; and like her mother she was for ever crying. In fact, life was a misery to her by the fact that she could never be herself but was always being her mother. She knew, however, that when she felt lonely, lost, frightened, and bewildered she was more her true self. She knew also that she gave her complicity to becoming angry, hating, screaming, crying, or querulous, for if she worked herself up into being like that (i.e. being her mother), she did not feel frightened any more (at the expense, it was true, of being no longer herself). However, the backwash of this manoeuvre was that she was oppressed, when the storm had passed, by a sense of futility (at not having been herself) and a hatred of the person she had been (her mother) and of herself for her self-duplicity. To some extent this patient, once she had become aware of this false way of overcoming the anxiety she was exposed to when she was herself, had to decide whether avoiding experiencing such anxiety, by avoiding being herself, was a cure worse than her dis-ease. The frustration she experienced with me, which called out intense hatred of me, was not fully to be explained by the frustration of libidinal or aggressive drives in the transference, but rather it was what one could term the existential frustration that arose out of the fact that I, by withholding from her the 'comfort' she sought to derive from me, in that *I did not tell her what she was to be*, was imposing upon her the necessity to make her own decision about the person she was to become. Her feeling that she had been denied her birthright because her parents had not

---

* That is, like her notion of what her mother was. I never met her mother and have no idea whether her phantasies of her mother bore any resemblance to her mother as a real person.

discharged their responsibility towards her by giving her a definition of herself that could act as her starting-point in life was intensified by my refusal to offer this 'comfort'. But only by withholding it was it possible to provide a setting in which she could take this responsibility into herself.

In this sense, therefore, the task in psychotherapy was to make, using Jaspers's expression, an appeal to the freedom of the patient. A good deal of the skill in psychotherapy lies in the ability to do this effectively.

Part 2

Thus far I have tried to characterize some of the anxieties that are aspects of a basic ontological insecurity. These anxieties arise in this particular existential setting and are a function of this setting. When a person is secure in his own being, they do not arise with anything like the same force or persistence, since there is no occasion for them to arise and persist in this way.

In the absence of such basic security, life must, nevertheless, go on. The question that one must now attempt to answer is what form of relation with himself is developed by the ontologically insecure person. I shall try to show how some such persons do not seem to have a sense of that basic unity which can abide through the most intense conflicts with oneself, but seem rather to have come to experience themselves as primarily split into a mind and a body. Usually they feel most closely identified with the 'mind'.

It is with certain of the consequences of this basic way in which one's own being can become organized within itself that the remainder of this book will be principally concerned. This split will be seen as an attempt to deal with the basic underlying insecurity. In some cases it may be a means of effectively living with it or even an attempt to transcend it; but it is also liable to perpetuate the anxieties it is in some measure a defence against and it may provide the starting position for a line of development that ends in psychosis. This last possibility is always present if the individual begins to identify himself too exclusively with that part of him which feels *unembodied*. In this chapter I shall first contrast schematically and in the most general terms the *embodied* to the *unembodied* self: then, in subsequent chapters, I shall leave aside all the possibilities of this position which do not bring anyone to a psychiatrist as a patient, and follow through in some detail those consequences of this position which result in severe disruption of the individual's being as a whole and can lead, therefore, to psychosis.

THE EMBODIED AND UNEMBODIED SELF

Everyone, even the most unembodied person, experiences himself as inextricably bound up with or in his body. In ordinary circumstances, to the extent that one feels one's body to be alive, real, and substantial, one feels oneself alive, real, and substantial. Most people feel they began when their bodies began and that they will end when their bodies die. We could say that such a person experiences himself as *embodied*.

This, however, need not be the case. Quite apart from those 'ordinary' people who feel in moments of stress partially dissociated from their bodies, there are individuals who do not go through life absorbed in their bodies but rather find themselves to be, as they always have been, somewhat detached from their bodies. Of such a person one might say that 'he' has never become quite incarnate and he may speak of himself as more or less *unembodied*.

Here we have a basic difference in the self's position in life. We would almost have, if the embodiment or unembodiment were ever complete in either direction, two different ways of being human. Most people may regard the former as normal and healthy and the latter as abnormal and pathological. Throughout this study such an evaluation is quite irrelevant. From certain points of view, one may regard embodiment as desirable. It is possible to suggest from another point of view that the individual should try to disentangle himself from his body and thereby achieve a desired state of discarnate spirituality.*

* Bultmann, for instance, in his *Primitive Christianity* (1956) gives an excellent short account of the gnostic ideal of divorce of soul (the real self) and body. Redemption was conceived of as a total breach of dissolution of soul and body. He quotes a gnostic text as follows: '[the body is] the dark prison, the living death, the sense-endowed corpse, the grave thou bearest about with thee, the grave which thou carriest around with thee, the thievish

What we have are two basic existential settings. The difference in setting does not preclude every basic issue, good and bad, life and death, identity, reality and irreality, from arising in the one context as in the other, but the radically different contexts in which they occur determine the basic ways in which they are lived. These two extreme possibilities require to be examined in terms of the way in which an individual whose position approximated to one or other of these possibilities would experience his relatedness to other persons and the world.

The embodied person has a sense of being flesh and blood and bones, of being biologically alive and real: he knows himself to be substantial. To the extent that he is thoroughly 'in' his body, he is likely to have a sense of personal continuity in time. He will experience himself as subject to the dangers that threaten his body, the dangers of attack, mutilation, disease, decay, and death. He is implicated in bodily desire, and the gratifications and frustrations of the body. The individual thus has as his starting-point an experience of his body as a base from which he can be a person with other human beings.

However, although his being is not cleft into himself as 'mind' and himself as body, he can, nevertheless, be divided against himself in many ways. In some ways, his position is more precarious than that of the individual who is somewhat divorced from his body, since the first individual lacks that sense of being inviolate from physical harm sometimes felt by the partially embodied person.

For instance, a man who had been a mental hospital patient for two long periods with schizophrenic breakdowns told me of his reactions on being attacked in an alleyway at night, at a time when he was quite sane. As he walked along the alley two men approached him from the opposite direction. When they were level with him, one of them suddenly hit at him with a cosh. The blow was not accurately aimed and stunned him only momentarily. He staggered but recovered enough to turn round and attack his

---

companion who hateth thee in loving thee, and envieth thee in hating thee . . .' (p. 169).

For studies of the mind-body split from a psychopathological viewpoint, see Clifford Scott (1949) and Winnicott (1945, 1949).

assailants although he himself was unarmed; after a brief scuffle they ran off.

What is interesting is this man's way of experiencing the incident. When he was struck his first reaction was of surprise; then, while he was still partially stunned, he thought how pointless it was for these men to hit him. He had no money on him. They could get nothing from him. '*They could only beat me up but they could not do me any real harm.*' That is, any damage to his body could not *really* hurt him. There is a sense of course, in which such an attitude could be the height of wisdom when, for example, Socrates maintains that no harm can possibly be done to a good man. In this case, 'he' and his 'body' were dissociated. In such a situation he felt much less afraid than the ordinary person, because from his position he had nothing to lose that essentially belonged to him. But, on the other hand, his life was full of anxieties that do not arise for the ordinary person. The embodied person, fully implicated in his body's desires, needs, and acts, is subject to the guilt and anxiety attendant on such desires, needs, and actions. He is subject to the body's frustrations as well as to its gratifications. Being in his body is no haven from possibly crushing self-condemnation. Being embodied as such is no insurance against feelings of hopelessness or meaninglessness. Beyond his body, he still has to know who he is. His body may come to be experienced as decayed, poisoned, dying. In short, the body-self is not an inviolable stronghold against the corrosion of ontological doubts and uncertainties: it is not in itself a bulwark against psychosis. Conversely, the split in the experience of one's own being into unembodied and embodied parts is no more an index of latent psychosis than is total embodiment any guarantee of sanity.

However, although it by no means follows that the individual genuinely based on his body is an otherwise unified and whole person, it does mean that he has a starting-point integral in this respect at least. Such a starting-point will be the precondition for a different hierarchy of possibilities from those open to the person who experiences himself in terms of a self-body dualism.

THE UNEMBODIED SELF

In this position the individual experiences his self as being more or less divorced or detached from his body. *The body is felt more as one object among other objects in the world than as the core of the individual's own being.* Instead of being the core of his true self, the body is felt as the core of a *false self*, which a detached, disembodied, 'inner', 'true' self looks on at with tenderness, amusement, or hatred as the case may be.

Such a divorce of self from body deprives the unembodied self from direct participation in any aspect of the life of the world, which is mediated exclusively through the body's perceptions, feelings and movements (expressions, gestures, words, actions, etc.). The unembodied self, as onlooker at all the body does, engages in nothing directly. Its functions come to be observation, control, and criticism *vis-à-vis* what the body is experiencing and doing, and those operations which are usually spoken of as purely 'mental'.

The unembodied self becomes hyper-conscious.

It attempts to posit its own imagos.

It develops a relationship with itself and with the body which can become very complex.

Now, whereas a great many studies in the psychopathology of the embodied person have been made, comparatively little has been written about the person whose being is radically split in this way. Temporary states of dissociation between the self and body have been studied, of course, but usually these dissociations are seen as arising from an original position wherein the self began as embodied, became temporarily dissociated under stress, and returned to its original embodied position when the crisis was over.

A 'BORDERLINE' CASE – DAVID

I shall give a straightforward account of David with the minimum of comment because I want the reader to be quite clear that such people and such problems exist in reality and are not matters of my invention. This case can also serve as a basis for much of the general discussion in the subsequent section.

David was eighteen when I saw him. He was an only child whose mother had died when he was ten. Since then he had lived with his father. From grammar school he had gone to university to study philosophy. His father could not see the point of his son consulting a psychiatrist as there was nothing, in his view, for him to see a psychiatrist about. His tutor, however, was worried about the boy because he seemed to be hallucinated and acted in various somewhat odd ways. For instance, he attended lectures in a cloak, which he wore over his shoulders and arms; he carried a cane; his whole manner was entirely artificial; his speech was made up largely of quotations.

His father's account of him was very meagre. He had always been perfectly normal, and he thought his present eccentricities were simply an adolescent phase. He had always been a very good child, who did everything he was told and never caused any trouble. His mother had been devoted to him. He was inseparable from her. He had been 'very brave' when she died and had done everything to help his father. He did the housework, cooked the meals, bought most of the food. He 'took over' from his mother or 'took after' her, even to the extent of showing her flair for embroidery, tapestry, and interior decoration. All this his father commended and spoke highly of.

The boy was a most fantastic-looking character – an adolescent Kierkegaard played by Danny Kaye. The hair was too long, the collar too large, the trousers too short, the shoes too big, and withall, his second-hand theatre cloak and cane! He was not simply eccentric: I could not escape the impression that this young man was *playing* at being eccentric. The whole effect was mannered and contrived. But why should anyone wish to contrive such an effect?*

He was indeed quite a practised actor, for he had been playing one part or other at least since his mother's death. Before that, he said, 'I had simply been what she wanted.' Of her death he said, 'As far as I can remember I was rather pleased. Perhaps I felt some sorrow; I would like to think so anyway.' Until his mother's death

---

* He was not unlike 'Tertian' in Lionel Trilling's brilliant short story,

he had simply been what she wanted him to be. After her death it was no easier for him to be himself. He had grown up taking entirely for granted that what he called his 'self' and his 'personality' were two quite separate things. He had never seriously imagined any other possibility and he took it equally for granted that everyone else was constructed along similar lines. His view of human nature in general, based on his own experience of himself, was that everyone was an actor. It is important to realize that this was a settled conviction or assumption about human beings which governed his life. This made it very easy for him to be anything his mother wanted, because all his actions simply belonged to some part or other he was playing. If they could be said to belong to his self at all, they belonged only to a 'false self', a self that acted according to *her* will, not his.

His self was never directly revealed in and through his actions. It seemed to be the case that he had emerged from his infancy with his '*own self*' on the one hand, and 'what his mother wanted him to be', his 'personality', on the other; he had started from there and made it his aim and ideal to make the split between his own self (which only he knew) and what other people could see of him, as complete as possible. He was further impelled to this course by the fact that despite himself he had always felt shy, self-conscious, and vulnerable. By always playing a part he found he could in some measure overcome his shyness, self-consciousness, and vulnerability. He found reassurance in the consideration that whatever he was doing he was not being himself. Thus, he used that same form of defence which has been already mentioned: in an effort to mitigate anxiety he aggravated the conditions that were occasioning it.

The important point he always kept in mind was that he was playing a part. Usually, in his mind, he was playing the part of someone else, but sometimes he played the part of himself (his own self): that is, he was not simply and spontaneously himself, but he *played* at being himself. His ideal was, *never to give himself away to others*. Consequently he practised the most tortuous equivocation towards others in the parts he played. Towards himself, however, his ideal was to be as utterly frank and honest as possible.

The whole organization of his being rested on the disjunction of his inner 'self' and his outer 'personality'. It is remarkable that this state of affairs had existed for years without his 'personality', i.e. his way of behaving with others, appearing unusual.

The outward appearance could not reveal the fact that his 'personality' was no true self-expression but was largely a series of *impersonations*. The part he regarded himself as having been playing most of his schooldays was that of a rather precocious schoolboy with a sharp wit, but somewhat cold. He said, however, that when he was fifteen he had realized that this part was becoming unpopular because '*It* had a nasty tongue'. Accordingly he decided to modify this part into a more likeable character, 'with good results'.

However, his efforts to sustain this organization of his being were threatened in two ways. The first did not trouble him too seriously. It was the risk of being spontaneous. As an actor, he wished always to be detached from the part he was playing. Thereby he felt himself to be master of the situation, in entire conscious control of his expressions and actions, calculating with precision their effects on others. To be spontaneous was merely stupid. It was simply putting oneself at other people's mercy.

The second threat was the more actual, and one upon which he had not calculated. If he had a personal source of complaint to bring to me, it was based on this threat, which indeed was beginning to disrupt his whole technique of living.

All through his childhood he had been very fond of playing parts in front of the mirror. Now in front of the mirror he continued to play parts, but in this one special instance he allowed himself to become absorbed into the part he played (to be spontaneous). This he felt was his undoing. The parts he played in front of the mirror were always women's parts. He dressed himself up in his mother's clothes, which had been kept. He rehearsed female parts from the great tragedies. But then he found he could not stop playing the part of a woman. He caught himself compulsively walking like a woman, talking like a woman, even seeing and thinking as a woman might see and think. This was his present position, and this was his explanation for his fantastic get-up. For, he said, he found that he was driven to dress up and act in his present manner as the only way to arrest the womanish part that threatened to engulf not only his actions but even his 'own' self as well, and to rob him of his much cherished control and mastery of his being. Why he was driven into playing this role, which he hated and which he knew everyone laughed at, he could not understand. But this 'schizophrenic' role was the only refuge he knew from being entirely engulfed by the woman who was inside him, and always seemed to be coming out of him.

This is the type of person who will be discussed in the following pages. It is evident that it will not be possible to understand the type of person of whom David is a most 'typical' example without considering in much more detail this type of schizoid organization. In David's case, we would have to describe in detail the nature of his 'own' self, its relation to his 'personality', the importance of being 'self-conscious' and 'vulnerable' to him, the meaning of his deliberate impersonations, and the way in which an alien 'personality' comes to intrude itself (herself) into his 'personality', apparently autonomously and outside his control, and to threaten the existence even of his 'own' self.

The central split is between what David called his 'own' self and what he called his 'personality'. This dichotomy is encountered again and again. What the individual variously terms his 'own', 'inner', 'true', 'real', self is experienced as divorced from all activity that is observable by another, what David called his 'personality'. One may conveniently call this 'personality' the individual's 'false self' or a 'false-self system'. The reason I suggest that one speaks of a *false-self system* is that the 'personality', false self, mask, 'front', or persona that such individuals wear may consist in an amalgam of various part-selves, none of which is so fully developed as to have a comprehensive 'personality' of its own. Close acquaintance with such a person reveals that his observable behaviour may comprise quite deliberate impersonations along with compulsive actions of every kind. One is evidently witness not to a single false self but to a number of only partially elaborated fragments of what might constitute a personality, if any single one had full sway. It seems best, therefore, to call the total of such elements a false-self system, or a system of false selves.

The 'self' in such a schizoid organization is usually more or less unembodied. It is experienced as a mental entity. It enters the

condition called by Kierkegaard 'shutupness'. The individual's
actions are not felt as expressions of his self. His actions, all that
David called his 'personality' and which I have proposed to call his
false-self system, become dissociated and partly autonomous. The
self is not felt to participate in the doings of the false self or selves,
and all its or their actions are felt to be increasingly false and
futile. The self, on the other hand, shut up with itself, regards
itself as the 'true' self and the persona as false. The individual
complains of futility, of lack of spontaneity, but he may be cultivating his lack of spontaneity and thus aggravating his sense of
futility. He says he is not real and is outside reality and not properly
alive. Existentially, he is quite right. The self is extremely aware of
itself, and observes the false self, usually highly critically. It is
characteristic of the organization of a false self or persona, on the
other hand, that one way in which it is usually incomplete is in its
very imperfect reflective awareness. But the self may feel itself in
danger from the overall spread of the false-self system or from one
particular part of it (cf. David's dread of female impersonation).

The individual in this position is invariably terrifyingly 'self-
conscious' (see Chapter 7) in the sense in which this word is used to
mean the exact opposite, namely, the feeling of being under observation by the *other*.

These changes in the relationship between the different aspects
of the person's relation to himself are constantly associated with
his *inter*-personal relationships. These are complex and never quite
the same from person to person.

The individual's self-relationship becomes a pseudo-inter-
personal one, and the self treats the false selves as though they were
other people whom it depersonalizes. David, for instance, referring
to a part he played which he found was disliked, said: '*It* had a
nasty tongue.' From within, the self now looks out at the false
things being said and done and detests the speaker and doer as
though he were someone else. In all this there is an attempt to
create relationships to persons and things within the individual
without recourse to the outer world of persons and things at all.
The individual is developing a microcosmos within himself; but,
of course, this autistic, private, intra-individual 'world' is not a
feasible substitute for the only world there really is, the shared

world. If this were a feasible project then there would be no need for psychosis.

Such a schizoid individual in *one* sense is trying to be omnipotent by enclosing within his own being, without recourse to a creative relationship with others, modes of relationship that require the effective presence to him of other people and of the outer world. He would appear to be, in an unreal, impossible way, all persons and things to himself. The imagined advantages are safety for the true self, isolation and hence freedom from others, self-sufficiency, and control.

The actual disadvantages that can be mentioned at this point are that this project is impossible and, being a false hope, leads on to persistent despair; secondly, a persistent, haunting sense of futility is the equally inevitable outcome, since the hidden shut-up self, in disowning participation (except, as David's case, by appearing as another persona) in the quasi-autonomous activities of the false-self systems, is living only 'mentally'. Moreover, this shut-up self, being isolated, is unable to be enriched by outer experience, and so the whole inner world comes to be more and more impoverished, until the individual may come to feel he is merely a vacuum. The sense of being able to do anything and the feeling of possessing everything then exist side by side with a feeling of impotence and emptiness. The individual who may at one time have felt predominantly 'outside' the life going on *there*, which he affects to despise as petty and commonplace compared to the richness he has *here*, inside himself, now longs to get *inside* life again, and get life *inside* himself, so dreadful is his inner deadness.

The crucial feature of the schizoid individual of this type that we have to understand is the nature of the anxieties to which he is subject. We have already outlined some of the forms these anxieties take under the terms engulfment, implosion, and the dread of losing inner autonomy, freedom; in short, being turned from a man with subjectivity to a thing, a mechanism, a stone, an it, being petrified.

We have yet to study how these anxieties are potentiated by the development of the schizoid organization.

When the self partially abandons the body and its acts, and withdraws into mental activity, it experiences itself as an entity perhaps localized somewhere in the body. We have suggested that this withdrawal is in part an effort to preserve its being, since relationship of any kind with others is experienced as a threat to the self's identity. The self feels safe only in hiding, and isolated. Such a self can, of course, be isolated at any time whether other people are present or not.

But this does not work.

No one feels more 'vulnerable', more liable to be exposed by the look of another person than the schizoid individual. If he is not acutely aware of being seen by others ('self-conscious'), he has temporarily avoided his anxiety becoming manifest by one or other of two methods. Either he turns the other person into a thing, and depersonalizes or objectifies his own feelings towards this thing, or he affects indifference. The depersonalization of the person and/or the attitude of indifference are closely related but not quite identical. The depersonalized person can be used, manipulated, acted upon. As we stated above (Chapter 1), the essential feature of a *thing* as opposed to a *person* is that a thing has no subjectivity of its own, and hence can have no reciprocal intentions. In the attitude of indifference the person or thing is treated with casualness, or callousness, as though he or it did not matter, ultimately as though he or it did not exist. A person minus subjectivity can still be important. A thing can still matter a great deal. Indifference denies to persons and to things their significance. Petrification, we remember, was one of Perseus's methods of killing his enemies. By means of the eyes in Medusa's head, he turned them into stones. Petrification is one way of killing. Of course, to feel that another person is treating or regarding one not as a person but as a thing need not itself be frightening if one is sufficiently sure of one's own existence. Thus, being a thing in someone else's eyes does not represent to the 'normal' person a catastrophic threat, but to the schizoid individual every pair of eyes is in a Medusa's head which he feels has power actually to kill or deaden something precariously vital in him. He tries therefore to forestall his own petrification by turning others into stones. By doing this he feels he can achieve some measure of safety.

Generally speaking, the schizoid individual is not erecting defences against the loss of a part of his body. His whole effort is rather to preserve his *self*. This, as we have pointed out, is precariously established; he is subject to the dread of his own dissolution into non-being, into what William Blake described in the last resort as 'chaotic non-entity'. His autonomy is threatened with engulfment. He has to guard himself against losing his subjectivity and sense of being alive. In so far as he feels empty, the full, substantial, living reality of others is an impingement which is always liable to get out of hand and become implosive, threatening to overwhelm and obliterate his self completely as a gas will obliterate a vacuum, or as water will gush in and entirely fill an empty dam. The schizoid individual fears a real live dialectical relationship with real live people. He can relate himself only to depersonalized persons, to phantoms of his own phantasies (imagos), perhaps to things, perhaps to animals.

We suggest, therefore, that the schizoid state we are describing can be understood as an attempt to preserve a being that is precariously structured. We shall suggest later that the initial structuralization of being into its basic elements occurs in early infancy. In normal circumstances, this occurs in such a way as to be so conclusively stable in its basic elements (for instance, the continuity of time, the distinction between the self and not-self, phantasy and reality), that it can henceforth be taken for granted: on this stable base, a considerable amount of plasticity can exist in what we call a person's 'character'. In the schizoid character structure, on the other hand, there is an insecurity in the laying down of the foundations and a compensatory rigidity in the superstructure.

If the whole of the individual's being cannot be defended, the individual retracts his lines of defence until he withdraws within a central citadel. He is prepared to write off everything he is, except his 'self'. But the tragic paradox is that the more the self is defended in this way, the more it is destroyed. The apparent eventual destruction and dissolution of these If in schizophrenic conditions is accomplished not by external attacks from the enemy (actual or supposed), from without, but by the devastation caused by the inner defensive manoeuvres themselves.

5 The inner self in the schizoid condition

In the schizoid condition here described there is a persistent scission between the self and the body. What the individual regards as his true self is experienced as more or less disembodied, and bodily experience and actions are in turn felt to be part of the false-self system.

It is now necessary to consider the two elements in this split in more detail, and also the relationship of the one to the other. First, we consider the mental or unembodied self.

It is well known that temporary states of dissociation of the self from the body occur in normal people. In general, one can say that it is a response that appears to be available to most people who find themselves enclosed within a threatening experience from which there is no physical escape. Prisoners in concentration camps *tried* to feel that way, for the camp offered no possible way out either spatially or at the end of a period of time. The only way out was by a psychical withdrawal 'into' one's self and 'out of' the body. This dissociation is characteristically associated with such thoughts as 'This is like a dream', 'This seems unreal', 'I can't believe this is true', 'Nothing seemed to be touching me', 'I cannot take it in', 'This is not happening to me', i.e. with feelings of estrangement and derealization. The body may go on acting in an outwardly normal way, but inwardly it is felt to be acting on its own, automatically.

However, despite the dream-nature or unreality of experience, and the automatic nature of action, the self is at the same time far from 'sleepy'; indeed, it is excessively alert, and may be thinking and observing with exceptional lucidity.

The temporary estrangement of the self from the body may be represented in dreams.

A girl of nineteen, the date of whose marriage was fast approaching, a marriage she had come to dread for various reasons, dreamed that she was in the back seat of a car, which was driving itself. This girl was not a basically schizoid person but was reacting by a schizoid defence to a particular situation.

R. had a dream shortly before starting treatment. He was on the footplate of a bus. The bus had no driver. He jumped off and the bus went on to crash. One is tempted to regard a dream he had after four months of psychotherapy as a measure of some change in a desirable direction. 'I am running after a bus. Suddenly I'm on the footplate of the bus, and at the same time, I'm running after it. I'm trying to join up with myself on the bus but I can't entirely catch up on the bus. I felt frightened at this.'

One could multiply instances of this common experience of temporary dissociation. Sometimes it is intentionally induced; more often, it occurs without the individual's control. But in the patients here considered, the splitting is not simply a temporary reaction to a specific situation of great danger, which is reversible when the danger is past. It is, on the contrary, a basic orientation to life, and if it is followed back through their lives one usually finds that they seem, in fact, to have emerged from the early months of infancy with this split already under way. The 'normal' individual, in a situation all can see to be threatening to his being and to offer no real sense of escape, develops a schizoid state in trying to get outside it, if not physically, at least mentally: he becomes a mental observer, who looks on, detached and impassive, at what his body is doing or what is being done to his body. If this is so in the 'normal', it is at least possible to suppose that the individual whose abiding mode of being-in-the-world is of this split nature is living in what to him, if not to us, is a world that threatens his being from all sides, and from which there is no exit. This is indeed the case for such people. For them the world is a prison without bars, a concentration camp without barbed wire.

The paranoic has specific persecutors. Someone is against him. There is a plot on foot to steal his brains. A machine is concealed in the wall of his bedroom which emits mind rays to soften his brain, or to send electric shocks through him while he is asleep. The person I am describing *feels* at this phase *persecuted by reality itself*. The world as it is, and other people as they are, are the dangers.

The self then seeks by being unembodied to transcend the world and hence to be safe. But a self is liable to develop which feels it is outside all experience and activity. It becomes a vacuum. Everything is there, outside; nothing is here, inside. Moreover, the constant dread of all that is there, of being overwhelmed, is potentiated rather than mitigated by the need to keep the world at bay. Yet the self may at the same time long more than anything for participation in the world. Thus, its greatest longing is felt as its greatest weakness and giving in to this weakness is its greatest dread, since in participation the individual fears that his vacuum will be obliterated, that he will be engulfed or otherwise lose his identity, which has come to be equated with the maintenance of the transcendence of the self even though this is a transcendence in a void.

This detachment of the self means that the self is never revealed directly in the individual's expressions and actions, nor does it experience anything spontaneously or immediately. The self's relationship to the other is always at one remove. The direct and immediate transactions between the individual, the other, and the world, even in such basic respects as perceiving and acting, all come to be meaningless, futile, and false. One can represent the alternative state of affairs schematically as shown opposite.

Objects perceived by the self are experienced as real. Thoughts and feelings of which the self is the agent are alive and are felt to have point. Actions to which the self is committed are felt as genuine.

If the individual delegates all transactions between himself and the other to a system within his being which is not 'him', then the world is experienced as unreal, and all that belongs to this system is felt to be false, futile, and meaningless.

Everyone is subject to a certain extent at one time or another to such moods of futility, meaninglessness, and purposelessness, but in schizoid individuals these moods are particularly insistent. These moods arise from the fact that the doors of perception and/or the

Figure 1

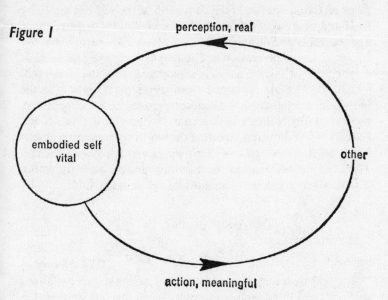

Figure 2

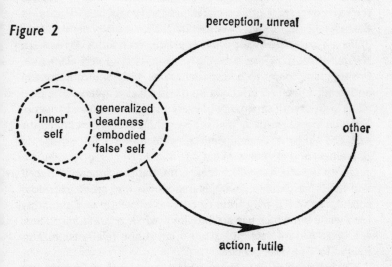

gates of action are not in the command of the self but are being
lived and operated by a false self. The unrealness of perceptions
and the falsity and meaninglessness of all activity are the necessary
consequences of perception and activity being in the command of
a false self – a system partially dissociated from the 'true' self,
which is, therefore, excluded from direct participation in the
individual's relatedness with other persons and the world. A
pseudo-duality is thus experienced in the individual's own being.
Instead of the individual meeting the world with an integral selfhood, he disavows part of his own being along with his dis-
avowal of immediate attachment to things and people in the world.
This can be represented schematically as follows:

Instead of

$$(self/body) \rightleftharpoons other$$

the situation is

$$self \rightleftharpoons (body\text{-}other)$$

The self, therefore, is precluded from having a direct relationship with real things and real people. When this has happened in
patients, one is witness to the struggle which ensues to preserve
the self's own sense of its own realness, aliveness, and identity. In
the first scheme, one has a benign circle. *The reality of the world and
of the self are mutually potentiated by the direct relationship between
self and other*. In *Figure 2*, there is a vicious circle. Every element in
this diagram comes to be experienced as more and more unreal
and dead. Love is precluded and dread takes its place. The final
effect is an overall experience of everything having come to a stop.
Nothing moves; nothing is alive; everything is dead, including the
self. The self by its detachment is precluded from a full experience
of realness and aliveness. What one might call *a creative relationship* with the other, in which there is mutual enrichment of the self
and the other (benign circle), is impossible, and an *interaction* is
substituted which may seem to operate efficiently and smoothly
for a while but which has no 'life' in it (*sterile relationship*). There
is a quasi-it-it interaction instead of an I-thou relationship. This
interaction is a dead process.

The inner self seeks to live by certain (apparently) compensating
advantages. Such a self cherishes certain ideals. One, which was

very clear in the schoolboy David, is an inner honesty. Whereas all the exchanges with the other may be fraught with pretence, equivocation, hypocrisy, the individual seeks to achieve a relationship with himself that is scrupulously sincere, honest, frank. Anything may be concealed from others, but nothing must be hidden from himself. In this, the self attempts to become 'a relationship which relates itself to itself'* to the exclusion of everything and anything. We have here the seeds of secondary splitting within the self. The individual's being having become cleft into a 'true' and a 'false' self, the true and false selves lose their realness as already indicated, but also they both in turn break into sub-systems within themselves. Thus, in the relationship that the self has with itself, one finds a second duality developing whereby the inner self splits to have a sado-masochistic relationship with itself. When this happens, the inner self, which had arisen, we suggested, in the first place as a means of clinging to a precarious sense of identity, begins to lose even what identity it had to begin with. (In the clinical illustrations, see particularly Rose, p. 150.)

The substitution of an interaction with the other results in the individual coming to live in a frightening world in which dread is unmitigated by love. The individual is frightened of the world, afraid that any impingement will be total, will be implosive, penetrative, fragmenting, and engulfing. He is afraid of letting anything of himself 'go', of coming out of himself, of losing himself in any experience, etc., because he will be depleted, exhausted, emptied, robbed, sucked dry.

The isolation of the self is a corollary, therefore, of the need to be in control. He prefers to *steal*, rather than to be given. He prefers to give, rather than have anything, as he feels, stolen from him; i.e. he has to be in control of who or what comes into him, and of who or what leaves him. This defensive system is elaborated, we suggest, to make up for the primary lack of ontological security. The individual who is sure of his own being does not require to adopt such measures. However, the effort to sustain a transcendent self, out of danger and in remote control of direct experiencing and

* Kierkegaard's phrase in *The sickness unto death* (1954), but used here with quite different connotations.

action, issues in unwished-for consequences that may far outweigh what apparent gains there seemed to be.

Since the self, in maintaining its isolation and detachment does not commit itself to a creative relationship with the other and is preoccupied with the figures of phantasies, thought, memories, etc. (imagos), which cannot be directly observable by or directly expressed to others, anything (in a sense) is possible. Whatever failures or successes come the way of the false-self system, the self is able to remain uncommitted and undefined. In phantasy, the self can be anyone, anywhere, do anything, have everything. It is thus omnipotent and completely free – but only in phantasy. Once commit itself to any real project and it suffers agonies of humiliation – not necessarily for any failure, but simply because it has to subject itself to necessity and contingency. It is omnipotent and free only in phantasy. The more this phantastic omnipotence and freedom are indulged, the more weak, helpless, and fettered it becomes in actuality. The illusion of omnipotence and freedom can be sustained only within the magic circle of its own shut-upness in phantasy. And in order that this attitude be not dissipated by the slightest intrusion of reality, phantasy and reality have to be kept apart.

Sartre expresses this split very well in his *Psychology of Imagination* (1950, pp. 165–6):

... we can recognize two distinct selves in us: the imaginary self with its tendencies and desires – and the real self. There are imaginary sadists and masochists, persons of violent imagination. At each moment our imaginary self breaks in pieces and disappears at contact with reality, yielding its place to the real self. For the real and the imaginary cannot coexist by their very nature. It is a matter of two types of objects, of feelings and actions that are completely irreducible.

Hence, we may think that individuals will have to be classified in two large categories, according to whether they prefer to lead an imaginary life or a real life. But we must understand what a preference for the imaginary signifies. It is not at all a matter of preferring one sort of object to another. For instance, we should not believe that the schizophrenic and morbid dreamers in general try to substitute an unreal and more seductive and brighter content for the real content of their life, and that they seek to forget the unreal character of their images by reacting to them as if they were actual objects actually present. To prefer the imaginary is not only to prefer a richness, a beauty, an imaginary luxury to the existing mediocrity *in spite of* their unreal nature. It is also to adopt 'imaginary' feelings and actions for the sake of their imaginary nature. It is not only this or that image that is chosen, but the imaginary state with everything it implies; it is not only an escape from the content of the real (poverty, frustrated love, failure of one's enterprise, etc.), but from the form of the real itself, its character of *presence*, the sort of response it demands of us, the adaptation of our actions to the object, the inexhaustibility of perception, their independence, the very way our feelings have of developing themselves.

This split between phantasy and reality is central to Minkowski's concept of autism.

But the person who does not act in reality and only acts in phantasy *becomes himself unreal*. The actual 'world' for that person becomes shrunken and impoverished. The 'reality' of the physical world and other persons ceases to be used as a pabulum for the creative exercise of imagination, and hence comes to have less and less significance in itself. Phantasy, without being either in some measure embodied in reality, or itself enriched by injections of 'reality', becomes more and more empty and volatilized. The 'self' whose relatedness to reality is already tenuous becomes less and less a reality-self, and more and more phantasticized as it becomes more and more engaged in phantastic relationships with its own phantoms (imagos).

Without an open two-way circuit between phantasy and reality anything becomes possible in phantasy. Destructiveness in phantasy goes on without the wish to make compensatory reparation, for the guilt that prompts towards preserving and making amends loses its urgency. Destructiveness in phantasy can thus rage on, unchecked, until the world and the self are reduced, in phantasy, to dust and ashes. In the schizophrenic state the world is in ruins, and the self is (apparently) dead. No amount of frantic activity seems to have the power to bring back life again.

Thus, what comes about has the very opposite effect to that desired. Real toads invade the imaginary gardens* and ghosts walk in the real streets. Thus, in another way, the identity of the self is again jeopardized.

* Marianne Moore, *Collected Poems.*

It is not quite correct to say that the self is related only to itself. It is necessary to qualify this in one respect and amplify it in another. We have already qualified this statement by making it clear that we are speaking of a direct and immediate relationship. It is this direct and immediate relationship with the other, and even with those aspects of the person's own being outside the enclave of the self, that becomes impossible.

A patient, for instance, who conducted his life along relatively 'normal' lines outwardly but operated this inner split, presented as his original complaint the fact that he could never have intercourse with his wife but only with his own image of her. That is, his body had physical relations with her body, but his mental self, while this was going on, could only look on at what his body was doing and/or *imagine* himself having intercourse with his wife as an object of his imagination. He gave the guilt he was subject to for doing this as his reason for seeking psychiatric advice.*

This is an example of what I mean by saying that phantasy and reality are kept apart. The self avoids being related directly to real persons but relates itself to itself and to the objects which it itself posits. *The self can relate itself with immediacy to an object which is an object of its own imagination or memory but not to a real person.* This is not always apparent, of course, even to the individual himself, still less to anyone else. The wife of the above patient was quite unaware that he felt that 'he' had never had intercourse directly with her; he had had intercourse only with his imago of her which happened to coincide sufficiently well with her in reality for no one but himself to know the difference.

One feature of this subterfuge is that the self is able to enjoy a sense of freedom which it fears it will lose if it abandons itself to the real. This applies both to perception and action. This patient, however lonely he was in the moments of greatest physical intimacy, was at any rate safe, as he felt: his mind remained free, albeit this freedom became something to which he felt condemned.

An equivalent issue arises in respect of action. The individual's actions may appear from another person's point of view to be un-

* The remarks on the guilt experienced by Peter (Chapter 8) are relevant to this form of schizoid guilt which, I believe, has not been sufficiently recognized.

equivocal and committed, but one finds that 'he' is going through the actions of doing something which 'he' feels he is not doing 'really'. Thus the above patient said that, although Kinsey might put down that he had intercourse two to four times per week for ten years, 'he' knew that he had never had intercourse 'really'. The transition from this type of statement to the statement of the psychotic millionaire who says he has no money 'really' is a decisive yet subtle one. As we shall see in Chapter 10, the transition seems to consist in a loss of the sense of the realness of the Kinsey Report reality so total that the individual expresses the 'existential' truth about himself with the same matter-of-factness that we employ about facts that can be consensually validated in a shared world.

This patient would have been psychotic, for instance, if, instead of saying that he never had intercourse with his wife 'really', he had insisted that the woman with whom he had intercourse was not his real wife. In a sense, this would be perfectly true: it would be existentially true because in this existential sense his 'real' wife was the object of his own imagination (a phantom or imago), rather than the other human being in bed with him.

The unembodied self of the schizoid individual cannot really be married to anyone. It exists in perpetual isolation. And yet, of course, this isolation and inner non-commitment are not without self-deception.

There is something final and definitive about an act, which this type of person regards with suspicion. Action is the dead end of possibility. It scleroses freedom. If it cannot be utterly eschewed, then every act must be of such an equivocal nature that the 'self' can never be trapped in it.

Hegel (1949, pp. 349–50) says this about the act:

The act is something simple, determinate, universal, to be grasped as an abstract, distinctive whole; it is murder, theft, a benefit, a deed of bravery, and so on, and what it *is* can be *said* of it. It *is* such, and such, and its being is not merely a symbol, it is the fact itself. It *is* this, and the individual human being *is* what the act *is*. In the simple fact that the act *is*, the individual is for others what he really is and with a certain general nature, and ceases to be merely something that is 'meant' or 'presumed' to be this or that. No doubt he is not put there in the form of mind; but when it is a question of his being *qua* being, and the two-fold being of bodily shape and act are pitted against one another, each claiming to be his true reality, the deed *alone* is to be affirmed as his genuine being – not his figure or shape, which would express what he 'means' to convey by his acts, or what anyone might 'conjecture' he merely could do. In the same way, on the other hand, when his performance and his inner possibility, capacity, or intention are opposed, the former *alone* is to be regarded as his true reality, even if he deceived himself on the point and, after he has turned from his action into himself, means to be something else in his 'inner world' than what he is in the act. Individuality, which commits itself to the objective element, when it passes over into a deed no doubt puts itself to the risk of being altered and perverted. But what settles the character of the act is just this – whether the deed is a real thing that holds together, or whether it is merely a pretended or 'supposed' performance, which is in itself null and void and passes away. Objectification does not alter the act itself; it merely shows what the deed *is*, i.e. whether it *is* or whether it is *nothing*.

It can readily be understood why the schizoid individual so abhors action as characterized by Hegel. The act is 'simple, determinate, universal . . .'. But his self wishes to be complex, indeterminate, and unique. The act is 'what can be said of it'. But he must *never* be what can be said of him. He must remain always ungraspable, elusive, transcendent. The act is 'such, and such . . . it is this, and the individual human being is what the act is'. But he must at all costs never be what his act is. If he were what his act was, then he would be helpless and at the mercy of any passer-by. 'In the simple fact that the act is, the individual is for others what he really is', but this again is precisely what he most fears might happen, and what he seeks to avoid by the use of a false self so that 'he' is never what he really is with others. 'He', his 'self', is endless possibility, capacity, intention. The act is always the product of a false self. The act or the deed is never his true reality. He wishes to remain perpetually uncommitted 'to the objective element' – hence the deed is always (or at least he believes it to be) a pretended, a supposed performance, and he may actively cultivate as far as he can that 'inner' negation of all that he does in an effort to declare everything that he does 'null and void', so that in the world, in reality, in 'the objective element', nothing of 'him' shall exist, and no footprints or fingerprints of the 'self' shall have been left. Thus the self withholds itself from 'the objective element' both in respect of perception and of action. There can be no spontaneous action as there can be no spontaneous perception. And just as commitment in action is avoided, so perception is felt as an act of commitment that endangers the freedom to be nothing that the self possesses.

The self, as long as it is 'uncommitted to the objective element', is free to dream and imagine anything. Without reference to the objective element it can be all things to itself – it has unconditioned freedom, power, creativity. But its freedom and its omnipotence are exercised in a vacuum and its creativity is only the capacity to produce phantoms. The *inner honesty*, *freedom*, *omnipotence*, and *creativity*, which the 'inner' self cherishes as its ideals, are can-celled, therefore, by a coexisting tortured sense of self-duplicity, of the lack of any real freedom, of utter impotence and sterility.

Here, of course, I am primarily concerned to follow through the schizoid position into psychosis and not to describe the possibilities inherent in it which may lead in other directions, but one must bear in mind that deterioration and disintegration are only one out-come of the initial schizoid organization. Quite clearly, authentic versions of freedom, power, and creativity can be achieved and lived out.

Many schizoid writers and artists who are relatively isolated from the other succeed in establishing a creative relationship with things in the world, which are made to embody the figures of their phantasy. But theirs is not our present story. Throughout this study, I am focusing on only one line of development, and the generalizations I am making are intended to cover only this very limited area.

Now, although the self has an attitude of freedom and omnipo-tence, its refusal to commit itself to 'the objective element' renders it impotent: it has no freedom *in* 'reality'. Moreover, even in its own enclave, in its detachment it is constantly subject to (as it feels) the threat of an implosive or engulfing 'reality', and whereas it is preoccupied by itself and its own objects, it is still hyper-acutely aware of itself as an object in the eyes of others. Thus, the para-doxical difficulties of the schizoid individual are aggravated by the special nature of the schizoid system of defences which we have described.

The individual has perhaps always the choice of endorsing his position of detachment, or of attempting to participate in life. The schizoid defence against 'reality' has, however, the grave disadvantage that it tends to perpetuate and potentiate the original threatening quality of reality. Participation of the self in life is possible, but only in the face of intense anxiety. Franz Kafka knew this very well, when he said that it was only through his anxiety that he could participate in life, and, for this reason, he would not be without it. For the schizoid individual direct participation 'in' life is felt as being at the constant risk of being destroyed by life, for the self's isolation is, as we said, its effort to preserve itself in the absence of an assured sense of autonomy and integrity.

The self of the schizoid has to be understood, therefore, as an attempt to achieve secondary security from the primary dangers facing him in his original ontological insecurity. One aspect of this original ontological insecurity not so far specifically related to the 'self' is the precariousness of the individual's subjective sense of his own aliveness, and the sense of others threatening this tentative feeling. This problem will be considered more fully in the chapter on 'Self-consciousness'.

In the absence of a spontaneous natural, creative, relationship with the world which is free from anxiety, the 'inner self' thus develops an overall sense of inner impoverishment, which is expressed in complaints of the emptiness, deadness, coldness, dryness, impotence, desolation, worthlessness, of the inner life. For instance, one presenting complaint was of the impoverishment of the imaginative and emotional life. The patient explained that he regarded this as a consequence of his own decision to shut himself out from reality. As a result, as he put it, he was getting no supplies from reality to enrich his imagination.

Another patient oscillated between moments when he felt as though he was bursting with power, and moments when he felt he had nothing inside and was lifeless. However, even his 'manic' feeling of himself was that he was a container full of air under tremendous pressure, in fact, nothing but hot air, and his sense of deflation came with this thought. The schizoid individual frequently speaks of himself in these terms, such that, phenomeno-logically, we are justified in speaking of the vacuum that the self feels itself to be.

If the patient contrasts his own inner emptiness, worthlessness, coldness, desolation, dryness, with the abundance, worth, warmth, companionship that he may yet believe to be elsewhere (a belief which often grows to fantastically idealized proportions, uncorrected as it is by any direct experience), there is evoked a welter of conflicting emotions, from a desperate *longing* and yearning for what others have and he lacks, to frantic *envy* and hatred of all that is theirs and not his, or a desire to destroy all the goodness, freshness, richness in the world. These feelings may, in turn, be offset by counter-attitudes of disdain, contempt, disgust, or indifference.

This emptiness, this sense of inner lack of richness, substantiality and value, if it overweighs his illusory omnipotence, is a powerful prompter to make 'contact' with reality. The soul or self thus desolate and arid longs to be refreshed and fertilized, but longs not simply for a relationship between separable beings, but to be completely drenched and suffused by the other.

James (see pp. 143 ff.) told of how, when walking on a summer evening in the park alone, watching the couples making love, he suddenly began to feel a tremendous oneness with the whole world, with the sky and trees and flowers and grass – with the lovers too. He ran home in panic, and immersed himself in his books. He told himself he had no right to this experience, but more than that, he was terrified at the threatened loss of identity involved in this merging and fusion of his self with the whole world. He knew of no half-way stage between radical isolation in self-absorption or complete absorption into all there was. He was afraid of being absorbed into Nature, engulfed by her, with irrevocable loss of his self; yet what he most dreaded, that also he most longed for. Mortal beauty, so Gerard Manley Hopkins said, is dangerous. If such individuals could take his advice to meet it, then let it alone, things would be easier. But it is just this which they cannot do.

The abundance *there* is longed for, in contrast to the emptiness *here*; yet participation without loss of being is felt to be impossible, and also is not enough, and so the individual must cling to his isolation – his separateness without spontaneous, direct related-ness – because in doing so he is clinging to his identity. His longing is for complete union. But of this very longing he is terrified, because it will be the end of his self. He does not wish for a relation-ship of mutual enrichment and exchange of give-and-take between two beings 'congenial' to each other. He does not conceive of a dialectical relationship.*

What may happen is that an experience of losing one's own individual isolated selfhood can be tolerated in certain circum-scribed situations without too much anxiety. It may be possible to lose oneself in listening to music, or in quasi-mystical experiences when the self feels it is merged with a not-self which may be called 'God', but not necessarily. However, the longing of the self to escape from the tedium of its own company encounters generally two insurmountable obstacles in the anxiety and guilt that this longing arouses. There has already been mention in various con-texts of the anxiety attendant on losing identity by being engulfed. One way, of course, of getting what one wants from someone, while retaining control of the process of acquisition, is by theft.

Schizoid phantasies of stealing and being robbed are based on this dilemma. If you steal what you want from the other, you are in control; you are not at the mercy of what is given. But every inten-tion is instantly felt to be reciprocated. The desire to steal breeds phobias of being robbed. The phantasy that one has got any worth that one possesses by stealing it is accompanied by the counter-phantasy that the worth that others have has been stolen from one-self (see Rose, Chapter 9), and that anything one has will be taken away finally: not only what one *has*, but what one *is*, one's very self. Hence the common schizophrenic complaint that the 'self' has been stolen, and the defences against this constant danger.

The final seal on the self-enclosure of the self is applied by its own guilt. In the schizoid individual guilt has the same paradoxical

* Plato postulates that friendship can exist only between 'congenial' beings. However, the discussion on the possibility of friendship in the *Lysis* gets stuck at the dilemma: if two beings are not 'wanting' in anything, why should they want anything from the other? It is on this central issue – is he self-sufficient or does he 'want' anything? – that the schizoid person's life is liable to founder.

quality about it that was encountered in his omnipotence and impotence, his freedom and his slavery, his self being anyone in phantasy and nothing in reality. There would seem to be various sources of guilt within the individual's being. In a being that is split into different 'selves' one has to know which self is feeling guilty about what. In other words, in a schizoid individual there is not and cannot be a non-contradictory unified sense of guilt. On general principles, one might suppose that one sense of guilt might have its source in the false self, and another source of guilt might arise in the inner self. If, however, we call any guilt that the false-self system might be capable of having, false guilt, one will have to be careful to avoid regarding the inner self as the source of 'genuine' or true guilt.

Here, I wish merely to prepare the ground for a discussion of this problem at greater length on the basis of clinical material (pp. 129 ff.)

If there is anything the schizoid individual is likely to believe in, it is his own destructiveness. He is unable to believe that he can fill his own emptiness without reducing what is there to nothing. He regards his own love and that of others as being as destructive as hatred. To be loved threatens his self; but his love is equally dangerous to anyone else. His isolation is not entirely for his own self's sake. It is also out of concern for others. A schizophrenic patient would not allow anyone to touch her, not because they would do her some harm, but because she might electrocute them. And this is simply a psychotic expression of what the schizoid individual feels daily. He says, 'It would not be fair to anyone I might love, to love him.' What he may then do is to destroy 'in his mind' the image of anyone or anything he may be in danger of becoming fond of, out of a desire to safeguard that other person or thing in reality from being destroyed. If, then, there is nothing to want, nothing to envy, there may be nothing to love, but there is nothing to be reduced to nothing by him. In the last resort he sets about murdering his 'self', and this is not as easy as cutting one's throat. He descends into a vortex of non-being in order to avoid being, but also to preserve being from himself.

6

The false-self system*

The 'inner self' is occupied in phantasy and in observation. It observes the processes of perception and action. Experience does not impinge (or at any rate this is the intention) directly on this self, and the individual's acts are not self-expressions. Direct relationships with the world are the province of a false-self system. It is the characteristics of this system that must now be examined.

One must be clear that the description of the false-self system given below is intended to relate specifically to the problem of the particular schizoid mode of being in the world under discussion. Every man is involved personally in whether or to what extent he is being 'true to his true nature'. In clinical practice, the hysterical and the hypomanic person, for instance, have their own ways of not being themselves. The false-self system to be described here exists as the complement of an 'inner' self which is occupied in maintaining its identity and freedom by being transcendent,

* The false self is one way of not being oneself. The following are a few of the more important studies within the existentialist tradition relevant to the understanding of the false self, as one way of living inauthentically: Kierkegaard, *The sickness unto death* (1954); Heidegger, *Sein und Zeit* (1953); Sartre's discussion on 'bad faith' in *Being and Nothingness* (1956); Binswanger, *Drei Formen missglückten Daseins* (1952) and 'The Case of Ellen West' (1958); and Roland Kuhn, *La Phénoménologie de masque* (1957). Within the psycho-analytic tradition the following are among the most relevant studies: Deutsch, 'Some forms of emotional disturbances and their relationship to schizophrenia' (1942); Fairbairn, *Psychoanalytic studies of the personality* (1952); Guntrip, 'A study of Fairbairn's theory of schizoid reactions' (1952); Winnicott, *Collected papers* (1958) (passim); Wolberg, 'The "borderline" patient' (1952); and Wolf in *Schizophrenia in psycho-analytic office practice* (pp. 135–9, 1957).

unembodied, and thus never to be grasped, pinpointed, trapped, possessed. Its aim is to be a pure subject, without any objective existence. Thus, except in certain possible safe moments the individual seeks to regard the whole of his objective existence as the expression of a false self. Of course, as already indicated, and as will be seen in more detail later, if a man is not two-dimensional, having a two-dimensional identity established by a conjunction of identity-for-others, and identity-for-oneself, if he does not exist objectively as well as subjectively, but has only a subjective identity, an identity-for-himself, he cannot be *real*.

'A man without a mask' is indeed very rare. One even doubts the possibility of such a man. Everyone in some measure wears a mask, and there are many things we do not put ourselves into fully. In 'ordinary' life it seems hardly possible for it to be otherwise.

The false self of the schizoid individual differs, however, in certain important respects from the mask worn by the 'normal' person, and also from the false front that is characteristically maintained by the hysteric. It will avoid confusion if we briefly discriminate between these three forms of false self.

In the 'normal' person a good number of his actions may be virtually mechanical. These areas of virtually mechanical behaviour do not, however, necessarily encroach on every aspect of everything he does, they do not absolutely preclude the emergence of spontaneous expressions, and they are not so completely 'against the grain' that the individual seeks actively to repudiate them as foreign bodies lodged in his make-up. Moreover, they do not assume an autonomous compulsive way of their own, such that the individual feels that they are 'living' or rather killing him, rather than he living them. The issue, at any rate, does not arise with such painful intensity that he must attack and destroy this alien reality within himself as though it had an almost separate (personal) existence. By contrast, however, these characteristics, absent in the 'normal', are very much present in the schizoid false-self system.

The hysteric characteristically dissociates himself from much that he does. The best description of this technique of evasion in action that I know is in Sartre's chapter on 'bad faith' in *Being and Nothingness*, where he gives a brilliant phenomenological account of ways of pretending to oneself that one is not 'in' what one is doing – this is a form of evasion of the full personal implication of one's actions which the hysterical character erects as a whole way of living. Sartre's concept of 'bad faith' is, of course, much more extensive than this.

Now, the hysteric is seeking to achieve gratification through his actions, the significance of which he is denying. The actions of the hysteric afford him 'gains' in the gratification of libidinal and/or aggressive wishes towards other persons, the significance of which he cannot acknowledge to himself. Hence the *belle indifference*, the casual detachment from the implications of what he says or does. One sees that this state of affairs is very different from the split in the schizoid individual's being. *His false self does not serve as a vehicle for the fulfilment or gratification of the self.* In the schizoid individual, the self may remain hungry and starved in a most primitive sense while the false self may be apparently genitally adapted. The actions of the false self do not, however, 'gratify' the 'inner self'.

The hysteric *pretends* that certain highly gratifying activities are just pretending, or do not mean anything, or have no special implications, or that he is merely doing such and such because he is being forced to, while secretly his own desires are being fulfilled in and through these very activities. The false self of the schizoid person is compulsively compliant to the will of others, it is partially autonomous and out of control, it is felt as alien; the unrealness, meaninglessness, purposelessness which permeate its perceptions, thoughts, feelings, and actions, and its overall deadness are not simply productions of secondary defences but are direct consequences of the basic dynamic structure of the individual's being.

For instance, a patient recalled that at school he was fond of mathematics but had a contempt for literature. A performance of *Twelfth Night* was given at school and the boys had to write an essay on the subject. At the time he felt he hated the play but wrote a most appreciative essay about it, by imagining what would be expected of him by the authorities and slavishly adhering to it. This essay won a prize. 'Not one word of it was the expression of how I felt. It was all how I felt I was expected to feel'. Or so he thought at the time. In fact, as he admitted to himself later, he had *really* enjoyed the play, and had *really* felt about it as he had described in the essay. But he had not dared to admit this possibility to himself because it would have precipitated him into a violent conflict with all the values that had been inculcated into him and entirely disrupted his own idea of who he was. This, however, was a neurotic and not a schizoid incident. This patient continued in other ways to do what he secretly wanted, while persuading himself he was only doing what other people wanted. In this way he succeeded in carrying through his desires, although he always had difficulty at the time in admitting this to himself. The neurotic may, therefore, pretend that he has a false-self system superficially resembling the schizoid's, but on closer inspection we see that the circumstances are, in fact, widely different.

The hysteric often begins by pretending he is *not* in his actions while really actualizing himself through them. If he is threatened with this insight in the face of too intense guilt, his actions are inhibited, e.g. he develops 'hysterical' paralysis, which prevents the guilty gratifying actions from being executed.

Particularly clear examples of schizoid false selves can be seen in the cases of James (p. 140), David (p. 69), and Peter (p. Ch.8).

In any one person, the false-self system is always very complex and contains many contradictions. We shall try in this chapter to make statements that are generally applicable, but in doing so we must build up the picture by considering one component of this system of many components at a time.

James, we remember, said that he was not a person in his own right. In his behaviour he had allowed himself to become a 'thing' for other people. His mother, he felt, had never recognized his existence. One can say, I suppose, that one can recognize the existence of another person perfectly well in Woolworth's, but this was quite clearly not what he had in mind. He felt that she never recognized his freedom and right to have a subjective life of his own from out of which his actions would emerge as an expression of his own autonomous and integral self-being. On the contrary, he was merely her puppet, 'I was simply a symbol of her reality'. What had happened was that he had developed his subjectivity inwardly without daring to allow it any objective expression. In his case, this was not total, since he could express his 'true' self very clearly and forcibly in *words*. He knew this: 'I can only make sounds.' There was, however, hardly anything else 'he' did, for all his other actions were ruled not by his will but by an alien will, which had formed itself within his own being; it was the reflection of the will of his mother's alien reality operating now from a source within his own being. The other, of course, must in the first instance always be the mother, that is, the 'mothering one'. The actions of this false self are not necessarily imitations or copies of the other, though its actions may come to be largely impersonations or caricatures of other personalities. The component we wish to separate off for the moment is the initial compliance with the other person's intentions or expectations for one's self, or what are felt to be the other person's intentions or expectations. This *usually* amounts to an excess of being 'good', never doing anything other than what one is told, never being 'a trouble', never asserting or even betraying any counter-will of one's own. Being good is not, however, done out of any positive desire on the individual's own part to do the things that are said by others to be good, but is a negative conformity to a standard that is the other's standard and not one's own, and is prompted by the dread of what might happen if one were to be oneself in actuality. This compliance is partly, therefore, a betrayal of one's own true possibilities, but it is also a technique of concealing and preserving one's own true possibilities, which, however, risk never becoming translated into actualities if they are entirely concentrated in an inner self for whom all things are possible in imagination but nothing is possible in fact.

We said that the false self arises in compliance with the intentions or expectations of the other, or with what are imagined to be the other's intentions or expectations. This does not *necessarily* mean that the false self is absurdly good. It may be absurdly bad. The essential feature of the compliant component in the false self is expressed in James's statement that he was 'a response to what other people say I am'. This consists in acting according to other people's definitions of what one is, in lieu of translating into action one's own definition of whom or what one wishes to be. It consists in becoming what the other person wants or expects one to become while only being one's 'self' in imagination or in games in front of a mirror. In conformity, therefore, with what one perceives or fancies to be the *thing* one is in the other person's eyes, the false self becomes that thing. This thing may be a phoney sinner as well as a phoney saint. In the schizoid person, however, the whole of his being does not conform and comply in this way. The basic split in his being is along the line of cleavage between his outward compliance and his inner withholding of compliance.

Iago pretended to be what he was not, and indeed *Othello* as a whole is occupied with what it means to 'seem one thing and to be another'. But we do not find in that play or elsewhere in Shakespeare a treatment of the dilemma of seeming and being as lived by the type of person upon whom we are here focusing. The characters in Shakespeare 'seem' in order to further their own purposes. The schizoid individual 'seems' because he is frightened not to seem to further what he imagines to be the purpose that someone else has in mind for him. Only in a negative sense is he furthering his own purpose in so far as this outward compliance is to a large extent an attempt to preserve himself from total extinction. But he may 'get his own back' by attacking his own compliance (see below p. 102).

The observable behaviour that is the expression of the false self is often perfectly normal. We see a model child, an ideal husband, an industrious clerk. This façade, however, usually becomes more and more stereotyped, and in the stereotype bizarre characteristics develop. Again, there are a number of strands that can only be followed through one at a time.

One of the aspects of the compliance of the false self that is most clear is the fear implied by this compliance. The fear in it is evident, for why else would anyone act, not according to his intentions, but according to another person's? Hatred is also necessarily present, for what else is the adequate object of hatred except that which endangers one's self? However, the anxiety to which the self is subject precludes the possibility of a direct revelation of its hatred, except, we shall see later, in psychosis. Indeed, what is called psychosis is sometimes simply the sudden removal of the veil of the false self, which had been serving to maintain an outer behavioural normality that may, long ago, have failed to be any reflection of the state of affairs in the secret self. Then the self will pour out accusations of persecution at the hands of that person with whom the false self has been complying for years.

The individual will declare that this person (mother, father, husband, wife) has been trying to kill him; or that he or she has tried to steal his 'soul' or his mind. That he/she is a tyrant, a torturer, an assassin, a child murderer, etc. For present purposes it is much more important to recognize the sense in which such 'delusions' are true than to see them as absurd.

This hatred, however, is revealed in another way which is quite compatible, up to a point, with sanity. There is a tendency for the false self to assume *more and more of the characteristics of the person or persons upon whom its compliance is based*. This assumption of the other person's characteristics may come to amount to an almost total impersonation of the other. The *hatred of the impersonation* becomes evident when the impersonation begins to turn into a *caricature*.

The impersonation of the other by the false self is not entirely the same as its compliance with the will of the other, for it may be directly counter to the other's will. The impersonation may be deliberate, as with some roles played by David. But, as also in David's case, the impersonation may be compulsive. The individual may not be aware of the extent to which his actions constitute an impersonation of someone else. The impersonation may be of a relatively constant and permanent nature or it may be quite transitory. Finally, the personality acted out may be more that of a figure of phantasy than of any actual person, just as the compliance may also be compliance with a figure of phantasy much more than with any real person.

Impersonation is a form of identification whereby a part of the individual assumes the identity of a personality he is not. In impersonation, the whole of the impersonator is not necessarily implicated. It is usually a sub-total identification limited to assuming the characteristics of another person's behaviour – his gestures, mannerisms, expressions; in general, his appearance and actions. Impersonation may be one component in a much more total identification with the other but one of its functions seems to be to prevent more extensive identification with the other (and hence a more complete loss of the individual's own identity) from occurring.

Referring back again to David, his actions seem from the beginning of his life to have been in almost total compliance and conformity with his parents' actual wishes and expectations, i.e. he was a perfect model child who was never a trouble. I have come to regard such an account of the earliest origins of behaviour as especially ominous, when the parents sense nothing amiss in it all, but on the contrary mention it with evident pride.

Following his mother's death when he was ten, David began to display an extensive identification with her; he dressed himself up in her clothes in front of the mirror and kept house for his father just as his mother had done, even to the extent of darning his socks, knitting, sewing, doing embroidery, tapestry, selecting chair covers and curtains. Although it is quite obvious to an outside observer, to neither the patient nor the father was it apparent to what an extent he had become his mother. It is also clear that in doing so the boy was complying with a wish on his father's part that had never been directly expressed and of whose existence his father was quite unaware. The false self of this schoolboy was already a most complex system by the time he was fourteen. He was unaware of the extent of his identification with his mother but he was intensely aware of his compulsive tendency to act in a feminine way and of his difficulty in shaking off the part of Lady Macbeth.

To keep himself from lapsing into one or other female persona, he had deliberately to set about cultivating others. Although he tried very hard to sustain the impersonation of a normal schoolboy whom people would like (which is the simple ideal of the compliant false self), his false self was now a whole system of personas, some 'possible' socially, others not, some compulsive, others deliberately developed. But over all there was a persistent tendency for the impersonation to be difficult to sustain without some disquieting element intruding.

In general, into the original appearance of perfect normality and adjustment there creeps a certain oddity, a certain compulsive excessiveness in unwonted directions which turns it into a caricature and creates in others a certain disquiet and unease, and even hatred.

For instance, James in some respects 'took after' his father. One of his father's irritating characteristics was a way of asking people at table if they had had enough to eat, and a tendency to press them to have more, even when they had said quite clearly that they were satisfied. James 'took after' his father in this respect: he always made a point of politely inquiring this of guests at table. At first it appeared as no more than a generous concern that others should have enough. But his solicitations then came to be compulsive and to be carried past all tolerable bounds, so that he made himself a complete nuisance and occasioned general embarrassment. In this, he took up what he sensed were the aggressive implications in his father's actions, and exposed these implications, through exaggerating them in his own adaptation, to general ridicule and anger. He, in fact, evoked from others the feelings he had towards his father but was unable to express directly to his face. Instead, he produced what amounted to a satirical comment on his father through the medium of a compulsive caricature of him.

Much of the eccentricity and oddity of schizoid behaviour has this basis. The individual begins by slavish conformity and compliance, and ends through the very medium of this conformity and compliance in expressing his own negative will and hatred.

The false-self system's compliance with the will of others reaches its most extreme form in the automatic obedience, echopraxia, echolalia, and flexibilitas cerea of the catatonic. Here obedience, imitation, copying, are carried to such excess that the grotesque parody produced becomes a concealed indictment of the manipulating examiner. The hebephrenic frequently employs guying and mimicry of the persons he hates and fears as his preferred and only available means of attacking them. This may be one of the patient's private jokes.

The most hated aspects of the person who is the object of the identification come to the fore by being exposed to ridicule, scorn, or hatred through the medium of the impersonation. David's identification with his mother turned into a compulsive impersonation of a vicious queen.

The 'inner' secret self hates the characteristics of the false self.

It also fears it, because the assumption of an alien identity is always experienced as a threat to one's own. The self fears being engulfed by the spread of the identification. To some extent, the false-self system would seem to act analogously to the body's reticulo-endothelial system, which walls off and encapsulates dangerous intruding foreign matter and thus prevents these alien intruders from spreading more diffusely throughout the body. But if such is its defensive function it must be judged a failure. The inner self is not more true than the outer. David's inner secret self turned into a most controlling manipulating agency which used his false self very much like the puppet he felt he had been for his mother. That is, the shadow of his mother had fallen across his inner self as well as his outer self.

An instructive version of this problem occurred in a girl of twenty whose complaint was of being 'self-conscious' because she had an ugly face. To her face she applied white powder and bright red lipstick, giving it, if not an ugly appearance, at least a startlingly unpleasant, clownish, mask-like expression, which decidedly did not exhibit to advantage the features she had. In her mind, she did this to cover up how ugly she was underneath her heavy make-up. On further examination it became evident that this girl's attitude to her face contained in nuclear form the central issue of her life: her relationship with her mother.

She was much addicted to scrutinizing her face in the mirror. One day it came to her mind how hateful she looked. It had been in the back of her mind for years that she had her mother's face. The word 'hateful' was pregnant with ambiguous meanings. She hated the face she saw in the mirror (her mother's). She saw, too, how full of hate for her was the face that looked back at her from the mirror; she, who was looking at the mirror, was identified with her mother. She was in this respect her mother seeing the hate in her daughter's face: that is, with her mother's eyes, she saw her hate for her mother in the face in the mirror, and looked, with hatred, at her mother's hatred of herself.

Her relationship with her mother was of over-protection on her mother's part, and over-dependence and compliance on her part. She could not tolerate the possibility, in reality, of hating her mother, nor could she allow herself to recognize the presence of hatred for herself in her mother. All that could not find direct expression and open acknowledgement in her was condensed in her presenting symptom. The central implication seemed to be that she saw her true face to be hateful (full of hate). She hated it for being so like her mother's. She was frightened of what she saw. In covering up her face she both disguised her own hatred and made a surrogate attack upon her mother's face. A similar principle operated throughout the rest of her life. In her, the child's normal obligingness and obedience not only turned into passive acquiescence in every wish of her mother, but became the complete effacement of herself and went on to become a parody of anything her mother consciously could have desired of her daughter. She turned her compliance into an attack, and exhibited for all to see this travesty of her true self, which was both a grotesque caricature of her mother and a mocking 'ugly' version of her own obedience.

Thus, the hatred of the other person is focused on the features of him which the individual has built into his own being, and yet at the same time the temporary or prolonged assumption of another's personality is a way of not being oneself which seems to offer security. Under the mantle of someone else's personality the person may act so much more competently, smoothly, 'reliably' – to use Mrs D.'s expression, the individual may prefer to pay the price of incurring the haunting sense of futility which is the necessary accompaniment of not being oneself, rather than hazard the frank experience of frightened helplessness and bewilderment which would be the inevitable start to being oneself. The false-self system tends to become more and more dead. In some people, it is as though they have turned their lives over to a robot which has made itself (apparently) indispensable.

Besides the more or less permanent 'personality' displayed by the false-self system, it may be, as we mentioned, the prey to innumerable *transitory identifications* on a small scale. The individual suddenly discovers that he has acquired a mannerism, a gesture, a turn of speech, an inflection in his voice that is not 'his' but belongs to someone else. Often it is a mannerism that he consciously particularly dislikes. The transitory acquisition of small fragments of other people's behaviour is not exclusively a schizoid problem, but it does tend to occur with particular insistence and compulsiveness on the basis of the schizoid false-self system. The whole behaviour of some schizophrenics is hardly anything else than a patchwork of other people's peculiarities made more peculiar by the incongruity of the setting in which they are reproduced. The following example is of a quite 'normal' person.

A girl student whose name was Macallum developed intensely ambivalent feelings towards a male lecturer called Adams. On one occasion she found to her horror that she had signed her name 'Macadams'. 'I could have cut off my hand with disgust.'

Such little fragments of others seem to get embedded in the individual's behaviour as pieces of shrapnel in the body. While maintaining an apparently happy smooth relationship with the outer world, the individual is for ever picking at those alien fragments which (as he experiences it) are unaccountably extruding from him. These behavioural fragments fill the subject very often with disgust and horror, as in the case of the girl student, and are hated and attacked. 'I could have cut my hand off.' But, of course, this destructive impulse is directed, in fact, against her own hand. This little 'introjected' *action fragment* or particle cannot be attacked without violence to the subject's own being. (Jean effaced her own features in attacking her mother-in-her-face.)

If all the individual's behaviour comes to be compulsively alienated from the secret self so that it is given over entirely to compulsive mimicry, impersonating, caricaturing, and to such transitory behavioural foreign bodies as well, he may then try to strip himself of all his behaviour. This is one form of catatonic withdrawal. It is as though one were to try to cure a general skin infection by sloughing off one's whole skin. Since this is impossible the schizophrenic may pick and tear away, as it were, at his behavioural skin.

7

Self-consciousness

Self-consciousness, as the term is ordinarily used, implies two things: an awareness of oneself by oneself, and *an awareness of oneself as an object of someone else's observation.*

These two forms of awareness of the self, as an object in one's own eyes and as an object in the other's eyes, are closely related to each other. In the schizoid individual both are enhanced and both assume a somewhat compulsive nature. The schizoid individual is frequently tormented by the compulsive nature of his awareness of his own processes, and also by the equally compulsive nature of his sense of his body as an object in the world of others. The heightened sense of being always seen, or at any rate of being always potentially seeable, may be principally referable to the body, but the preoccupation with being seeable may be condensed with the idea of the mental self being penetrable, and vulnerable, as when the individual feels that one can look right through him into his 'mind' or 'soul'. Such 'plate-glass' feelings are usually spoken about in terms of metaphor or simile, but in psychotic conditions the gaze or scrutiny of the other can be experienced as an actual penetration into the core of the 'inner' self.

The heightening or intensifying of the awareness of one's own being, both as an object of one's own awareness and of the awareness of others, is practically universal in adolescents, and is associated with the well-known accompaniments of shyness, blushing, and general embarrassment. One readily invokes some version of 'guilt' to account for such awkwardness. But to suggest, say, that the individual is self-conscious 'because' he has guilty secrets (e.g. masturbation) does not take us far. Most adolescents masturbate, and not uncommonly they are frightened that it will show in some way in their faces. But why, if 'guilt' is the key to this phenomenon, does guilt have these particular consequences and not others, since there are many ways of being guilty, and a heightened sense of oneself as an embarrassed or ridiculous object in the eyes of others is not the only way. 'Guilt' in itself is inadequate to help us here. Many people with profound and crushing guilt do not feel unduly self-conscious. Moreover, it is possible, for instance, to tell a lie and feel guilt at doing so without being frightened that the lie will show in one's face, or that one will be struck blind. It is indeed an important achievement for the child to gain the assurance that the adults have no means of knowing what he does, if they do not see him; that they cannot do more than guess at what he thinks to himself if he does not tell them; that actions that no one has seen and thoughts that he has 'kept to himself' are in no way accessible to others unless he himself 'gives the show away'. The child who *cannot* keep a secret or who *cannot* tell a lie because of the persistence of such primitive magical fears has not established his full measure of autonomy and identity. No doubt in most circumstances good reasons can be found against telling lies, but the *inability* to do so is not one of the best reasons.

The self-conscious person feels he is more the object of other people's interest than, in fact, he is. Such a person walking along the street approaches a cinema queue. He will have to 'steel himself' to walk past it: preferably, he will cross to the other side of the street. It is an ordeal to go into a restaurant and sit down at a table by himself. At a dance he will wait until two or three couples are already dancing before he can face taking the floor himself, and so on.

Curiously enough, those people who suffer from intense anxiety when performing or acting before an audience are by no means necessarily 'self-conscious' in general, and people who are usually extremely self-conscious may lose their compulsive preoccupations with this issue when they are performing in front of others – the very situation, on first reflection, one might suppose would be most difficult for them to negotiate.

Further features of such self-consciousness may seem again to point to guilt being the key to the understanding of the difficulty.

The look that the individual expects other people to direct upon him is practically always imagined to be unfavourably critical of him. He is frightened that he will look a fool, or he is frightened that other people will think he wants to show off. When a patient expresses such phantasies it is easy to suppose that he has a secret unacknowledged desire to show off, to be the centre of attraction, to be superior, to make others look fools beside him, and that this desire is charged with guilt and anxiety and so is unable to be experienced as such. Situations, therefore, which evoke phantasies of this desire being gratified lose all pleasure. The individual would then be a concealed exhibitionist, whose body was unconsciously equated with his penis. Every time his body is on show, therefore, the neurotic guilt associated with this potential avenue of gratification exposes him to a form of castration anxiety which 'presents' phenomenologically as 'self-consciousness'.

An understanding of self-consciousness in some such terms eludes, I believe, the central issue facing the individual whose basic existential position is one of ontological insecurity and whose schizoid nature is partly a direct expression of, and occasion for, his ontological insecurity, and partly an attempt to overcome it; or, putting the last remark in slightly different terms, partly an attempt to defend himself against the dangers to his being that are the consequences of his failure to achieve a secure sense of his own identity.

Self-consciousness in the ontologically insecure person plays a double role:

1. Being aware of himself and knowing that other people are aware of him are a means of assuring himself that he exists, and also that they exist. Kafka clearly demonstrates this in his story called 'Conversation with a Suppliant': the suppliant starts from the existential position of ontological insecurity. He states, 'There has never been a time in which I have been convinced from within myself that I am alive.' The need to gain a conviction of his own aliveness and the realness of things is, therefore, the basic issue in his existence. His way of seeking to gain such conviction is by feeling himself to be an object in the real world; but, since *his* world is unreal, he must be an object in the world of someone else, for objects to other people seem to be real, and even calm and beauti-

ful. At least, '. . . it must be so, for I often hear people talking about them as though they were'. Hence it is that he makes his confession '. . . don't be angry if I tell you that *it is the aim of my life to get people to look at me*' (italics mine).

A further factor is the discontinuity in the temporal self. When there is uncertainty of identity in time, there is a tendency to rely on spatial means of identifying oneself. Perhaps this goes some way to account for the frequently pre-eminent importance to the person of being *seen*. However, sometimes the greatest reliance may be placed on the awareness of oneself in time. This is especially so when time is experienced as a succession of moments. The loss of a section of the linear temporal series of moments through inattention to one's time-self may be felt as a catastrophe. Dooley (1941) gives various examples of this temporal self-awareness arising as part of the person's 'struggle against fear of obliteration' and his attempt at the preservation of his integrity 'against threats of being engulfed, crushed, of losing . . . identity. . . '. One of her patients said: 'I forgot myself at the Ice Carnival the other night. I was so absorbed in looking at it that I forgot what time it was and who and where I was. When I suddenly realized I hadn't been thinking about myself I was frightened to death. The unreality feeling came. I must never forget myself for a single minute. I watch the clock and keep busy, or else I won't know who I am' (p. 17).

2. In a world full of danger, to be a potentially seeable object is to be constantly exposed to danger. Self-consciousness, then, may be the apprehensive awareness of oneself as potentially exposed to danger by the simple fact of being visible to others. The obvious defence against such a danger is to make oneself invisible in one way or another.

In an actual instance, the issue is thus always necessarily complex. Kafka's suppliant makes it the aim of his life to get people to look at him, since thereby he mitigates his state of depersonalization and derealization and inner deadness. He needs other people to experience him as a real live person because he has never been convinced from within himself that he was alive. This, however, implies a trust in the benign quality of the other person's apprehension of him which is not always present. Once he becomes aware of something it becomes unreal, although 'I always feel that

they were once real and are now flitting away'. One would not be
surprised to find that such a person would have in some measure a
distrust of other people's awareness of him. What, for instance, if
they had, after all, the same 'fugitive awareness' of him as he had
of them? Could he place any more reliance on their consciousness
than on his own to lend him a conviction that he was alive? Quite
often, in fact, the balance swings right over so that the individual
feels that his greatest risk is to be the object of another person's
awareness. The myth of Perseus and the Medusa's head, the 'evil
eye', delusions of death rays and so on are I believe referable to
this dread.

Indeed, considered biologically, the very fact of being visible
exposes an animal to the risk of attack from its enemies, and no
animal is without enemies. Being visible is therefore a basic
biological risk; being invisible is a basic biological defence. We all
employ some form of camouflage. The following is a written
description given by a patient who employed a form of magical
camouflage to help her over her anxiety when she was twelve years
old.

I was about twelve, and had to walk to my father's shop through a
large park, which was a long, dreary walk. I suppose, too, that I was
rather scared. I didn't like it, especially when it was getting dark. I
started to play a game to help to pass the time. You know how as a
child you count the stones or stand on the crosses on the pavement –
well, I hit on this way of passing the time. *It struck me that if I stared
long enough at the environment that I would blend with it and disappear
just as if the place was empty and I had disappeared. It is as if you get
yourself to feel you don't know who you are or where you are.* To blend
into the scenery so to speak. Then, you are scared of it because it begins
to come on without encouragement. I would just be walking along and
felt that I had blended with the landscape. Then I would get frightened
and repeat my name over and over again to bring me back to life, so to
speak.

It may be that here is a biological analogue for many anxieties
about being obvious, being out of the ordinary, being distinctive,
drawing attention to oneself, where the defences employed against
such dangers so often consist in attempts to merge with the human
landscape, to make it as difficult as possible for anyone to see in

what way one differs from anyone else. Oberndorf (1950), for instance, has suggested that depersonalization is a defence analogous to 'playing possum'. We shall consider these defences in some detail in the case of Peter (Chapter 8).

Being like everyone else, being someone other than oneself, playing a part, being incognito, anonymous, being nobody (psychotically, pretending to have no body), are defences that are carried through with great thoroughness in certain schizoid and schizophrenic conditions.

The above patient became frightened when she had blended with the landscape. Then, in her words: 'I would repeat my name over and over again to bring me back to life, so to speak.' This raises an important issue. I think that it would be a correct conjecture to suppose that the particular form of defence against anxiety in this little girl could only have arisen from a shaky ontological foundation. A securely established sense of identity is not easily lost, not as readily as this girl of twelve was able to lose hers in her game. It is, therefore, probable that this very ontological insecurity at least partly occasioned her anxiety in the first place and that she then used her source of weakness as her avenue of escape. This principle has been seen operating already in the cases of James, David, Mrs D., and others. In blending with the landscape, she lost her autonomous identity, in fact she lost her self and it was just her 'self' that was endangered by being alone in the gathering dusk in an empty expanse.

The most general expression of this principle is that when the risk is loss of being, the defence is to lapse into a state of non-being with, however, all the time the inner reservation that this lapsing into non-being is just a game, just pretending.

As Tillich (1952, p. 62) writes: 'Neurosis is the way of avoiding non-being by avoiding being.' The trouble is that the individual may find that the pretence has been in the pretending and that, in a more real way than he had bargained for, he has actually lapsed into that very state of non-being he has so much dreaded, in which he has become stripped of his sense of autonomy, reality, life, identity, and from which he may not find it possible to regain his foothold 'in' life again by the simple repetition of his name. In fact this little girl's game got out of hand in this way. When the patient wrote her account of her life, from which the above quotation is taken, she had remained severely depersonalized for a number of years.

In this region everything is paradoxical. In Chapter 5 we stated that the self dreads as well as longs for real aliveness. The self dreads to become alive and real because it fears that in so doing the risk of annihilation is immediately potentiated. 'Self-consciousness' is implicated in this paradox.

Our little girl blended with the landscape. Now, someone who only too easily blends with other people (we have described ways in which this occurs in the previous chapter), and is frightened of losing his identity thereby, uses his awareness of his self as a means of remaining detached and aloof. Self-consciousness comes to be relied upon to help sustain the individual's precarious ontological security. This insistence on awareness, especially awareness of the self, ramifies in many directions. For instance, whereas the hysteric seems only too glad to be able to forget and to 'repress' aspects of his being, the schizoid individual characteristically seeks to make his awareness of himself as intensive and extensive as possible.

Yet it has been remarked how charged with hostility is the self-scrutiny to which the schizoid subjects himself. The schizoid individual (and this applies still more to the schizophrenic) does not bask in the warmth of a loving self-regard. Self-scrutiny is quite improperly regarded as a form of narcissism. Neither the schizoid nor the schizophrenic is narcissistic in this sense. As a schizophrenic put it (see p. 204), she was scorched under the glare of a black sun. The schizoid individual exists under the black sun, the evil eye, of his own scrutiny. The glare of his awareness kills his spontaneity, his freshness; it destroys all joy. Everything withers under it. And yet he remains, although profoundly *not* narcissistic, compulsively preoccupied with the sustained observation of his own mental and/or bodily processes. In Federn's language, he cathects his ego-as-object with mortido.

A very similar point was made in different terms when it was said earlier that the schizoid individual depersonalizes his relationship with himself. That is to say, he turns the living spontaneity of his being into something dead and lifeless by inspecting it. This he does to others as well, and fears their doing it to him (petrification).

We are now in a position to suggest that whereas he is afraid *not* to be dead and lifeless – as stated, he dreads real aliveness – so also he is afraid *not* to continue being aware of himself. Awareness of his self is still a guarantee, an assurance of his continued existence, although he may have to live through a death-in-life. Awareness of an object lessens its potential danger. Consciousness is then a type of radar, a scanning mechanism. The object can be felt to be under control. As a death ray, consciousness has two main properties: its power to petrify (to turn to stone: to turn oneself or the other into things); and its power to penetrate. Thus, if it is in these terms that the gaze of others is experienced, there is a constant dread and resentment at being turned into someone else's thing, of being penetrated by him, and a sense of being in someone else's power and control. Freedom then consists in being inaccessible.

The individual may attempt to forestall these dangers by turning the other into stone. Unfortunately, since one cannot be seen by a stone, one becomes, in so far as others have been successfully reduced to things in one's own eyes, the only person who can see oneself. The process now swings in the reverse direction, culminating in the longing to be rid of the deadening and intolerable self-awareness so that the prospect of being a passive thing penetrated and controlled by the other may come as a welcome relief. Within such oscillation there is no position of peace, since the individual has no choice between feasible alternatives.

The compulsive preoccupation with being seen, or simply with being visible, suggests that we must be dealing with underlying phantasies of not being seen, of being invisible. If, as we saw, being visible can be both in itself persecutory and also a reassurance that one is still alive, then being invisible will have equally ambiguous meanings.

The 'self-conscious' person is caught in a dilemma. He may *need* to be seen and recognized, in order to maintain his sense of realness and identity. Yet, at the same time, the other represents a threat to his identity and reality. One finds extremely subtle efforts expended in order to resolve this dilemma in terms of the secret inner self and the behavioural false-self systems already described. James, for instance, feels that 'other people provide me with my existence'. On his own, he feels that he is empty and nobody. 'I can't feel real unless there is someone there. . . .' Nevertheless, he cannot feel at ease with another person, because he feels as 'in danger' with others as by himself.

He is, therefore, driven compulsively to seek company, but never allows himself to 'be himself' in the presence of anyone else. He avoids social anxiety by never really *being with* others. He never quite says what he means or means what he says. The part he plays is always not quite himself. He takes care to laugh when he thinks a joke is *not* funny, and look bored when he is amused. He makes friends with people he does not really like and is rather cool to those with whom he would 'really' like to be friends. No one, therefore, really knows him, or understands him. He can be *himself* in safety only in isolation, albeit with a sense of emptiness and unreality. With others, he plays an elaborate game of pretence and equivocation. His social self is felt to be false and futile. What he longs for most is the possibility of 'a moment of recognition', but whenever this by chance occurs, when he has by accident 'given himself away', he is covered in confusion and suffused with panic.

The more he keeps his 'true self' in hiding, concealed, unseen, and the more he presents to others a false front, the more compulsive this false presentation of himself becomes. He appears to be extremely narcissistic and exhibitionistic. In fact he hates himself and is terrified to reveal himself to others. Instead, he compulsively exhibits what he regards as mere extraneous trappings to others; he dresses ostentatiously, speaks loudly and insistently. He is constantly drawing attention to himself, and at the same time drawing attention *away* from his self. His behaviour is compulsive. All his thoughts are occupied with being seen. His longing is to be known. But this is also what is most dreaded.

Here the 'self' has become an invisible transcendent entity, known only to itself. The body in action is no longer the expression of the self. The self is not actualized in and through the body. It is distinct and dissociated. The implicit meaning of Mrs R.'s (p. 54) actions was: 'I am only what other people regard me as being.' James played on the opposite possibility. 'I am not what anyone can see.' His apparent exhibitionism was, therefore, a way of avoiding people discovering what or who he felt he really was.

The adult is not able to use either being seen or being invisible as a stable defence against the other, since each holds dangers of its own as well as affording its own form of safety. How complicated are the issues at stake can be gauged by considering the complexity even of the earliest and simplest infantile situations.

It is a common game for children to play at being invisible and at being seen. This game has several variations. It can be played alone; in front of a mirror; or with the collusion of adults.

In a footnote to his famous description (1920) of the little boy's play with the reel and string, Freud gives a description of one version of this game. It is worth while recalling the whole passage although it is to the footnote that I wish to direct particular attention.

The child was not at all precocious in his intellectual development. At the age of one and a half he could say only a few comprehensible words; he could also make use of a number of sounds which expressed a meaning intelligible to those around him. He was, however, on good terms with his parents and their one servant-girl, and tributes were paid to his being a 'good boy'. He did not disturb his parents at night, he conscientiously obeyed orders not to touch certain things or go into certain rooms, and above all he never cried when his mother left him for a few hours. At the same time, he was greatly attached to his mother, who had not only fed him herself but had also looked after him without any outside help. This good little boy, however, had an occasional disturbing habit of taking any small objects he could get hold of and throwing them away from him into a corner, under the bed, and so on, so that hunting for his toys and picking them up was often quite a business. As he did this he gave vent to a loud, long-drawn-out 'o-o-o-o', accompanied by an expression of interest and satisfaction. His mother and the writer of the present account were agreed in thinking that this was not a mere interjection but represented the German word *fort* (gone). I eventually realized that it was a game and that the only use he made of any of his toys was to play 'gone' with them. One day I made an observation which confirmed my view. The child had a wooden reel with a piece of string tied round it. It never occurred to him to pull it along the floor behind him, for instance, and play at its being a carriage. What he did was to hold the reel by the string and very skilfully throw it over the edge of his curtained cot, so that it disappeared into it, at the same time uttering his expressive 'o-o-o-o'. He then pulled the reel out of the cot again by the string and hailed its reappearance with a joyful 'da' (there). This then was the complete game:

disappearance and return. As a rule one only witnessed the first act which was repeated untiringly as a game in itself though there is no doubt that greater pleasure was attached to the second act.

Freud adds this significant footnote to his account of this game:

A further observation subsequently confirmed this interpretation fully. One day, the child's mother had been away for several hours and on her return was met with the words, 'Baby o–o–o–o!' which was at first incomprehensible. It soon turned out, however, that during this long period of solitude *the child had found a method of making himself disappear* [italics mine]. He had discovered his reflection in a full-length mirror which did not quite reach to the ground so that by crouching down he could make his mirror-image 'gone'.

Thus, this little boy not only plays at making his mother disappear, but plays also at making himself disappear. Freud suggests that both games are to be understood as attempts to master the anxiety of a danger situation by repeating it again and again in play.

If this is so, the fear of being invisible, of disappearing, is closely associated with the fear of his mother disappearing. It seems that loss of the mother, at a certain stage, threatens the individual with loss of his self. The mother, however, is not simply a *thing* which the child can see, but a *person* who sees the child. Therefore, we suggest that a necessary component in the development of the self is the experience of oneself as a person under the loving eye of the mother. The ordinary infant lives almost continually under the eyes of adults. But being seen is simply one of innumerable ways in which the infant's total being is given attention. He is attended to, by being noticed, petted, rocked, cuddled, thrown in the air, bathed: his body is handled to an extent that it never will be again. Some mothers can recognize and respond to the child's 'mental' processes but cannot responsively accept its concrete bodily actuality and vice versa. It may be that a *failure of responsiveness* on the mother's part to one or other aspect of the infant's being will have important consequences.

A further consideration of what this boy was achieving by his game suggests that he was able, as Freud presumes, to make *himself* disappear by not being able to see his reflection in the mirror.

That is to say, if he could not see himself *there*, he himself would be 'gone'; thus he was employing a schizoid presupposition by the help of the mirror, whereby there were two 'hims', one *there* and the other *here*. That is to say, in overcoming or attempting to overcome the loss or absence of the real other in whose eyes he lived and moved and had his being, he becomes another person to himself who could look at him from the mirror.

However, although the 'person' whom *he* could see in the mirror was neither his own self nor another person but only a reflection of his own person, when he could no longer see that other reflected image of his own person in the mirror he himself disappeared, possibly in the way he felt that he disappeared when he could no longer feel that he was under scrutiny or in the presence of his mother. Now, whether the threat from the real other arises out of the contingency of the fact that the other may at any time go away or die or not reciprocate one's feelings for him, or whether the other represents more directly a threat in the form of implosion or penetration, the schizoid person seeks in the boy's way of being a mirror to himself, to turn his self, a quasi-duality with an overall unity, into two selves, i.e. into an actual duality. In this little boy, of the 'two selves', his own actual self outside the mirror was the one which one could imagine would most readily be identified with his mother. This *identification of the self with the phantasy of the person by whom one is seen* may contribute decisively to the characteristics of the observing self. As stated above, this observing self often kills and withers anything that is under its scrutiny. The individual has now a persecuting observer in the very core of his being. It may be that the child becomes possessed by the alien and destructive presence of the observer who has turned bad in his absence, occupying the place of the observing self, of the boy himself outside the mirror. If this happens, he retains his awareness of himself as an object in the eyes of another by observing himself as the other: he lends the other his eyes in order that he may continue to be seen; he then becomes an object in his own eyes. But the part of himself who looks into him and sees him, has developed the persecutory features he has come to feel the real person outside him to have.

The mirror game can have peculiar variants. The manifest

onset of one man's illness occurred when he looked into a mirror and saw someone else there (in fact, his own reflection): 'him'. 'He' was to be his persecutor in a paranoid psychosis. 'He' (i.e. 'him') was the instigator of a plot to kill him (i.e. the patient) and he (the patient) was determined to 'put a bullet through "him"' (his alienated self).

In the game of this little boy, he, in the position of the person who was perceiving him, that is, his mother, was in a sense killing himself in a magical way: he was killing the mirror image of himself. We shall have occasion to return later to this peculiar state of affairs when studying schizophrenia. Making *himself* disappear and return again must have had a similar significance to that of his other game, of making his mother (symbolically) disappear and reappear. The game makes sense in this way, however, only if we can believe that there is a danger situation for him not only in not being able to see his mother but also in not feeling himself to be seen by her. At this stage, *esse = percipi*, not only as regards others but also as regards the self.

At two years six months, one of my daughters played a similar game. I had to cover my eyes with my hands on the command, 'Don't see us.' Then, on the command, 'See me', I had suddenly to take my hands away, and express surprise and delight at seeing her. I also had to look at her and pretend I could not see her. I have been made to play this game with other children. There is no question of not seeing them doing something naughty. The whole point seems to lie in the child experiencing himself temporarily as not being seen. It is not a question of the child not seeing *me*. One notices also that no actual physical separation occurs in the game. Neither the adult nor the child, in this game, has to hide or actually to disappear. It is a magical version of the peek-a-boo game.

The child who cries when its mother disappears from the room is threatened with the disappearance of his own being, since for him also *percipi = esse*. It is only in the mother's presence that he is able fully to *live* and *move* and *have his being*. Why do children want the light on at night, and want their parents so often to sit with them until they fall asleep? It may be that one aspect of these needs is that the child becomes frightened if he can no longer see himself, or feel himself to be seen by someone else; or to hear others and be heard by them. Going to sleep consists, phenomeno-logically, in a loss of one's own awareness of one's being as well as that of the world. This may be in itself frightening, so the child needs to feel seen or heard by *another* person, while he is losing his own awareness of his being in the process of falling asleep. In sleep the 'inner' light that illumines one's own being is out. Leaving on the light not only provides assurance that if he wakes there are no terrors in the dark, but provides a magical assurance that during sleep he is being watched over by benign presences (parents, good fairies, angels). Even worse, perhaps, than the possible presence of bad things in the dark is the terror that in the dark is *nothing* and *no one*. Not to be conscious of oneself, therefore, may be equated with nonentity. The schizoid individual is assuring himself that he exists by always being aware of himself. Yet he is persecuted by his own insight and lucidity.

The need to be perceived is not, of course, purely a visual affair. It extends to the general need to have one's presence endorsed or confirmed by the other, the need for one's total existence to be recognized; the need, in fact, to be loved. Thus those people who cannot sustain from within themselves the sense of their own identity or, like Kafka's suppliant, have no inner conviction that they are alive, may feel that they are real live persons only when they are experienced as such by another, as was the case with Mrs R. (p. 54), who was threatened with depersonalization when she could not be recognized or imagine herself recognized and re-sponded to by someone who knew her sufficiently well for their recognition of and response to her to be significant. Her need to be seen was based on the equation that 'I am the person that other people know and recognize me to be'. She required the tangible reassurance of the presence of another who knew her, in whose presence her own uncertainties about whom she was could be temporarily allayed.

> *I am not fond of the word psychological. There is no such thing as the psychological. Let us say that one can improve the biography of the person.*
> JEAN-PAUL SARTRE

In the following case, one can see many of the issues discussed in the last two chapters being lived out.

Peter was a large man of twenty-five, and he looked the picture of health. He came to see me complaining that there was a constant unpleasant smell coming from him. He could smell it clearly, but he was not too sure whether it was the sort of smell that others could smell. He thought that it came particularly from the lower part of his body and the genital region. In the fresh air, it was like the smell of burning, but usually it was a smell of something sour, rancid, old, decayed. He likened it to the sooty, gritty, musty smell of a railway waiting-room; or the smell that comes from the broken-down 'closets' of the slum tenements of the district in which he grew up. He could not get away from this smell although he had taken to having several baths a day.

The following information about his life was given to me by his father's brother:

His parents were not happy people but they stuck close to each other. They had been married ten years before he was born. They were inseparable. The baby, the only child, made no difference to their life. He slept in the same room as his parents from birth until he left school. His parents were never openly unkind to him and he seemed to be with them all the time and yet they simply *treated him as though he wasn't there*.

His mother, his uncle went on, never could give him affection since she had never had any herself. He was bottle-fed and put on weight well, but he was never cuddled or played with. As a baby, he was always crying. His mother, however, did not openly reject him or neglect him. He was adequately fed and clothed. He passed through his subsequent childhood and adolescence without any noticeable peculiarities. His mother, however, his uncle said, hardly noticed him at all. She was a pretty woman, and was always fond of dressing up and admiring herself. His father liked to see this, bought her clothes when he could, and was very proud to be seen with his attractive wife.

The uncle thought that though the father was very fond of the boy in his way, something seemed to stop him from being able to show his affection to him. He tended to be gruff, to pick on faults, occasionally to thrash him for no good reason, and to belittle him with such remarks as, 'Useless Eustace', 'You're just a big lump of dough'. The uncle thought this was a pity because when he did well at school and later when he got a job in an office, which was a big step-up socially for this very poor family, he really was 'terribly proud of that boy'; it was 'a terrible blow to him' when his son seemed later just not to want to make anything of himself.

He was a lonely child, and he was always very good. When he was nine, a little girl of his own age who lived beside him was blinded in an air-raid in which both her parents were killed. For several years he spent most of his time with this little girl; he had inexhaustible patience and kindness, he taught her how to get around the district, took her to pictures, sat with her and talked with her. This girl later partially recovered her sight. She told his uncle that she owed her life to the little boy of nine, because he was the only person who had really had time for her when she was blind, helpless, and friendless, with no one who either could or would step into the place of her dead parents.

In his last years at school, his uncle took a special interest in him and with his prompting, and through arrangements he made, he went into a solicitor's office. The boy left this office after a few months because of lack of interest but, again through his uncle, he obtained work in a shipping office. He stayed with this firm till his call-up to the Army. In the Army, at his own wish, he looked after patrol dogs and when he left, after serving his two years without incident, he 'broke his father's heart' by, literally, 'going to the dogs', in that he obtained a job as a kennelman at a dog track. He left this, however, after a year, and after five months doing various unskilled odd jobs he simply did nothing for the seven months before he went to his general practitioner complaining of smell. There was, in fact, no smell from him so his G.P. referred him for psychiatric help.

The patient described his life in the following way:

His own feeling about his birth was that neither his father nor his mother had wanted him and, indeed, that they had never forgiven him for being born. His mother, he felt, resented his presence in the world because he had messed up her figure and damaged and hurt her in being born. He maintained that she had cast this up to him frequently during his childhood. His father, he felt, resented him simply for existing at all, 'He never gave me any place in the world. . . .' He thought too that his father probably hated him because the damage and pain he had caused his mother by his birth had put her against having sexual intercourse. He entered life, he felt, as a thief and criminal.

One recalls his uncle's statement to the effect that his parents remained largely engrossed in themselves, and that they treated him as though he was not there. The relation of being ignored to self-consciousness is well brought out in the following transcript of a tape-recording of an exchange during our second interview:

PETER: . . . ever since I can remember I was sort of aware of myself, a sort of self-conscious – obvious in a way, you know.

ME: Obvious?

PETER: Well, yes, obvious. Simply being there . . . it was just being aware of myself.

ME: Being there?

PETER: Oh, just being at all, I suppose. He [his father] used to say that I had been an eyesore since the day I was born.

ME: An eyesore?

PETER: Yes, Useless Eustace was another name for me, and a big lump of dough.

ME: You felt guilty about just being there.

PETER: Well, yes, I don't know really . . . *it was simply for being in the world in the first place*, I suppose.

He said he was not lonely as a child although he was on his own a good deal, but 'lonely is not the same as being alone'.

He had what was probably a 'screen' memory from about four

or five years of his mother telling him, when she caught him playing with his penis, that it wouldn't grow if he did that: when he was about seven or eight there were a few episodes of a sexual nature with a girl of his own age, but he did not start masturbating until the age of about fourteen. All this was of major importance to him and served to intensify his self-consciousness. The only early memories he told me to begin with were of these sexual incidents. They were told without any warmth. It was many months before he mentioned, in a casual way, the blind little girl, Jean.

At secondary school his feelings about himself were becoming more definitely crystallized. As far as it is now possible to reconstruct them, he was beginning to have a growing sense that he was being put by everyone in a false position. He felt under an obligation to his teacher and his parents to be somebody and to make something of himself, whereas all the time he felt that this was on the one hand impossible and on the other hand unfair. He felt that he had to spend all his time and energy in being a credit to his father, his mother, his uncle, or his teacher. However, he was convinced in himself that he was nobody and worthless, that all this effort to be somebody was a deception and a pretence. His teacher, for instance, wanted him to 'speak properly' and to wear 'middle-class clothes'. But all this was trying to make him be what he was not. She had him, the secret masturbator, reading Bible lessons to the other children at school and held him up as a paragon. When people said how good he must be to be able to read the Bible so well he laughed sardonically to himself. 'It just showed what a good actor I was.' Yet he himself, beyond feeling that he was not the person he was playing at being, did not know what he wanted to be. Alongside the feeling that he was worthless, there was also the growing impression that he was someone very special, sent by God for a special mission, but who, or what . . . he could not say. In the meantime, he deeply resented what he felt were everybody's efforts to make him into a saint which were 'more or less just for credit to themselves'. It was without joy, therefore, that he worked in his office job. He came to hate more and more, and women in particular. He was aware of hating others, but it had not occurred to him that he feared them. Why should he, when 'they couldn't stop me thinking what I liked'? This, of course, implies that 'they' had some power to coerce him to do what 'they' wanted, but as long as he was outwardly compliant to 'their' wishes, he avoided experiencing the anxiety which we must suppose led him to conform to others and hardly ever reveal himself to them.

It was at the second office that he first experienced attacks of anxiety. By then, the central issue for him had crystallized in terms of being sincere or being a hypocrite; being genuine or playing a part. For himself, he knew he was a hypocrite, a liar, a sham, a pretence, and it was largely a matter of how long he could kid people before he would be found out. At school, he had believed that he had been able, to a large extent, to get away with it. But the more he dissembled what he regarded as his real feelings and did things and had thoughts that had to be kept hidden and secret from every other, the more he began to scan people's faces in order to try to make out, from what he could read in them, what he imagined they either thought about him or knew about him. At the office what he regarded as his 'real feelings' were largely sadistic sexual phantasies about his female colleagues, particularly one woman there who, he thought, looked respectable enough but who, he imagined, was probably a hypocrite like himself. He used to masturbate in the office lavatory while evoking these phantasies and once, as had previously happened with his mother, just after he had been doing this, he emerged and encountered the very woman whom he had been raping in his mind. She was looking directly at him so that she seemed to look straight through him into his secret self and to see there what he had been doing to her. He was filled with panic. He now could no longer believe with any assurance that he could conceal his actions and his thoughts from other people. In particular, as he said, he could no longer feel confidence that his face would not 'give him away'. At the same time, he became frightened lest a smell of semen should betray him.

He was in this state when he entered the Army. He completed his service, however, without exhibiting outward signs of his inner distress. Indeed, he seems to have achieved an outward appearance or normality and a measure of freedom from anxiety. His sense of achieving this was most interesting and important. His apparent normality was the consequence of a deliberate intensification of the split between his 'inner' 'true' self and outer 'false' self in a quite

calculated way. This was expressed by a dream he had at that time.
He was in a fast-moving car: he jumped off, hurting himself but not
seriously, while the car went on to crash. He thus took to the
logical but disastrous conclusion the game that he had been playing
with himself for some while. He finally opted out as completely as
he knew how; he dissociated himself both from himself and from
other people. The immediate effect of this was to lessen his anxiety
and to allow him to appear normal. But this was not all he did and
these were not the only consequences.

His sense of pointlessness, of lack of direction, of futility, was
enhanced, as was his conviction that he was nobody 'really'. He
felt that it was pointless to pretend any more. He formulated this
to himself in these words: 'I am nobody, so I'll do nothing.' He
was now bent not only on dissociating himself from his false self
but on destroying everything he seemed to be. 'I derived,' as he
said, 'a certain sardonic satisfaction out of becoming even less
than I had thought I was or they had thought me to be. . . .'

He had all along felt that he was, in his own words (which inci-
dentally are also Heidegger's), 'on the fringe of being', with only
one foot in life and with no right even to that. He felt that he was
not really alive and that anyway he was of no value and had hardly
the right to the pretension of having life. He imagined himself to
be outside it all, yet he cherished for a while one shred of hope.
Women might still have the secret. If he could somehow be loved
by a woman, then he felt he might be able to overcome his sense of
worthlessness. But this possible avenue was blocked for him by his
conviction that any woman who had anything to do with him
could only be as empty as he was, and that anything that he might
be able to get from women, whether he took it or whether they gave
it to him, could only be as worthless as the stuff of which he himself
was made. Any woman who was not as futile as he was could,
therefore, never have anything to do with him, least of all in a
sexual sense. All his actual sexual relationships with women were
entirely promiscuous and through them he was never able to break
through his 'shut-upness'. With the one girl whom he regarded as
'pure', he maintained a tenuous and platonic relationship for some
years. But he was unable to translate his relationship with this girl
into anything more than this. Perhaps he would have agreed with

Kierkegaard had he read him, which he had not, that if he had had faith he would have married his Regina.

One has to ask why he took so long to tell me about this friendship, which was undoubtedly one of the most significant things in his life, and may well have helped to prevent him from becoming openly schizophrenic in his teens. It was quite characteristic of Peter, and of this type of person, that it should be this sort of thing in his life that he tended to keep most concealed from others, whereas he had no inhibitions about speaking about infantile promiscuous sexual incidents, masturbation, and adult sadistic sexual phantasies.

DISCUSSION

As far as I could gather Peter had never been 'at home' either in his body or in the world. He felt clumsy, awkward, obvious. One recalls his uncle's account of his narcissistic mother, who did not cuddle or play with him. Even his physical presence in the world was hardly recognized. 'He was treated as though he wasn't there.' For his part, not only did he feel awkward and obvious, he felt guilty simply at 'being in the world in the first place'.

His mother had, it seems, eyes only for herself. She was blind to him. He was not *seen*. It was no mere accident that he became such a good companion, a 'mother' rather, to the little blind girl who could not see him. There were many facets of this friendship but one important aspect of it was that he felt safe with her, since he could see her and she could not see him. Moreover, she desperately needed him; he gave her his eyes; and he, of course, could afford to be sorry for her in a way he could not for his mother. This girl, the patrol dogs, and the kennel dogs were the only living creatures towards whom he could show and from whom he could receive affection spontaneously.

With almost everyone he began to operate with a false-self system, based on compliance with their wishes and ambitions for him. As he continued to do so, he came more and more to hate others and himself. As his feeling of what properly belonged to his 'true' self contracted more and more, this self began to feel more and more vulnerable and he came to be more and more frightened that other people could penetrate through his sham personality into the inner sanctum of his secret phantasies and thoughts.

He was able to carry on in an outwardly normal way the deliberate employment of two techniques which he called 'disconnexion' and 'uncoupling'. By disconnexion, he meant widening the existential distance between his self and the world. By uncoupling he meant the severance of any relationship between his 'true' self and his repudiated false self. These techniques were basically to avoid being discovered and had many variants. For instance, when he was at home or among people he knew, he was awkward and ill at ease, until he could get himself set into some role or part which was not him, and which he felt was a suitable disguise. Then he could, he said, 'uncouple' his 'self' from his actions, and function smoothly, without anxiety. This was not a satisfying resolution of his difficulties, however, for various reasons. If he was consistently not able to put his self into his actions for a long period of time, he felt with growing intensity the falsity of his life, a lack of desire to do anything, an unrelieved sense of boredom. Moreover, the defence was not foolproof because from time to time he would be caught off his guard and feel a look or remark to penetrate into the core of his 'self'. His sense of being 'in danger' from the gaze of others became more persistent and less easily allayed by the device of not letting them see his 'self'. He would feel at times, and have difficulty in dissolving the impression, that they could see through his pretences.

His preoccupation with being seen was, I believe, an attempt to recoup himself from his underlying feeling that he was nobody (had no body). There was a primary inadequacy in the reality of his own experience of himself as embodied and it was out of this that his preoccupation with his body-for-others arose, i.e. his body as seeable, hearable, smellable, touchable by the other. No matter how painful this 'self'-consciousness was to him, it arose inevitably out of the fact that his own body experiences were so uncoupled from his self that he needed the awareness of himself as a real object to others to assure himself, by this roundabout route, that he had a tangible existence.

Furthermore, his delusion of smell from himself also became less easily shakeable.

He found, however, another way of adjusting himself to his particular anxieties, which had exactly the opposite advantages and the opposite disadvantages. He could, he felt, be himself with others if they knew nothing about him. This was, however, a requirement that demanded exacting fulfilment. It meant that he had to go to another part of the country where he was a 'stranger'. He would go from place to place, never staying long enough to be known, each time under a different name. Under these conditions he could be (almost) happy – for a while. He was 'free' and could be 'spontaneous'. He could even have sexual relations with girls. He was not 'self-conscious' and had no 'ideas of reference'. These no longer arose because the inner uncoupling of his self from his body was no longer necessary. He could be an embodied person if he was really incognito. If, however, *he* was known, he had to revert to the disembodied position.

The phantasy he put into action of being anonymous, or incognito, or a stranger in a strange land, is a common one in people with ideas of reference. They feel that if they could get away from their workmates, or leave their town, and start afresh, everything would be all right. They are often found to move from job to job, or from place to place. This defence works for a short while, but can last only as long as they are anonymous; it is very difficult not to be 'discovered': and they are liable to become as suspicious and cautious as any spy in enemy territory that others are trying to 'catch them out' into 'giving themselves away'.*

Peter, for instance, hesitated even in a strange town to go to a barber's shop. His anxiety about a barber's was not primarily an expression of castration anxiety, at any rate in any usual sense of the term. Rather, he was uneasy about having to answer any questions about himself that the barber might possibly ask, however 'innocent', for example, 'Do you like football?', 'What do you think of that chap who won seventy-five thousand pounds?', etc. In the barber's chair he was caught: for him it was a nightmare situation in which while his hair was being shorn, he would be shorn of his anonymity by having to commit himself, by becoming

* I do not suggest that all ideas of reference are to be understood in these terms.

congealed for a moment into someone definite. 'Whereas people are commonly found to say that they come from this or that place, or work at this or that job, or know such and such a person, I try as far as possible not to let it be known where I'm from, what I do, or who I know. . . .'

Similarly, he was unable to patronize one public library and hold a single ticket in his own name. Instead, he borrowed books from various libraries all over the city, at each of which he held tickets under an assumed name and a false address. If he thought that the librarian had come to 'recognize' him, he did not return to that library.

Although this defence was difficult to sustain, since it indeed demanded for its success as much effort, skill, and vigilance as would be required of a spy in enemy territory, so long as he could feel that he was not 'discovered' or 'recognized', this method did serve to rid him of the need to be constantly 'uncoupled' and 'disconnected'. But it required a constant anxious alertness since he could never be out of danger. At this point, however, his situation, although difficult, was not utterly desperate. It was, of course, rendered critical by the way his schizoid defence system, which was his whole *modus vivendi*, his attempt to find some feasible way of living in the world, became *an intentional project of self-annihilation*. It was when this happened that his precarious sanity began to pass a critical point and become a psychosis.

True and false guilt.

We must now consider more closely the guilt Peter was subject to and its consequences. We remember that not only did he feel awkward and obvious, but he felt guilty 'simply at being in the world in the first place'. On this level, his guilt was not attached to anything he had thought or done; he felt he had *no right to occupy space*. Not only this; he had a deep-seated conviction that the stuff he was made of was rotten. The phantasies he had of anal intercourse and the production of children made of faeces were expressions of this conviction. The details of these phantasies are not our present concern except in so far as they contributed to his apperception of his self as made up of muck and dung. If his father had said he was a 'big lump of dough', he himself went much further. Under the conviction that he was a worthless lump of muck and dung, *he felt guilty at seeming to be anything worth while to others.*

He felt bad for masturbating. However, the crux of his sense of guilt is, I believe, revealed in the curious finding that *when he gave up masturbating his feeling of worthlessness was intensified*, and when he really set about doing and being nothing, his smell of himself became intolerable. As he said later of this smell, 'It was more or less the regard I had for myself. It was really a form of self-dislike.' That is to say, he stank so badly in his own nostrils that he could hardly endure it.

He had, in fact, two entirely antithetical and opposed sources of guilt; one urged him to life, the other urged him to death. One was constructive, the other destructive. The feelings they induced were different but both were intensely painful. If he did things that were an expression of self-affirmation, of being a worth-while valuable person, real and alive, he would be told 'this is a sham, a pretence. You are worthless.' However, if he persisted and refused to endorse this false counsel of conscience, he did not feel so futile, unreal, or dead, and he did not smell so badly. On the other hand if he resolutely tried to *be* nothing, he still felt he was a pretence or a sham; he still experienced anxiety; and he was just as compulsively aware of his body as an object of other people's perception.

The worst effect of all efforts to be nothing was the deadness that settled over his whole existence. This deadness permeated his experience of his 'uncoupled self', his experience of his body, and his perception of the 'disconnected' world. Everything began to come to a stop. The world came to lose what reality it had for him and he had difficulty in imagining that he had any existence-for-others. Worst of all, he began to feel 'dead'. From his subsequent description of this feeling of being 'dead', it was possible to see that it involved a loss of the feeling of realness and aliveness of his body. The core of this feeling was the *absence* of the experience of his body as a real object-for-others. He was coming to exist only for himself (intolerably), and ceasing to feel that he had any existence in the eyes of the world.

It seems probable that in all this he was contending with a primary gap in the two-dimensional experience of himself of which his parents' handling, or rather failure to handle him, had deprived him. His compulsive preoccupation (which he felt as extremely unpleasant) with being touchable, smellable, etc., to others was a desperate attempt to retain that very dimension of a living body: that it has a being-for-others. But he had to 'pump up' a sense of this dimension to his body in a secondary, artificial, and compulsive way. This was a dimension of his experience that had not become established in a primary sense out of the original infantile situation, and the gap was filled, not by any later development of a feeling of being loved and respected as a person, but by a feeling that practically all love was disguised persecution, since it aimed to turn him into a thing of the other – a feather in the hat of his school teacher, as he put it.

Yet although this patient had had difficulties at school and at his work, although he felt that he was a pretence and a sham at school, and experienced panic at the office, it was more particularly when he himself began deliberately to cultivate the splits in his being that his condition took an ominous turn. He said that he tried to 'disconnect himself from everything' and this is true; and to this he added his method of 'uncoupling'. In this, he tried to sever the ties that related different aspects of his being together. In particular, he tried not to be 'in' his actions or in his expressions: not to be what he was doing. One sees that here he was playing on the transitional position of body actions and expression between oneself and the world. Now he tried to say, 'All of me that can be an object-for-the-other is not me.'

The body clearly occupies an ambiguous transitional position between 'me' and the world. It is, on the one hand, the core and centre of my world, and on the other, it is an object in the world of the others. Peter tried to uncouple himself from anything of him that could be perceived by anyone else. In addition to his effort to repudiate the whole constellation of attitudes, ambitions, actions, etc., which had grown up in compliance with the world, and which he now tried to uncouple from his inner self, he set about trying to reduce his whole being to non-being; he set about as systematically as he could to become nothing. Under the conviction that he was nobody, that he was nothing, he was driven by a terrible sense of honesty to *be* nothing. He felt that if he was nobody he ought to become nobody. Being anonymous was one way of magically translating this conviction into fact. When he gave up his work he wandered through the country, constantly on the move. He belonged nowhere. He was going from anywhere to anywhere: he had no past, no future. He had no possessions, no friends. Being nothing, knowing nobody, being known by none, he was creating the conditions which made it more easy for him to believe that he *was* nobody.

Onan's sin in spilling his seed on the ground was that thereby he wasted his productivity and creativity. Peter's guilt, as he later expressed it, was not simply that he masturbated and had sadistic phantasies but that he did not have the courage to do with others what he imagined himself in phantasy to be doing with them; and when he tried and to some extent succeeded in curbing, if not repressing, his phantasies, his guilt became not only that he had these phantasies but that he was repressing them. When he set out to be nothing, his guilt was not only that he had no right to do all the things that an ordinary person can do, but that he had not the courage to do these things over and against and despite his conscience which sought to tell him that everything he did or could do in this life among other people was wrong. His guilt was in endorsing by his own decision this feeling that he had no right to life, and in denying himself access to the possibilities of this life.

He felt guilty, that is, not so much at his desires, drives, or impulses in themselves, but because he had not the courage to become a real person by doing real things with real people in reality. His guilt was not simply at his wishes but that they remained only wishes. His sense of futility arose from the fact that his wishes were fulfilled only in phantasy, and not in reality. Masturbation was an activity in which *par excellence* he had substituted a sterile relationship to the phantoms of phantasy for a creative relationship with a real other; instead of the possible guilt that he might have had arising out of real desire for a real person, his guilt was that his desires were only phantastic ones.

Guilt is the call of Being for itself in silence, says Heidegger. What one might call Peter's *authentic guilt* was that he had capitulated to his *unauthentic guilt*, and was making it the aim of his life not to be himself.

There was also in this patient, however, the division of his inner self mentioned earlier. From his earliest days, he had been haunted by the sense of being nobody and now he was grimly bent on creating the conditions that would confirm this feeling. Yet at the same time he felt he was someone very special, with a special mission and purpose, sent by God to this earth. This empty omnipotence and sense of mission were frightening to him, and he set them aside as 'a sort of mad feeling'. He sensed that if he gave this feeling indulgence that way lay, in Empson's expression, 'madhouse and the whole thing there'. Yet a severe penalty was exacted from him for indulging the alternative. Since he had tried to be nobody by not living in and through his body, his body became, in a sense, dead.

When he dropped the pretence, therefore, it forced itself on his notice as he was recalled to it as something musty, rancid, uncanny – in fact, unlived and dead. He had severed himself from his body by a psychic tourniquet and both his unembodied self and his 'uncoupled' body had developed a form of existential gangrene.

One of his later remarks states the crux of the matter in a nut-shell:

I've been sort of dead in a way. I cut myself off from other people and became shut up in myself. And I can see that you become dead in a way when you do this. You have to live in the world *with* other people. If you don't something dies inside. It sounds silly. I don't really understand it, but something like that seems to happen. It's funny.

Part 3

> *Things fall apart, the centre cannot hold,*
> *Mere anarchy is loosed upon the world.*
>   W. B. YEATS

Already, especially in the cases of David and Peter, we have considered schizoid manifestations that have come perilously close
to frank psychosis. In this chapter, we shall study some of the
ways of crossing the borderline into a psychotic condition. Here,
it is, of course, not always possible to make sharp distinctions
between sanity and insanity, between the sane schizoid individual
and the psychotic. Sometimes the onset of psychosis is so dramatic
and abrupt, and its manifestations are so unequivocal, that there
can be no question or doubt about the diagnosis. However, in
many cases there is no such sudden apparently qualitative change,
but a transition extending over years, at no single point in which
may it be at all clear whether any critical point has been passed.

In order to understand the nature of the transition from sanity
to insanity when the point of departure is the particular form of
a schizoid existential position described in the foregoing pages,
it is necessary to consider the psychotic possibilities that arise out
of this particular existential context. In this position, we stated
that the self, in order to develop and sustain its identity and
autonomy, and in order to be safe from the persistent threat and
danger from the world, has cut itself off from direct relatedness
with others, and has endeavoured to become its own object: to
become, in fact, related directly only to itself. Its cardinal functions become phantasy and observation.

Now, in so far as this is successful, one necessary consequence
is that the self has difficulty in sustaining any *sentiment du réel* for
the very reason that it is not 'in touch' with reality, it never actually
'meets' reality. As Minkowski (1953) puts it, there is loss of 'vital

contact' with the world. Instead, relationship with others and the world is, as we saw, delegated to a false-self system whose perceptions, feelings, thoughts, actions, possess a relatively low 'coefficient' of realness.

The individual in this position may appear relatively normal, but he is maintaining his outward semblance of normality by progressively more and more abnormal and desperate means. The self engages in phantasy in the private 'world' of 'mental' things, i.e. of its own objects, and observes the false self, which alone is engaged in living in the 'shared world'. Since direct communication with others in this real shared world has been turned over to the false-self system, it is only through this medium that the self can communicate with the outside shared world. Hence what was designed in the first instance as a guard or barrier to prevent disruptive impingement on the self, can become the walls of a prison from which the self cannot escape.

Thus the defences against the world fail even in their primary functions: to prevent persecutory impingements (implosion) and to keep the self alive, by avoiding being grasped and manipulated as a thing by another. Anxiety creeps back more intensely than ever. The unrealness of perception and the falsity of the purposes of the false-self system extend to feelings of deadness of the shared world as a whole, to the body, in fact, to all that is, and infiltrate even to the 'true' self. Everything becomes suffused with nothingness. The inner self itself becomes entirely unreal or 'phantasticized', split, and dead, and no longer able to sustain what precarious sense of its own identity it started with. This is aggravated by the use of the very possibilities that are most ominous as defences, e.g. the avoidance of being identified to preserve identity (since, as we have indicated above, identity is reached and sustained two-dimensionally, it requires recognition of oneself by others as well as the simple recognition one accords to oneself); or the deliberate cultivation of a state of death-in-life as a defence against the pain of life.

Efforts both at further withdrawal of the self and towards restitution of the self come to combine in the same direction of psychosis. In one way, the schizoid individual may be desperately trying to be himself, to regain and preserve his being; yet it is very difficult to disentangle the desire to be from the desire for non-being, since so much that the schizoid person does is in its nature inextricably ambiguous. Can one say unequivocally of Peter that he was seeking to destroy himself or to preserve himself? The answer cannot be provided if we think of the two terms of either/or as mutually exclusive. Peter's defences against life were, in large measure, the creation of a form of death within life, which seemed to afford within itself a measure of freedom from anxiety, at least for a time. In order to survive he had, like the possum, to feign a measure of death. Peter could either 'be himself' when he was anonymous or incognito, i.e. when he was not known to others, or he could let himself be known to others if he was not being himself. This equivocation could not be sustained indefinitely, since *the sense of identity requires the existence of another by whom one is known*; and a conjunction of this other person's recognition of one's self with self-recognition. It is not possible to go on living indefinitely in a sane way if one tries to be a man disconnected from all others and uncoupled even from a large part of one's own being.

Such a mode of being-with-others would presuppose the capacity to maintain one's reality by means of a basically autistic identity. It would presuppose that it is finally possible to be human without a dialectical relationship to others. It seems that the whole aim of this manoeuvring is the preservation of an 'inner' identity from phantasied destruction from outer sources, by eliminating any direct access from without to this 'inner' self. But without the 'self' ever being qualified by the other, committed to the 'objective' element, and without being lived in a dialectical relationship with others, the 'self' is not able to preserve what precarious identity or aliveness it may already possess.

The changes that the 'inner' self undergoes have already in part been described. They may be listed here as follows:

1. It becomes 'phantasticized' or 'volatilized' and hence loses any firmly anchored identity.
2. It becomes unreal.
3. It becomes impoverished, empty, dead, and split.

4. It becomes more and more charged with hatred, fear, and envy.

These are four aspects of one process, as looked at from different points of view.

James carried this process to the limits of sanity, perhaps indeed beyond it. This young man of twenty-eight had, as is so often the case, deliberately cultivated the split between what he regarded as his 'true self' and his false-self system.

In his mind hardly any way of looking at anything, or any thought or action, was not false and unreal. Seeing, thinking, feeling, acting, were merely 'mechanical' and 'unreal' because they were simply the way 'they' saw things, thought, felt, or acted. When he walked to his train in the morning, if he met anyone, he had to fall in step with the other person, talk, laugh, about the things everyone talked and laughed about. 'If I open the door of the train and allow someone to enter before me, this is not a way of being considerate, it is simply a means of acting as much as I can the same as everyone else.' Yet his effort to appear to be like everyone else was made with such resentment of others and contempt for self that his actual behaviour was a bizarre product of conflict between concealing and revealing his 'true' feelings.

He attempted to assert his identity by eccentricity of ideas. He was a pacifist, a theosophist, an astrologer, a spiritualist, an occultist, a vegetarian. It seems that the fact that *he could share with others* at least his odd ideas was perhaps the most important single factor in preserving his sanity. For in those limited areas he was sometimes able to be *with* others with whom he shared his ideas and peculiar experiences. Such ideas and experiences tend to isolate a man from his fellows in our present Western culture and, unless they serve at the same time to draw him into a small group of similar 'eccentrics', his isolation is greatly in danger of passing over into psychotic alienation. For instance, his 'body schema' extended from before birth to after death, and dissolved the usual limitations of time and place. He had various 'mystical' experiences in which he felt himself united with the Absolute, with the One Reality. The laws by which he secretly 'knew' the world was governed were entirely magical ones. Although by profession a chemist, his 'true' belief was not in the laws of chemistry and science but in alchemy, black and white magic, and astrology. His 'self', as it was only partially real-ized even in and through relationship with others who shared his views, became more and more caught up in, and itself a part of, the world of magic. The objects of phantasy or imagination obey magical laws; they have magical relationships, not real relationships. When the 'self' becomes more and more a participant in phantasy relationships, less and less a direct participant in real relationships, in doing so it loses its own reality. It becomes, like the objects to which it is related, a magical phantom. One implication of this is that, for such a 'self', everything and anything become possible, unqualified, as even every wish must be sooner or later, by reality, necessity, the conditioned and finite. If this is not so, the 'self' can be anyone, be anywhere, and live at any time. With James this was coming to be the case. 'In imagination' the conviction was growing and gathering of having phantastic powers (occult, magical, mystical), characteristically vague and undefined but nevertheless contributing to the idea that he was not simply James of this time and this place, of such parents, but someone very special, with an extraordinary mission, a reincarnation perhaps of the Buddha or Christ.

That is to say, the 'true' self, being no longer anchored to the mortal body, becomes 'phantasticized', volatilized into a changeable phantom of the individual's own imagining. By the same token, isolated as is the self as a defence against the dangers from without which are felt as a threat to its identity, it loses what precarious identity it already has. Moreover, the withdrawal from reality results in the 'self's' own impoverishment. Its omnipotence is based on impotence. Its freedom operates in a vacuum. Its activity is without life. The self becomes desiccated and dead.

In his dream world James experienced himself as even more alone in a desolate world than in his waking existence, for example:

1. I found myself in a village. I realize it has been deserted: it is in ruins; there is no life in it. . . .
2. . . . I was standing in the middle of a barren landscape. It was absolutely flat. There was no life in sight. The grass was hardly growing. My feet were stuck in mud. . . .

3. ... I was in a lonely place of rocks and sand. I had fled there from something; now I was trying to get back to somewhere but didn't know which way to go. ...

The tragic irony is that even finally no anxiety is avoided, whereas every anxiety and all else besides becomes even more tormenting by the infusion into all experiences in waking life and in dreams of an abiding sense of nothingness and deadness.

The self can be 'real' only in relation to real people and things. But it fears that it will be engulfed, swallowed up in any relationships. If the 'I' only comes into play *vis-à-vis* objects of phantasy, while a false self manages dealings with the world, various profound phenomenological changes occur in all elements of experience.

Thus the point we have already got to is that the self, being transcendent, empty, omnipotent, free in its own way, comes to be anybody in phantasy, and nobody in reality.

This self is related primarily to objects of its own phantasies. Being so much a self-in-phantasy, it becomes eventually volatilized. In its dread of facing the commitment to the objective element, it sought to preserve its identity; but, no longer anchored to fact, to the conditioned and definitive, it comes to be in danger of losing what it was seeking above all to safeguard. Losing the conditioned, it loses its identity; losing reality, it loses its possibility of exercising effective freedom of choice in the world. In the escape from the risk of being killed, it becomes dead. The individual may now no longer be experiencing the world as other people experience it, though he may still know how it is for others if not for him. But the immediate sense of the realness of the world cannot be sustained by a false-self system. Moreover, the false-self system cannot put reality to the test, for the testing of reality demands a mind of one's own that can choose the better of alternatives and so on, and it is the lack of such a mind of its own that makes the false self false.

When experience from the outer world is filtered to the inner self, this self can no longer either experience or give expression to its own desires in a way that is socially acceptable.

Social acceptability has come to be merely a trick, a technique. His own view of things, the meaning they have for him, his feelings, his expression, are now likely to be at least odd and eccentric, if not bizarre and crazy. The self remains encapsulated more and more within its own system, while adaptation and adjustment to changing experiences have to be conducted by the false self. This false-self system is apparently plastic: it operates with new people, and adapts to changing surroundings. But the self does not keep up with changes in the real world. The objects of its phantasy relationships remain the same basic figures although they undergo modification, for instance, in the direction of idealization, or they become more persecutory. There is no thought of checking, testing, correcting these phantom figures (imagos) in terms of reality. There is in fact no occasion to do so. The individual's self by now is not making any effort to act upon reality, to effect real changes in it.

While the self and its imagos are undergoing the above modification, the false-self system undergoes parallel changes.

We recall the original position, which was represented schematically thus:

$$\text{Self} \rightleftharpoons (\text{body-world})$$

The body is the *niveau* of the false-self system but this system is conceived by the individual to reify and extend beyond solely bodily activity. It consists in large measure of all those aspects of his 'being' which the inner 'self' repudiates as not an expression of his self. Thus, as with James, while the self retreats into more and more exclusive phantasy relationships and 'detached', non-participant observation of the transactions of the false self and others, the false-self system is felt to encroach more and more, to make deeper and deeper inroads into the individual's being until practically everything is conceived to belong to this system. James finally could hardly perceive any object by sight, sound, touch, particularly,* nor do anything without his feeling it was 'not himself'. We have already given some examples. They could be multiplied indefinitely, since in this way he experienced his actions at home, at work, and with friends. The consequences of this mode

---

* The relation of splits in one's being to the various sense modalities remains very inadequately understood.

of being to the nature of the false-self system can now be summarized as follows:

1. The false-self system becomes more and more extensive.
2. It becomes more autonomous.
3. It becomes 'harassed' by compulsive behaviour fragments.
4. All that belongs to it becomes more and more dead, unreal, false, mechanical.

The dissociation of the self from the body and the close link between the body and others, lends itself to the psychotic position wherein the body is conceived not only as operating to comply with and placate others, but as being in the actual possession of others. The individual is beginning to be in a position to feel not only that his perceptions are false because he is continually looking at things through other people's eyes, but that they are playing him tricks because people are looking at the world through his eyes.

James had almost come to this point. He already felt that the thoughts in his 'brain', as he always put it, were not really *his*. Much of his intellectual activity was an attempt to gain possession of his thoughts; to bring his thoughts and feelings under *his* control. For instance, his wife would give him a cup of milk at night. Without thinking, he would smile and say, 'Thank you'. Immediately he would be overcome with revulsion at himself. His wife had simply acted mechanically and he had responded in terms of the same 'social mechanics'. Did *he* want the milk, did *he* feel like smiling, did *he* want to say 'Thank you'? No. Yet he did all these things.

The situation facing the individual in James's position is critical. He has become in large measure unreal and *dead*. Realness and life may not any more be directly felt or experienced, although the sense of their possibility is not lost. Others *have* realness and life. Realness and life exist, perhaps, in Nature (more concretely, inside the body of Mother Nature), or they can be grasped in certain types of experience: they can be regained by intellectual disciplines and control. The self is, however, charged with hatred in its envy of the rich, vivid, abundant life which is always elsewhere; always there, never here. The self, as we said, is empty and dry. One might call it an oral self in so far as it is empty and longs to be and dreads being filled up. But its orality is such that it can never be satiated by any amount of drinking, feeding, eating, chewing, swallowing. It is unable to incorporate anything. It remains a bottomless pit; a gaping maw that can never be filled up. In a world of wet, it cannot quench its thirst. Guilt, which might arise if it were possible to take in and destroy the world as food (in a sense), for constructive purposes, cannot arise. The self tries to destroy the world by reducing it to dust and ashes, without assimilating it. Its hatred reduces the object to nothing, without digesting it. Thus, although the 'self' is desolate, and desperately envies the goodness (life, realness) it imagines to reside in others, it must destroy it rather than take it in. It becomes a question of 'getting' life and realness in some way that will not result in the annihilation of the self. But the destruction of reality and the surreptitious acquisition of it are largely magical procedures by this time. These magical ways of surreptitiously acquiring reality include:

1. Touching,
2. Copying, imitating,
3. Magical forms of stealing it.

The individual may even find some measure of reassurance if he can evoke in himself an immediate impression of realness in others. (These methods are illustrated in the case of Rose, pp. 150 ff.)

A further attempt to experience real alive feelings may be made by subjecting oneself to intense pain or terror. Thus, one schizophrenic woman who was in the habit of stubbing out her cigarettes on the back of her hand, pressing her thumbs hard against her eyeballs, slowly tearing out her hair, etc., explained that she did such things in order to experience something 'real'. It is most important to understand that this woman was not courting masochistic gratification; nor was she anaesthetic. Her sensations were not less intense than normal. She could feel everything except being alive and real. Minkowski reports that one of his patients set fire to her clothing for similar reasons. The cold schizoid person may 'go for kicks', court extreme thrills, push himself into extreme risks in order to 'scare some life into himself', as one patient put it. Hoelderlin* wrote: 'O thou, daughter of the ether, appear to me from your father's gardens and if you may not promise me mortal happiness, then frighten, O frighten my heart with something else.' However, these attempts cannot come to anything. As James put it, in almost the same words as Kafka's suppliant: 'Reality recedes from me. Everything I touch, everything I think, everyone I meet, becomes unreal as soon as I approach. . . .'

In the progressive loss of the real presence of the other, and hence loss of the sense of me-and-you-together, of we-ness, women may become more remote and threatening than men. The last hope of a point of break-through of what Binswanger (1942) calls a dual mode of being-in-the-world may be through a homosexual attachment, or the last loving bond may be with the other as child or animal. Boss (1949) describes the role that a form of homosexual love played in a man whose self and world were becoming shrunken and narrowed in his isolation:

This human being, in whom even 'scalp and heart-muscle' contract, is less and less able to 'reach out' for a broadening and deepening of existential fullness of a male-female love union. He can no longer attain the 'heavenly bliss', the 'passion and enlightenment', which the love for the cousin had once meant to him. The first step in the process of increasing barrenness of his existence was that the woman lost her love transparency, being a completely different, remote 'foreign' pole of existence; she became 'pale', a 'mirage', then she represented 'undigestible food' and finally she dropped entirely out of the frame of his world. When his progressing schizophrenia 'depleted his masculinity', when most of his own male feelings 'had run out', he suddenly and for the first time in his life felt driven to 'open himself' to a certain form of homosexual love. He described most vividly how in this homosexual love he succeeded in experiencing at least half of the fullness of existence. He did not have to 'exert' himself very much to attain this semifullness, there was little danger of 'losing himself' and of 'running out' into boundlessness in this limited extent and depth. On the contrary, the homosexual love could 'replenish' his existence 'to a whole man'.

Boss states, I think rightly, that

this observation throws a new light upon Freud's important statement

* 'Entreaty (to Hope)', quoted by Binswanger (1958), p. 311.

that homosexual tendencies are regularly encountered in all paranoics. Freud believed that this homosexuality was the cause of the development of persecution thoughts. We, however, see in both phenomena, in this sort of homosexuality and in the persecution ideas, nothing but two parallel forms of expression of the same schizophrenic shrinkage and destruction of human existence, namely two different attempts at regaining the lost parts of one's personality (pp. 122–4).

The individual is in a world in which, like some nightmare Midas, everything he approaches becomes dead. There are now perhaps only two further possibilities open to him at this stage:

1. He may decide to 'be himself' despite everything, or
2. He may attempt to murder his self.

Both these projects, if carried through, are likely to result in manifest psychosis. We shall consider them separately.

The individual whose false-self system has remained intact and has not become devastated by attacks from the self, or from the accumulation of transitory fragments of alien behaviour, may present the appearance of complete normality. However, behind this sane façade an interior psychotic process may be going on secretly and silently.

The individual's apparently normal and successful adjustment and adaptation to ordinary living is coming to be conceived by his 'true' self as a more and more shameful and/or ridiculous pretence. *Pari passu* his 'self', in its own phantasied relationships, has become more and more volatilized, free from the contingencies and necessities that encumber it as an object among others in the world, where he knows he would be committed to be of this time and this place, subject to life and death, and embedded in this flesh and these bones. If the 'self' thus volatilized in phantasy now conceives the desire to escape from its shut-upness, to end the pretence, to be honest, to reveal and declare and let itself be known without equivocation, one may be witness to the onset of an acute psychosis.

Such a person though sane outside has been becoming progressively insane inside. Cases of this kind may present on superficial examination a most baffling problem since, on reviewing the 'objective' history, one may find no understandable precipitating stresses or, even in retrospect, any obvious indications that such a sudden abrupt form of events was imminent. It is only when one is able to gather from the individual himself the history of his *self*, and *not what a psychiatric history in these circumstances usually is, the history of the false-self system*, that his psychosis becomes explicable.

The following are two quite everyday accounts of the onset of psychosis 'out of a blue sky', of a kind that is familiar to any psychiatrist, given from the 'outside'. From this point of view they must remain quite baffling.

A young man of twenty-two was regarded by his parents and friends as entirely 'normal'. While on holiday by the sea, he took a boat out to sea. He was picked up some hours later, having drifted far from the land. He resisted being rescued, saying that he had lost God, and had set out on the ocean to find him. This incident marked the onset of a manifest psychosis that required his hospitalization for many months.

A man in his fifties who never before had had any 'nervous' trouble, at least not to his wife's knowledge, and who had seemed to her, up to the acute onset of the psychosis, to be his 'usual self', went with his wife and children on a picnic beside a river, on a hot summer's afternoon. After the meal, he undressed completely, although there were other picnickers in view, and entered the water. This was perhaps not more than unusual. Having waded waist deep, he threw the water over himself. He now refused to come out, saying that he was baptizing himself for his sins, which were that he had never loved his wife or his children, and that he would not leave the water until he was cleansed. He eventually had to be dragged from the river by the police and admitted to a mental hospital.

In both these cases, and in the others described elsewhere, sanity, i.e. outwardly 'normal' appearance, dress, behaviour, motor and verbal (everything observable), was maintained by a false-self system while the 'self' had come to be more and more engaged not in a world of its own but in the world as seen by the self.

I am quite sure that a good number of 'cures' of psychotics consist in the fact that the patient has decided, for one reason or other, once more to *play at being sane*.

It is not uncommon for depersonalized patients, whether or not they are schizophrenic, to speak of having murdered their selves and also of having lost or been robbed of their selves.

Such statements are usually called delusions, but if they are delusions, they are delusions which contain existential truth. They are to be understood as statements that are literally true within the terms of reference of the individual who makes them.

The schizophrenic who says he has committed suicide, may be perfectly clear about the fact that he has not cut his throat open or thrown himself into a canal, and he may expect this to be equally clear to the person whom he is addressing, otherwise that person is regarded as a fool. In fact, he makes many statements of this order, which may be expressly intended as snares for those he regards as idiots and the whole herd of the uncomprehending. For such a patient it would probably be a complete *non sequitur* to attempt to kill his *self*, by cutting his throat, since his *self* and his *throat* may be felt to bear only a tenuous and remote relationship to each other, sufficiently remote for what happens to the one to have little bearing on the other. That is, his self is virtually unembodied. The self is probably conceived as immortal or made of nearly imperishable non-bodily substance. He may call it 'life substance' or his 'soul', or even have his own name for it, and feel that he can be robbed of it. This was one of the ideas most central to Schreber's (1955) famous psychosis.

We may approach this rather difficult psychotic material by comparing the fear of loss of the 'self' to a more familiar neurotic anxiety that may lie behind a complaint of impotence. In impotence, one may find the following latent phantasy. The individual is afraid of losing his genital function, so he preserves its use (avoids castration), by appearing to be castrated. He fends off the threat of castration by pretending to himself that he is castrated, and acting as though he were so. The psychotic has employed a defence on the same principles, but it is carried out, not in respect of penial functions but in respect of the self. It is the ultimate and most paradoxically absurd possible defence, beyond which magic defences can go no further. And it, in one or other of its forms, is the basic defence, so far as I have been able to see, in every form of psychosis. It can be stated in its most general form as: *the denial of being, as a means of preserving being*. The schizophrenic feels he has killed his 'self', and this appears to be in order to avoid being killed. He is dead, in order to remain alive.

A variety of factors may converge to prompt the individual in one way or other to be rid of his self. Even the efforts of the self to become separable and non-identified with the body and practically every thought, feeling, action, or perception, have failed to free it in the long run from being subject to anxiety; it is left with none of the possible advantages of detachment, and is subject to all the anxiety it originally sought to evade.

The following two cases demonstrate the great distress of an individual involved in such issues.

I saw Rose when she was twenty-three years of age. When I saw her she said that she was frightened she was going insane, as in fact she was. She said that horrible memories had been coming back to her, which she could not forget no matter how hard she tried. But now she had discovered the answer to this. She was now trying, she said, to forget these memories by *forgetting herself*. She tried to do this by looking all the time at other people and hence never noticing herself. At first it was something of a relief for her to feel that she was going down and down and that she didn't want to fight. But something in her fought against this. She was depressed and continued to try to do things, but this became a greater and greater effort, until every thought or movement felt as though it had to be initiated by a deliberate act of will. But then she began to feel that she had no more will-power – she had used it all up. Moreover, she was frightened to do anything on her own behalf or take personal responsibility for anything she did. At the same time, she said that she was distressed by the feeling that her life was no longer hers to lead. 'My own being is in everyone else's hands than my own.' She had no life of her own, she was just existing. She had no purpose, no 'go', no point to herself. She felt, as she said, that 'she' had recently 'gone right down' and she wanted to get out of 'it' now, before it was too late, and yet she had a feeling that things had gone too far and that she 'could not hold on to herself' for much longer and that 'it' was 'slipping away' from her. If she could like people she would be better.

A few days later she was expressing herself in the following way:

These thoughts go on and on, I'm going over the border. My real self is away down – it used to be just at my throat, but now it's gone further down. I'm losing myself. It's getting deeper and deeper. I want to tell you things, but I'm scared. My head's full of thoughts, fears, hates, jealousies. My head can't grip them; I can't hold on to them. I'm behind the bridge of my nose – I mean, my consciousness is there. They're splitting open my head, oh, that's schizophrenic, isn't it? I don't know whether I have these thoughts or not. I think I just made them up last time in order to get treated. Oh, if I could like and love again instead of this hate. I would like to like people, yet I want to hate them. I'm just killing myself too.

She continued to talk in the subsequent weeks in this way. The impression that she was killing herself came to be translated into the conviction that she *had* killed 'herself'. She maintained almost constantly that she had actually killed herself or sometimes that she had lost herself. On the occasions when she did not feel that she was entirely 'lost' or 'dead' she felt 'strange' to herself, and both she and other things no longer had the same realness about them. She was painfully aware of the loss of some capacity to experience things in a real way, and the capacity to think thoughts which were real. She was aware with equal intensity that other people had this capacity, and she described various techniques which either intentionally or unintentionally she now practised in order 'to recapture reality'. For instance, if anyone said anything to her which she classified as 'real', she would say to herself, 'I'll think that'; and she would keep repeating the word or phrase over and over again to herself in the hope that some of the realness of the expression would rub off on her. She felt doctors were real so she tried to keep the name of a doctor in her mind all the time. She tried to produce effects in other people such as saying something which she hoped would embarrass them. She found this quite easy to do since she felt quite detached from what feelings they might have. If then, looking at the other person, she saw signs of embarrassment she told herself that she must be real because she could produce a real effect in a real other person. As soon as anyone 'came into her mind', she would tell herself that she was that person. She now felt that in so far as she could like a person, to that extent she would be *like* that person. She followed behind people, imitated their walk, copied their phrases, and mimicked their gestures. In a way that was frequently infuriating to others, she agreed with absolutely everything that was said. All this time, however, she kept saying that she was getting farther and farther away from her real self. She wanted to be able to 'reach' other people and let other people reach her, but this was becoming more and more impossible. As she felt more desperate she came to feel less panicky, but nevertheless remained haunted by a persistent dread. She became unable to know what anything was for. She saw people doing things, but she said that she 'could not real-ize them. It is a blank feeling.' She was convinced that everyone was more clever than she was. They were all doing clever things but she could not make out what their simplest actions were intended to accomplish. She had no future. Time had stopped moving. She couldn't look forward and all her memories were dense and solid things, jostling around in her head. It was clear that she was losing any sense of the differentiation of events in time as past, present, or future, of 'lived' time, in Minkowski's sense.

It was a most significant fact that the more she felt she could not reach other people, that other people could not reach her, and the more she felt herself to be in a world of her own – 'They can't get in and I can't get out' – the more this private and closed world of hers became invaded by psychotic dangers from outside, i.e. the more 'public' in a sense it became. She became more suspicious of other people and began to hide things in her locker; she had a notion that some person was stealing things from her. She would check her handbag and personal possessions frequently to make sure that she had not been robbed of anything. This paradox of being more withdrawn and at the same time more vulnerable found its clearest expression in the statement that she was murdering herself on the one hand, and her fear that her 'self' might be lost or stolen on the other. She had only other people's thoughts and could think only what other people had said.

She now talked of being two. 'There are two mes.' 'She's me, and I'm her all the time.' She heard a voice telling her to murder her mother and she knew that this voice belonged to 'one of my mes'. 'From up here [indicating her temples] it's just cotton wool. I've no thoughts of my own; I'm awfully confused, me, me, me all the time, me and me, me and myself, when I say myself, I know there's something wrong, something's happening to me, I don't know what.'

Thus, despite the fear of losing her self, all her efforts to 'recapture reality' involved not being herself, and attempts to escape from her self or to kill her self continued to be used as basic defences, indeed, they became intensified.

The individual is led to 'kill himself' not only under pressure from anxiety, but out of his sense of guilt, which in such people is of a particularly radical and crushing kind, and seems to leave the subject with no room to manoeuvre.

We have already seen how, under such pressure of guilt, Peter was led to *be no thing*, to be no body. Here is another instance, of a patient who was pursuing a somewhat similar course, which happily was apparently arrested, or, it would be more correct to say, she arrested it before she had led herself into a psychotic state from which return would have been difficult.

Marie, aged twenty, had been a college student for one year without passing any of her examinations. She arrived to sit an exam either several days too early or too late. If she ever turned up on time or while the exam was still in progress, it seemed more or less by accident, and she could not be bothered to answer the questions. In her second year, she stopped attending classes altogether, and appeared to be doing nothing at all. It was extraordinarily difficult to find out any concrete facts of this girl's life. She came to me at the suggestion of someone else. I set a regular time for her to see me twice a week. It was never possible to predict when she might arrive. To say she was unpunctual would be a vast understatement. The definitive time for the interview was a point in time which served only vaguely to orientate her. She would turn up on a Saturday morning for an interview on Thursday afternoon or she would phone at 5 p.m. to say that she had just awakened and so could not manage her interview at four o'clock but would it be suitable if she came along in an hour or so. She missed five consecutive sessions without giving notice, and arrived punctually for the sixth without comment and continued where she had left off before this break.

She was a pale, thin, wan creature with unkempt straight hair. She dressed in an indeterminately vague and odd way. She was extraordinarily elusive and secretive about herself. As far as I could gather, not a single one among the many people with whom she came into fleeting contact ever knew how she spent her life. Her home was outside London but since going to college she had taken digs in town and changed her digs frequently. Her parents never knew where she was staying; she would call on them at odd moments and pass the time of day as though she was a casual acquaintance of the family. She was in fact the only child. She walked swiftly and silently, almost on tiptoe. Her speech was soft and distinct, but listless, far-away, still and stilted without any animation. She preferred not to speak about herself but of topics such as politics and economics. She treated me with apparent indifference. Usually she made it clear to me that she regarded me as no more than a further one of her numerous casual acquaintances, on whom she dropped to have a chat. She once told me, however, that I was a fascinating person; but that my nature was vicious and dirty. She did not betray any desire or expectation to get anything from me and it was never completely clear what she did feel that she derived from me. When she felt herself to be so indifferent to me she could not understand why she travelled considerable distances in order to see me.

One would have thought that the outlook in this girl's case was pretty hopeless, as she presented unequivocally the clinical psychiatric picture of dementia praecox or schizophrenia simplex.

However, one day she arrived punctually and amazingly transformed. For the first time in my experience of her she was dressed with at least ordinary care and without that disturbingly odd appearance in dress and manner that is so characteristic of this type of person but so difficult to define. Her movements and her expression had, unmistakably, *life* in them. She began the session by saying that she realized that she had been cutting herself off from any real relationship with other people, that she was scared by the way she had been living, but, apart from that, she knew in herself that this wasn't the right way to live. Obviously something very decisive had happened. According to her, and I see no reason to doubt this, it had arisen out of going to see a film. She had gone every day for a week to see the film *La Strada*. This is an Italian film about a man and a girl. The man is an itinerant strong man who travels from town to town performing his act, which consists in bursting by chest expansion a chain fastened round him. He acquires a girl from her parents to act as his assistant. He is strong, cruel, dirty, and vicious. He treats the girl as dirt. When he chooses, he rapes her, beats her, abandons her. He seems to be without conscience or remorse: he accords her no recognition as a person, shows not the slightest gratitude when she tries to please him or when she is loyal to him. He makes it clear to her that there is nothing that she can do for him that someone else couldn't do better. She cannot see what use her life is since it has been given over to this man, and to him she is worthless and useless. Although in her sadness and desolation there is no persistent bitterness, yet she is in despair that she is of no significance. She makes friends with a tight-rope walker in a circus. She laments to him her insignificance. However, when this funambulist asks her to come away with him she refuses, saying that if she does so the man will have nobody to put up with him. The funambulist picks up a pebble and says that he can't believe that she is *absolutely* useless since she must be worth at least as much as the pebble, and the pebble at least exists. Moreover, he points out that she must also have some use though she does not know it, since she knows that she is the only person whom this man does not drive away from him. Much of the charm of the film derives from this girl. She is utterly without guile or deception. Every shade of feeling shows itself simply and immediately through her every action. When the strong man kills the funambulist before her eyes, and evades justice rather than confess his crime, she becomes silent except to whimper, 'The fool is sick, the fool is sick.' She does nothing and eats nothing. When she seems not to be getting any better the man abandons her asleep beside a wintry road, leaving her to chance.

This patient identified herself with the girl and at the same time she saw herself in contrast to this girl. The strong man with his viciousness, indifference, and cruelty embodied her phantasy of her father and to some extent her phantasy of me. But what struck her most forcibly was that, though so despairing and unhappy, this girl did not cut herself off from life, no matter how terrible it was. She never became an agent of her own destruction. Nor did she try to distort her simplicity. The girl was not specifically religious; she seemed not to have had, any more than Marie, a faith in a Being whom she could call God; yet, although her faith was nameless her way of living was somehow an affirmation of life rather than a negation of it. Marie saw all this in horrified contrast to her own way of living her life. For she felt she had been denying herself access to the freshness and forgivingness of creation. Even the girl in the film could laugh at circus clowns, be thrilled by a tight-rope walker, find comfort in a song, and be worth no less than a pebble.

From the 'objective', clinical psychiatric point of view, one would say that there was an arrest in the process of progressive schizophrenic deterioration probably on an organic basis. From the existential point of view one could say that she had stopped trying to murder herself. She saw that her life had become a systematic attempt to destroy her own identity and to become nobody. She avoided everything whereby she could be specifically defined as an actual person engaged in specific tasks with others. She had tried to act in such a way that her acts had not any real consequences, and so by that token could hardly be real acts at all. Instead of using action as we normally do to achieve real ends and thus to become more and more defined in and through our actions as the specific persons we are, she attempted to reduce herself to vanishing-point by never doing anything specific, never seeming to be in any particular place at any particular time, with any particular person, doing any particular thing. She was always, as we all are, at a particular place at a particular time, but she attempted to avoid the implications of this by always being abstracted, being 'somewhere else as it were'. She acted as though it was possible not 'to put herself into' her actions. The effort to dissociate herself from her actions comprised everything she did, the work she seemed to be doing, the friendships she seemed to form, and all her gestures and expressions. By these means she sought to become nobody. Her position, therefore, was very similar to Peter's. Both these patients had come to feel more and more convinced that it was a mere pretence for them to be somebody and that the only honest course they could take was to become nobody, since that was all that they could feel themselves 'really' to be. What this process of self-annihilation presented to the observing clinician was nothing else than the dementing process of schizophrenia simplex.

As with Peter and Marie, the patients at the stage now being described do not experience guilt so much in respect to specific thoughts or acts they have or have not entertained or committed. If they have guilt in these respects it is superseded by a much more inclusive sense of badness or worthlessness which attacks their very right to *be* in any respect. The individual feels guilty at daring to be, and doubly guilty at not being, at being too terrified to be, and attempting to murder himself if not biologically, then existentially. His guilt is the urgent factor in preventing active participation in life, and in maintaining the 'self' in isolation, in pushing it into further withdrawal. Thereupon, guilt becomes attached to this very manoeuvre, which was prompted by guilt originally.

James, for instance, had the following dream:

'Two atoms were travelling in a parallel direction and then they turned in their courses backwards to come to rest almost contiguously.' He indicated their courses with his hands. He woke up from this dream abruptly, in a panic, and with a sense of awful foreboding.

His reading of this dream was that the two atoms were himself: instead of continuing on their 'natural course' they 'turned in on themselves'. In doing so, 'they violated the natural order of things'. Further associations to this dream revealed that James felt profoundly guilty at his own 'turned-in-backwards' relationship to himself, since it was:

1. A form of Onanism, i.e. wasting his powers of creativity and productiveness.
2. A withdrawal from actual heterosexual relationships, and establishing a relationship between two parts of his own being, in which the one was male and the other female.

3. Withdrawal from relationships with other men, and the setting up within himself of an exclusive homosexual relationship with himself.

This illuminates the further difficult problem, that in these circumstances the relationship of the self to itself is a guilty one, since, as we indicated earlier, it gathers into itself, or seeks to, a mode of relationship that 'in the natural order of things' can exist only between *two* persons and cannot be lived out in actuality by the self exclusively.

The splitting of the self (Rose's 'two mes', the state represented by James's two atoms) forms the basis of one type of hallucination. One of the fragments of the self generally seems to retain the sense of 'I'. The other 'self' might then be called 'her'. But this 'her' is still 'me'. Rose says, '*She*'s *me*, and *I*'m *her* all the time.' One schizophrenic told me, '*She*'s an *I* looking for a *me*.' (The self in chronic schizophrenic states seems to fragment into several foci each with a certain I-sense, and each experiencing the other fragments as partially not-me.) A 'thought' belonging to the 'other' self tends to have some of the quality of a perception since it is received by the experiencing self neither as a product of its imagination nor as belonging to it. That is, the *other self* is the basis of an hallucination. An hallucination is an as-if perception of a fragment of the disintegrated 'other' self by a remnant (self-focus) retaining residual I-sense; this becomes more apparent in manifestly psychotic patients. Moreover, the self-self relationship provides the internal setting for violent attacks between warring phantoms inside, experienced as having a sort of phantom concreteness (see following chapter). It is in fact such attacks from such inner phantoms that compel the individual to say he has been murdered, or that 'he' has murdered his 'self'. In the last resort, however, even speaking in 'schizophrenese', it is in fact impossible to murder the inner phantom 'self' although it is possible to cut one's throat. A ghost cannot be killed. What may happen is that the place and function of the inner phantom 'self' become almost completely 'taken over' by archetypal agencies which appear to be in complete control and dominate all aspects of the individual's being. The task in therapy then comes to be to make contact with the original 'self' of the individual which, or who, we must believe is still a *possibility*, if not an actuality, and can still be nursed back to a feasible life. But this is a story that we can take up and make explicable only after we have studied psychotic processes and phenomena at greater length; and this task we shall now undertake.

We shall now attempt to consolidate our account by selected
descriptions of a schizophrenic illness given by an American
patient in the phase of recovery. This case is reported by two
American authors, Hayward and Taylor (1956), and was in
psychotherapy with one of them. They state:

Joan is a twenty-six-year-old white woman. Her illness first appeared
early in 1947 when she was seventeen. In the ensuing two years she
was treated in four private hospitals with a regimen of psychotherapy,
accompanied by a total of thirty-four electric shock and sixty insulin
treatments. Fifty comas occurred. She showed 'little, if any, improvement' and was finally referred to one of the writers (M.L.H.), since she
appeared to be hopelessly ill.

At the start of the writer's treatment, Joan was cold, withdrawn,
seclusive, and suspicious. Visual and auditory hallucinations were
active. She would enter into no hospital activities and frequently
became so stuporous that it was difficult to elicit any response from her.
If pressed about the need for treatment, she would become sullenly
resistive or maintain angrily that she wanted to be left alone. Three
suicidal attempts were made, by slashing herself with broken glass or
taking an overdose of sedation. At times, she became so violently
belligerent that she had to be placed on the agitated ward.

I have chosen to draw on this material for a number of reasons.
This girl's account of her psychosis seems to afford striking confirmation of the views here presented. The confirmation is strengthened by the fact that the present book was originally written
before the American material was published. The American
authors write in the classical psycho-analytic terminology of ego,

superego, id, which I feel puts unnecessary limitations on one's understanding of the material: the patient's own account seems to be very much her own way of looking at herself, and not to have been imposed upon her or suggested to her by the authors. In this case, therefore, the possible fallacy in presenting material from one of my own patients that the patient was merely repeating parrot-wise my own theories about her is avoided.

Finally, this patient has given as clear and insightful an account of herself in 'ordinary' language as any within my knowledge. I hope that it will show that, if we look at the extraordinary behaviour of the psychotic from his own point of view, much of it will become understandable.

First, I would like to summarize briefly the views I have so far presented.

The divorce of the self from the body is both something which is painful to be borne, and which the sufferer desperately longs for someone to help mend, but it is also utilized as the basic means of defence. This in fact defines the essential dilemma. The self wishes to be wedded to and embedded in the body, yet is constantly afraid to lodge in the body for fear of there being subject to attacks and dangers which it cannot escape. Yet the self finds that though it is outside the body it cannot sustain the advantages that it might hope for in this position. We have already mentioned what happens:

1. Its orientation is a primitive oral one, concerned with the dilemma of sustaining its aliveness, while being terrified to 'take in' anything. It becomes parched with thirst, and desolate.
2. It becomes charged with hatred of all that is *there*. The only way of destroying and of not destroying what is there may be felt to be to destroy itself.
3. The attempt to kill the self may be undertaken intentionally. It is partly defensive ('If I'm dead, I can't be killed'); partly an attempt to endorse the crushing sense of guilt that oppresses the individual (no sense of a right to be alive).
4. The 'inner' self becomes itself split, and loses its own identity and integrity.

5. It loses its own realness and direct access to realness outside itself.

6. (*a*) The place of safety of the self becomes a prison. Its would-be haven becomes a hell.

(*b*) It ceases even to have the safety of a solitary cell. Its own enclave becomes a torture chamber. The inner self is persecuted within this chamber by split concretized parts of itself or by its own phantoms which have become uncontrollable.

A certain amount of the incomprehensibility of a schizophrenic's speech and action becomes intelligible if we remember that there is the basic split in his being carried over from the schizoid state. The individual's being is cleft in two, producing a disembodied self and a body that is a thing that the self looks at, regarding it at times as though it were just another thing in the world. The total body and also many 'mental' processes are severed from the self, which may continue to operate in a very restricted enclave (phantasying and observing), or it may appear to cease to function altogether (i.e. be dead, murdered, stolen). This account is, of course, highly schematic and has the failings of any preliminary over-simplification.

We have already outlined some of the ways in which this split may fail to support sane experience, and can become the kernel of psychosis.

In many schizophrenics, the self-body split remains the basic one. However, when the 'centre' fails to hold, neither self-experience nor body-experience can retain identity, integrity, cohesiveness, or vitality, and the individual becomes precipitated into a condition the end result of which we suggested could best be described as a state of 'chaotic nonentity'.* In its final form, such complete disintegration is a hypothetical state which has no verbal equivalents. We feel justified, however, in postulating such a

* The best description of any such condition I have been able to find in literature is in the Prophetic Books of William Blake. In the Greek descriptions of Hell, and in Dante, the shades or ghosts, although estranged from life, still retain their inner cohesiveness. In Blake, this is not so. The figures of his Books undergo division in themselves. These books require prolonged study, not to elucidate Blake's psychopathology, but in order to learn from him what, somehow, he knew about in a most intimate fashion, while remaining sane.

hypothetical condition. In its most extreme form it is perhaps not compatible with life. The thoroughly dilapidated, chronic catatonic-hebephrenic is presumably the person in whom this process has gone on to the most extreme degree in one who remains biologically viable.

One of the greatest barriers against getting to know a schizophrenic is his sheer incomprehensibility: the oddity, bizarreness, obscurity in all that we can perceive of him. There are many reasons why this is so. Even when the patient is striving to tell us, in as clear and straightforward a way as he knows how, the nature of his anxieties and his experiences, structured as they are in a radically different way from ours, the speech content is necessarily difficult to follow. Moreover, the formal elements of speech are in themselves ordered in unusual ways, and these formal peculiarities seem, at least to some extent, to be the reflection in language of the alternative ordering of his experience, with splits in it where we take coherence for granted, and the running together (confusion) of elements that we keep apart.

Yet these irreducible difficulties are practically certain to be much increased, at least in one's first encounters with the patient, by his or her deliberate use of obscurity and complexity as a smokescreen to hide behind. This creates the ironical situation that the schizophrenic is often playing at being psychotic, or pretending to be so. In fact, as we have said, pretence and equivocation are greatly used by schizophrenics. The reasons for doing this are, in any single case, likely to serve more than one purpose at a time. The most obvious one is that it preserves the secrecy, the privacy, of the self against intrusion (engulfment, implosion). The self, as one patient put it, feels crushed and mangled even at the exchanges in an ordinary conversation. Despite his longing to be loved for his 'real self' the schizophrenic is terrified of love. Any form of understanding *threatens* his whole defensive system. His outward behaviour is a defensive system analogous to innumerable openings to underground passages which one might imagine would take one to the inner citadel, but they lead nowhere or elsewhere. The schizophrenic is not going to reveal himself for casual inspection and examination to any philandering passer-by. If the self is not known it is safe. It is safe from penetrating remarks; it is safe from being smothered or engulfed by love, as much as from destruction from hatred. If the schizophrenic is incognito, his body can be handled and manipulated, petted, caressed, beaten, given injections or what have you, but 'he', an onlooker, is inviolable.

The self at the same time longs to be understood; indeed, longs for one whole person who might accept his total being, and in doing so, just 'let him be'. But it is necessary to proceed with great caution and circumspection. 'Don't try', as Binswanger puts it, 'to get too near, too soon.'

Joan says, 'We schizophrenics say and do a lot of stuff that is unimportant, and then we mix important things in with all this to see if the doctor cares enough to see them and feel them.'

A variant of this technique of mixing in important things among 'a lot of stuff that is unimportant' was explained to me by one schizophrenic. He gave an actual example. During a first meeting with a psychiatrist he conceived an intense contempt for him. He was terrified to reveal this contempt in case he was ordered to have a leucotomy and yet he desperately wanted to express it. As the interview was going on he felt it more and more to be a pretence, and futile, since he was only pretending a false front and the psychiatrist seemed to take this false presentation perfectly seriously. He thought the psychiatrist was more and more a fool. The psychiatrist asked him if he heard a voice. The patient thought what a stupid question this was since he heard the psychiatrist's voice. He therefore answered that he did, and to subsequent questioning, that the voice was male. The next question was, 'What does the voice say to you?' To which he answered, 'You are a fool.' By playing at being mad, he had thus contrived to say what he thought of the psychiatrist with impunity.

A good deal of schizophrenia is simply nonsense, red-herring speech, prolonged filibustering to throw dangerous people off the scent, to create boredom and futility in others. The schizophrenic is often making a fool of himself and the doctor. He is playing at being mad to avoid at all costs the possibility of being held *responsible* for a single coherent idea, or intention.

Joan gives other examples:

Patients laugh and posture when they see through the doctor who says he will help but really won't or can't. Posturing, for a girl, is seductive, but it's also an effort to distract the doctor away from all her pelvic functions. The patients try to divert and distract him. They try to please the doctor but also confuse him so he won't go into anything important. When you find people who will really help, you don't need to distract them. You can act in a normal way. I can sense if the doctor not only wants to help but also can and will help.

This provides striking confirmation of Jung's statement that the schizophrenic ceases to be schizophrenic when he meets someone by whom he feels understood. When this happens most of the bizarrerie which is taken as the 'signs' of the 'disease' simply evaporates.

Meeting you made me feel like a traveller who's been lost in a land where no one speaks his language. Worst of all, the traveller doesn't even know where he should be going. He feels completely lost and helpless and alone. Then, suddenly, he meets a stranger who can speak English. Even if the stranger doesn't know the way to go, it feels so much better to be able to share the problem with someone, to have him understand how badly you feel. If you're not alone, you don't feel hopeless any more. Somehow it gives you a life and a willingness to fight again.

Being crazy is like one of those nightmares where you try to call for help and no sound comes out. Or if you can call, no one hears or understands. You can't wake up from the nightmare unless someone does hear you and helps you to wake up.

The main agent in uniting the patient, in allowing the pieces to come together and cohere, is the physician's love, a love that recognizes the patient's total being, and accepts it, with no strings attached.

This, however, is simply the threshold and not the end of the relationship with the doctor. The patient remains psychotic in terms of the persisting splits in his or her being, even though the more obtrusive outward 'signs' may not be so much in evidence.

We noted that the self has lost contact with realness, and cannot feel itself real or alive.

Joan gives examples of some ways in which the schizophrenic tries to conjure up assurances of being real from the awareness of being seen, and hence at least being *there*. The schizophrenic cannot sustain this conviction from inner sources.

Patients kick and scream and fight when they aren't sure the doctor can see them. It's a most terrifying feeling to realize that the doctor can't see the real you, that he can't understand what you feel and that he's just going ahead with his own ideas. I would start to feel that I was invisible or maybe not there at all. I had to make an uproar to see if the doctor would respond to me, not just to his own ideas.

Throughout her account this patient repeatedly contrasts her real self with a compliant self which was false. The split between her 'real self' and her body is expressed vividly in the following passage:

If you had actually screwed me it would have wrecked everything. It would have convinced me that you were only interested in pleasure with my animal body and that you didn't really care about the part that was a person. It would have meant that you were using me like a woman when I really wasn't one and needed a lot of help to grow into one. It would have meant you could only see my body and couldn't see the real me which was still a little girl. The real me would have been up on the ceiling watching you do things with my body. You would have seemed content to let the real me die. When you feed a girl, you make her feel that both her body and her self are wanted. This helps her get joined together. When you screw her she can feel that her body is separate and dead. People can screw dead bodies, but they never feed them.

Her 'real self' had to be the starting-point for the development of genuine integral status. This 'real self', however, was not readily accessible, both because of the dangers threatening it:

My interviews were the only place where I felt safe to be myself, to let out all my feelings and see what they were really like without fear that you would get upset and leave me. I needed you to be a great rock that I could push and push, and still you would never roll away and leave me. It was safe for me to be bitchy with you. With everyone else I was trying to change myself to please them,

but also because it was felt to be so charged with hatred and destructive potential that nothing could survive that entered into it:

Hate has to come first. The patient hates the doctor for opening the wound again and hates himself for allowing himself to be touched again. The patient is sure it will just lead to more hurt. He really wants to be dead and hidden in a place where nothing can touch him and drag him back.

The doctor has to care enough to keep after the patient until he does hate. If you hate, you don't get hurt so much as if you love, but still you can be alive again, not just cold and dead. People mean something to you again.

The doctor must keep after the patient until he does hate, that is the only way to get started. But the patient must never be made to feel guilty for hating. The doctor has to feel sure he has the right to break into the illness, just as a parent knows he has the right to walk into a baby's room, no matter what the baby feels about it. The doctor has to know he's doing the right thing.

The patient is terribly afraid of his own problems, since they have destroyed him, so he feels terribly guilty for allowing the doctor to get mixed up in the problems. The patient is convinced that the doctor will be smashed too. It's not fair for the doctor to ask permission to come in. The doctor must fight his way in; then the patient doesn't have to feel guilty. The patient can feel that he has done his best to protect the doctor. The doctor must say by his manner, 'I'm coming in no matter what you feel.'

Again:

The problem with schizophrenics is that they can't trust anyone. They can't put their eggs in one basket. The doctor will usually have to fight to get in no matter how much the patient objects. It is wonderful to be beaten up or killed because no one ever does that to you unless they really care and can be made very upset. A person kills because he really wants the other to be resurrected, not just lie dead.

Loving is impossible at first because it turns you into a helpless little baby. The patient can't feel safe to do this until he is absolutely sure the doctor understands what is needed and will provide it.

The dread of taking in anything or anyone thus extends to good as well as bad. The bad will destroy the self, the self will destroy the good.

The self is therefore at the same time empty and starving. The whole orientation of the self is in terms of longing to eat, yet destroying the food or being destroyed by it.

Some people go through life with vomit on their lips. You can feel their terrible hunger but they defy you to feed them.

It's hellish misery to see the breast being offered gladly with love, but to know that getting close to it will make you hate it as you hated your mother's. It makes you feel hellish guilt because before you can love, you have to be able to feel the hate too. The doctor has to show that he can feel the hate but can understand and not be hurt by it. It's too awful if the doctor is going to be hurt by the sickness.

It's hell to want the milk so much but to be torn by guilt for hating the breast at the same time. Consequently, the schizophrenic has to try to do three things at once. He's trying to get to the breast but he's also trying to die. A third part of him is trying not to die.

We shall return to the issues involved in this last sentence later. For the moment, we have to continue with this effort of the self to avoid anything entering it in case it (the self and/or the object) will be destroyed.

The self, as we said, tries to be outside everything. All being is *there*, none is *here*.

This finally comes even to the position that everything the patient *is* is felt to be 'not-me'. He rejects all that he is, as a mere mirror of an alien reality. This total rejection of his being makes 'him', his 'true' self, a mere vanishing point. 'He' can't be real, substantial; he can have no actual identity, or actual personality. Everything he is comes by definition, therefore, under the scope of his false-self system. This may go beyond actions and words and extend to thoughts, ideas, even memories and phantasies. This false-self system is the breeding-ground of paranoid fears, since it follows easily that the false-self system, which has spread to include everything and is disavowed by the self as a mere mirror of alien reality (an object, a thing, mechanical, a robot, dead), can be regarded as an alien presence or person in possession of the individual. The 'self' has disavowed participation in it, the false-self system becomes enemy-occupied territory, felt to be controlled and directed by an alien, hostile, a destructive agency. As for the self, it exists in a vacuum. But this vacuum becomes encapsulated, albeit at first perhaps in moments in a relatively benign and protective way.

I felt as though I were in a bottle. I could feel that everything was outside and couldn't touch me.

But this turns into a nightmare. The walls of the bottle become a prison excluding the self from everything while, contrariwise, the self is persecuted as never before even within the confines of its own prison. The end result is thus at least as terrible as the state against which it was originally a defence. Thus:

> There is no gentleness, no softness, no warmth
>> in this deep cave.
> My hands have felt along the cave's stony sides,
>> and, in every crevice, there is only black depth.
> Sometimes, there is almost no air.
> Then I gasp for new air,
>> though, all the time, I am breathing
>> the very air that is in this cave.
> There is no opening, no outlet,
> I am imprisoned.
> But not alone.
> So many people crowd against me.
> A narrow shaft of light streams into this cave,
>> from a minute space between two rocks.
> It is dark in here.
> It is damp and the air is so very stale.
> The people, in here, are large, enormous.
> They echo themselves when they talk.
> And their shadows, on the cave walls,
>> follow them, as they move.
> I don't know what I look like,
>> nor how these people look.
> These people step on me,
>> sometimes, by careless mistake,
> I think. I hope.
> They are heavy people.
> It is getting tighter and tighter in here.
> I am frightened.
> If I get out of here, it may be terrible.
> More of these people would be outside.
> They would crush me, altogether,
> For they are even heavier than those,
>> in here, I think.
> Soon, the people, in here, will step on me
>> (by mistake, I think) so often, that
>> there won't be much left of me,
>> and I shall become part of the cave walls.

Then, I shall be an echo and a shadow,
   along with the other people, in here,
   who have become echoes and shadows.
I am not very strong any more.
I am frightened.
There is nothing for me, outside of here.
The people are bigger and would push me
   back into this cave.
The people, outside, don't want me.
The people, in here, don't want me.
I don't care.
The cave walls are so very rough and hard.
Soon, I shall be a part of them, hard and
Immovable, also. So very hard.

*

I ache from being stepped on by the people,
   in here, but they don't mean to step on me,
   and it's just a careless mistake that they do,
I think, I hope.
It might be interesting to see what I look like.
But I can never get into that shaft of light
   that creeps in this cave, because the people
   block my way, by mistake, I think, I hope.
But it might be terrible to see what I look like.
Because, then, I might see that I am like
   the other people, in here.
I am not.
I hope.

*

Strip this cave!
Strip it of all its cruel edges,
That bruise and cut my limbs.
Pour light into it.
Cleanse it!
Get the echoes and shadows out!
Drown the people's murmurs!
Blow the cave up! With dynamite!

*

> No, I don't – not yet.
> Wait, until I stand up, in this corner.
> Now, I am walking.
> There, I have stepped on you,
>   and you, and you, and you!!
> Do you feel my heel?
> Do you suffer from a kick?
> Ha! Now, I'm stepping on you!
> Are you crying?
> Good.

The bottle has become a cave, with cruel edges that bruise and cut her limbs, peopled by persecuting echoes and shadows, which she in turn persecutes.

Yet she still is frightened to give up the cave even with its attendant horrors, for only in the cave does she feel she can retain some sense of identity.

> There! There is no cave.
> It is gone.
> But when did I go?
> I cannot find me.
> Where am I?
> Lost.
> And all I know is that I am cold,
>   and it is colder, than when I was in the cave.
> So very, very cold.
> And, the people – they have walked on me,
>   as though I wasn't there, among them –
>   by mistake, I think. I hope.
> Yes, I want the cave,
> There, I know where I am.
> I can grope, in the dark,
>   and feel the cave walls.
> And the people, there, know I'm there,
>   and they step on me, by mistake –
> I think, I hope.
> But, outside –
> Where am I?

In the last resort, it is perhaps never true to say that the 'self' has been utterly lost, or destroyed, even in the most 'dilapidated hebephrenic', to use H. S. Sullivan's appropriately horrible term. There is still an 'I' that cannot find a 'me'. An 'I' has not ceased to exist, but it is without substance, it is disembodied, it lacks the quality of realness, and it has no identity, it has no 'me' to go with it. It may seem a contradiction in terms to say that the 'I' lacks identity but this seems to be so. The schizophrenic either does not know who or what he is or he has become something or someone other than himself. At any rate, without such a last shred or scrap of a self, an 'I' therapy of any kind would be impossible. There seems insufficient reason to believe that there is not such a last shred in any patient who can talk, or at least execute some integrated movements.

We can see also, in Joan's case, that it was her identity which she most desperately wished to preserve. Yet she felt either that she could not, ought not, or dare not be herself as an embodied person. The problems of her characteristically courting a sense of guilt, her unintegration, the nature of her false-self system, and her insecurely established capacity to differentiate her being from others, were intimately interrelated.

Everyone should be able to look back in their memory and be sure he had a mother who loved him, all of him; even his piss and shit. He should be sure his mother loved him just for being himself; not for what he could do. Otherwise he feels he has no right to exist. He feels he should never have been born.

No matter what happens to this person in life, no matter how much he gets hurt, he can always look back to this and feel that he is lovable. He can love himself and he cannot be broken. If he can't fall back on this, he can be broken.

You can only be broken if you're already in pieces. As long as my baby-self has never been loved then I was in pieces. By loving me as a baby, you made me whole.

Again:

I kept asking you to beat me because I was sure you could never like my bottom but, if you could beat it, at least you would be accepting it in a sort of way. Then I could accept it and make it part of me. I wouldn't have to fight to cut it off.

Being mad conferred a certain distinction on her which was not entirely unacceptable:

It was terribly hard for me to stop being a schizophrenic. I knew I didn't want to be a Smith (her family name), because then I was nothing but old Professor Smith's granddaughter. I couldn't be sure that I could feel as though I were your child, and I wasn't sure of myself. The only thing I was sure of was being a 'catatonic, paranoid and schizophrenic'. I had seen that written on my chart. That at least had substance and gave me an identity and personality. [What led you to change?] When I was sure that you would let me feel like your child and that you would care for me lovingly. If you could like the real me, then I could too. I could allow myself just to be me and didn't need a title.

I walked back to see the hospital recently, and for a moment I could lose myself in the feeling of the past. In there I could be left alone. The world was going by outside, but I had a whole world inside me. Nobody could get at it and disturb it. For a moment I felt a tremendous longing to be back. It has been so safe and quiet. But then I realized that I can have love and fun in the real world and I started to hate the hospital. I hated the four walls and the feeling of being locked in. I hated the memory of never being really satisfied by my fantasies.

She had been unable to sustain from her own resources a self-sufficient right to be herself, and be autonomous.

She was unable to sustain real autonomy because all she could be *vis-à-vis* her parents was a compliant thing.

My doctors just tried to make me a 'good girl' and patch things up between me and my parents. They tried to make me fit in with my parents. This was hopeless. They couldn't see that I was longing for new parents and a new life. None of the doctors seemed to take me seriously, to see how sick I was and what a big change I needed in life. No one seemed to realize that if I went back to my family I would be sucked back and lose myself. It would be like the photograph of a big family group taken from far away. You can see that there are people there but you can't be sure who is who. I would just be lost in a group.

Yet the only way she could disentangle herself was by means of an empty transcendence, into a 'world' of phantoms. Even when she began to 'be herself', she could at first only dare to do so by completely mirroring the doctor's reality. She could do this, however, since although his reality (his wishes for her) were still another's, they were not alien to her: they were congruent with her own authentic desire to be herself.

I only existed because you wanted me to and I could only be what you wanted to see. I only felt real because of the reactions I could produce in you. If I had scratched you and you didn't feel it, then I'd be really dead.

I could only be good if you saw it in me. It was only when I looked at myself through your eyes that I could see anything good. Otherwise, I only saw myself as a starving, annoying brat whom everyone hated and I hated myself for being that way. I wanted to tear out my stomach for being so hungry.

At this point, she has no genuine autonomy. One can see here very clearly how the schizophrenic's guilt stands in the way of his being himself. The simple act of achieving autonomy and separateness is for him an act arrogating to himself something that properly is not his: an act of Promethean *hubris*. We remember, indeed, that Prometheus' punishment was to have his entrails devoured by an eagle ('I wanted to tear out my stomach for being so hungry'), while he was chained to a rock. Indeed, in one version of the myth, Prometheus partially loses his separate identity in that he becomes fused with the rock to which he is chained. Without attempting a balanced interpretation of the whole myth, it seems that the rock and the eagle can be seen as two aspects of the mother, to whom one is chained (the rock: 'the granite breast of despair'), and by whom one is devoured (the eagle). The devouring eagle and the entrails, renewed only to be devoured again, are together a nightmarish inversion of the normal cycle of feeding.

To the schizophrenic, liking someone equals *being like* that person: being like a person is equated with being the same as that person, hence with losing identity. Hating and being hated may therefore be felt to threaten loss of identity less than do loving and being loved.

We postulated that the basic split in the schizoid personality was a cleft that severed the self from the body:

self/(*body-world*)

Such a scission cleaves the individual's own being in two, in such a way that the I-sense is disembodied, and the body becomes the centre of a false-self system.

The totality of experience has been differentiated by a line of cleavage within the individual's being into self/body.

When this is the primary split or when it exists along with the further vertical split of self/body/world, the body occupies a particularly ambiguous position.

The two basic segments of experience can be taken as

here   *there*

which are further differentiated in the normal way into

inside   *outside*

(*me*)   (*not-me*)

The schizoid cleavage disrupts the normal sense of self by disembodying the sense of 'I'. The seed is thus sown for a persisting running together, mergence, or confusion at the interface between here and there, inside and outside, because the body is not firmly felt as me in contrast to the not-me.

It is only when the body can be thus differentiated from others that all the problems involved in relatedness/separateness, between separate whole persons, can begin to be worked through in the usual way. The self does not need so desperately to remain bottled up in its defensive transcendence. The person can be like someone without being that other person; feelings can be *shared* without their being confused or merged with those of the other. Such sharing can begin only through an establishment of a clear distinction between here-me, there-not-me. At this stage it is critically important for the schizophrenic to test out the subtleties and niceties that lie at the interface between inside and outside, and all that is involved in the expression and revealing of what belongs truly to the real self. In this way does the self become a genuinely *embodied* self.

The first time I cried, you made a terrible mistake; you wiped away my tears with a handkerchief. You had no idea how I wanted to feel those tears roll down my face. At least I had some feelings that were on the outside. If only you could have licked my tears with your tongue, I would have been completely happy. Then you would have shared my feelings.

Joan refers a number of times to becoming dead, and to the desire to be dead. The patient, she says, 'really wants to be dead and hidden in a place where nothing can touch him and drag him back'.

We have referred to the desire to be dead, the desire for non-being, as perhaps the most dangerous desire that can be pursued In the schizophrenic, two main motives form into one force operating in the direction of promoting a state of death-in-life. There is the primary guilt of having no right to life in the first place, and hence of being entitled at most only to a dead life. Secondly, it is probably the most extreme defensive posture that can be adopted. One no longer fears being crushed, engulfed, overwhelmed by realness and aliveness (whether they arise in other people, in 'inner' feelings or emotions, etc.), since one is already dead. Being dead, one cannot die, and one cannot kill. The anxieties attendant on the schizophrenic's phantastic omnipotence are undercut by living in a condition of phantastic impotence.

Joan, since she could not be anything other than what her parents wanted her to be, and since they wanted her to be a boy, could only be – nothing.

I needed to be controlled and know what you wanted me to be. Then I'd be sure you would want me. With my parents I couldn't be a boy and they never made it clear what else they wanted me to be except that. So I tried to die by being catatonic.

She puts the whole matter extremely succinctly in the following passage:

When I was catatonic, I tried to be dead and grey and motionless. I thought mother would like that. She could carry me around like a doll.
I felt as though I were in a bottle. I could feel that everything was outside and couldn't touch me.
I had to die to keep from dying. I know that sounds crazy but one time a boy hurt my feelings very much and I wanted to jump in front of a subway. Instead I went a little catatonic so I wouldn't feel anything. (I guess you had to die emotionally or your feelings would have killed you.) That's right. I guess I'd rather kill myself than harm somebody else.

There are, of course, other ways of looking at the foregoing material and many other aspects to it. I have deliberately focused primarily on the nature of Joan's experience of her 'true' self, and her 'false' self, and I have hoped to show that this way of looking at it does not seem to impose distortion upon the patient's own testimony nor require us to deny aspects that do not 'fit'. In Joan's case, the minimum of reconstructing is required on our part, since she herself provides us with a clear statement of the phenomenology of her psychosis in straightforward simple language. When, however, one is dealing with a patient who is actively psychotic, one has to take the risk of translating the patient's language into one's own, if one is not to give an account that is itself in schizophrenese. This is our problem in the following case.

The ghost of the weed garden:
a study of a chronic schizophrenic

> ... *for the Truth is past all commiseration*
> MAXIM GORKY

Julie, at the time I knew her, had been a patient in a ward of a
mental hospital since the age of seventeen, that is, for nine years.
In these years, she had become a typical 'inaccessible and withdrawn' chronic schizophrenic. She was hallucinated, given to
posturing, to stereotyped, bizarre, incomprehensible actions;
she was mostly mute and when she did speak it was in the most
'deteriorated' 'schizophrenese'. On admission, she had been
diagnosed as a hebephrenic and given a course of insulin, without
improvement, and no other specific attempts had been made to
recall her to sanity. Left to herself, there is little doubt she would
quickly have become physically entirely 'dilapidated', but her
outward appearance was maintained by the almost daily attentions
of her mother, in addition to the work of the nursing staff.

On account of various odd and somewhat alarming things she
said and did at the time, her parents had taken her to see a psychiatrist when she was seventeen. In her interview with the psychiatrist, he recorded that there was nothing particularly unusual
about her non-verbal behaviour in itself but that the things
she said were enough to establish the diagnosis of schizophrenia.
In clinical psychiatric terminology, she suffered from depersonalization; derealization; autism; nihilistic delusions; delusions of
persecution, omnipotence; she had ideas of reference and end-of-
the-world phantasies; auditory hallucinations; impoverishment of
affects, etc.

She said the trouble was that she was not a real person; she was
trying to become a person. There was no happiness in her life
and she was trying to find happiness. She felt unreal and there was

an invisible barrier between herself and others. She was empty and worthless. She was worried lest she was too destructive and was beginning to think it best not to touch anything in case she caused damage. She had a great deal to say about her mother. She was smothering her, she would not let her live, and she had never wanted her. Since her mother was prompting her to have more friends, and to go out to dances, to wear pretty dresses, and so on, on the face of it these accusations seemed palpably absurd.

However, the basic psychotic statement she made was that 'a child had been murdered'. She was rather vague about the details, but she said she had heard of this from the voice of her brother (she had no brother). She wondered, however, if this voice may not have been her own. The child was wearing her clothes when it was killed. The child could have been herself. She had been murdered either by herself or by her mother, she was not sure. She proposed to tell the police about it.

Much that Julie was saying when she was seventeen is familiar to us from the preceding pages. We can see the existential truth in her statements that she is not a person, that she is unreal, and we can understand what she was getting at when she said that she was trying to become a person, and how it may have come about that she felt at once so empty and so powerfully destructive. But beyond this point, her communications become 'parabolic'. Her accusations against her mother, we suspect, must relate to her failure to become a person but they seem, on the surface, rather wild and far-fetched (see below). However, it is when she says that 'a child has been murdered' that one's common sense is asked to stretch further than it will go, and she is left alone in a world that no one will share.

Now, I shall want to examine the nature of the psychosis, which appeared to begin about the age of seventeen, and I think this can best be approached by first considering her life until then.

CLINICAL BIOGRAPHY OF A SCHIZOPHRENIC

It is *never* easy to obtain an adequate account of a schizophrenic's early life. Each investigation into the life of any single schizophrenic patient is a laborious piece of original research. It cannot be too strongly emphasized that a 'routine' or even a so-called dynamically orientated history obtained in the course of several interviews can give very little of the crucial information necessary for an existential analysis. In this particular case, I saw the mother once a week over a period of several months and interviewed (each on a number of occasions) her father, her sister, three years older, who was her only sibling, and her aunt (father's sister). However, no amount of fact-gathering is proof against bias. Searles (1958), for instance, is I think absolutely correct to emphasize the existence of positive feelings between the schizophrenic and his mother, a finding that has been singularly 'missed' by most other observers. I have no illusions that the present study is immune from bias which I cannot see.

Father, mother, sister, aunt were the effective personal world in which this patient grew up. It is the patient's life in her own interpersonal microcosmos that is the kernel of any psychiatric clinical biography. Such clinical biography is therefore self-consciously limited in scope. The socio-economic factors of the larger community of which the patient's family is an integral part are not *directly* relevant to the subject matter that is our concern. This is not to say that such factors do not profoundly influence the nature of the family and hence of the patient. But, just as the cytologist puts, *qua* cytologist, his knowledge of macroanatomy in parentheses in his description of cellular phenomena, while at the same time being in possession of this knowledge, so we put the larger sociological issues in parentheses as not of direct and immediate relevance to the understanding of how this girl came to be psychotic. Thus I think the clinical biography that I shall present could be of a working-class girl from Zürich, of a middle-class girl from Lincoln, or of a millionaire's daughter from Texas. Very similar human possibilities arise in the inter-personal relationships of people as differently placed within society as these. I am, however, describing something that occurs in our twentieth-century Western world, and perhaps not, in quite the same terms, anywhere else. I do not know what are the essential features of this world that allow of such possibilities to arise. But we, as clinicians, must not forget that what goes on beyond our self-imposed horizons may make a great difference to the patterns to be made out within the boundaries of our clinical interpersonal microcosmos.

I have felt it necessary to state this briefly here because I feel that clinical psychiatry in the West tends towards what a schizophrenic friend of mine called 'social gaucherie', whereas Soviet psychiatry seems to be rather gauche in the interpersonal sphere. Although a clinical biography must, I believe, focus on the interpersonal sphere, this should be in such a way as not to be a closed system which excludes the relevance in principle of what one may temporarily place in parentheses for convenience.'

Now, although each of the various people interviewed had his or her own point of view on Julie's life, they all agreed in seeing her life in three basic states or phases. Namely, there was a time when,

1. The patient was a *good*, normal, healthy child; until she gradually began
2. to be *bad*, to do or say things that caused great distress, and which were on the whole 'put down' to naughtiness or badness, until
3. this went beyond all tolerable limits so that she could only be regarded as completely *mad*.

Once the parents 'knew' she was mad, they blamed themselves for not realizing it sooner. Her mother said,

I was beginning to hate the terrible things she said to me, but then I saw she couldn't help it . . . she was such a good girl. Then she started to say such awful things . . . if only we had known. Were we wrong to think she was responsible for what she said? I knew she really could not have meant the awful things she said to me. In a way, I blame myself but, in a way, I'm glad that it was an illness after all, but if only I had not waited so long before I took her to a doctor.

What is meant precisely by good, bad, and mad we do not yet know. But we do now know a great deal. To begin with, as the parents remember it now, of course, Julie acted in such a way as to appear to her parents to be everything that was right. She was good, healthy, normal. Then her behaviour changed so that she acted in terms of what *all* the significant others in her world unanimously agreed was 'bad' until, in a short while, she was 'mad'.

This does not tell us anything about what the child did to be good, bad, or mad in her parents' eyes, but it does supply us with the important information that the original pattern of her actions was entirely in conformity with what her parents held to be good and praiseworthy. Then, she was for a time 'bad', that is, those very things her parents most did not want to see her do or hear her say or to believe existed in her, she 'came out with'. We cannot at present say why this was so. But that she was capable of saying and doing such things was almost incredible to her parents. All that emerged was totally unsuspected. They tried at first to discount it, but as the offence grew they strove violently to repudiate it. It was a great relief, therefore, when, instead of saying that her mother wouldn't let her live, she said that her mother had murdered a child. Then all could be forgiven. 'Poor Julie was ill. She was not responsible. How could I ever have believed for one moment that she meant what she said to me? I've always tried my best to be a good mother to her.' We shall have occasion to remember this last sentence.

These three stages in the evolution of the idea of psychosis in members of a family occur very commonly. Good – bad – mad. It is just as important to discover the way the people in the patient's world have regarded her behaviour as it is to have a history of her behaviour itself. I shall try to demonstrate this conclusively below, but at this point I would like to observe one important thing about the story of this girl as told me by her parents.

They did not suppress facts or try to be misleading. Both parents were anxious to be helpful and did not deliberately, on the whole, withhold information about actual facts. The significant thing was the way facts were discounted, or rather the way obvious possible implications in the facts were discounted or denied. We can probably best present a brief account of this girl's life by first grouping the events together within the parents' framework. My account is given predominantly in the mother's words.

Phase I: A normal and good child

Julie was never a demanding baby. She was weaned without

difficulty. Her mother had no bother with her from the day she took off nappies completely when she was fifteen months old. She was never 'a trouble'. She always did what she was told.

These are the mother's basic generalizations in support of the view that Julie was always a 'good' child.

Now, this is the description of a child who has in some way never come alive: for a really alive baby is demanding, is a trouble, and by no means always does what she is told. It may well be that the baby was never as 'perfect' as the mother would like me to believe, but what is highly significant is that it is just this 'goodness' which is Mrs X's ideal of what perfection is in a baby. Maybe this baby was not as 'perfect' as all that; maybe in maintaining this the mother is prompted by some apprehensiveness lest I blame her in some way. The crucial thing seems to me to be that Mrs X evidently takes just those things which I take to be expressions of an inner deadness in the child as expressions of the utmost goodness, health, normality. The significant point, therefore, if we are thinking not simply of the patient abstracted from her family, but rather of the whole family system of relationships of which Julie was a part, is not that her mother, father, aunt all describe an existentially dead child, but that none of the adults in her world know the difference between existential life and death. On the contrary, being existentially dead receives the highest commendation from them.

Let us consider each of the above statements of the mother in turn:

1. *Julie was never a demanding baby*. She never cried really for her feeds. She never sucked vigorously. She never finished a bottle. She was always 'whinie and girnie'; she did not put on weight very rapidly. 'She never wanted for anything but I felt she was never satisfied.'

Here we have a description of a child whose oral hunger and greed have never found expression. Instead of a healthy vigorous expression of instinct in lusty, excited crying, energetic suckling, emptying the bottle, followed by contented satiated sleep, she fretted continually, seemed hungry, yet, when presented with the bottle, sucked desultorily, and never satisfied herself. It is tempting to try to reconstruct these early experiences from the infant's point of view, but here I wish to restrict myself only to the observable facts as remembered by the mother after over twenty years, and to make our constructions from these alone.

As stated above, and this is I believe an important point when thinking of aetiological factors, one of the most important aspects of this account is not simply that we get the picture of a child who, however physically alive, is not existentially becoming alive, but that the mother so far misunderstands the situation that she continues to rejoice in the memory of just those aspects of the baby's behaviour which were most dead. The mother is not alarmed that the baby did not cry 'demandingly' nor drain the bottle. That Julie did not do so, is not sensed by her as an ominous failure of basic oral instinctual drives to find expression and fulfilment but solely as token of 'goodness'.

Mrs X repeatedly emphasized that Julie had never been a 'demanding' baby. This did not mean that she was not a generous person herself. In fact, she had 'given her life' for Julie, as she put it. As we shall see, Julie's sister had been a demanding, greedy baby. Her mother had never had much hope for her: 'I just let her go her own way.' However, it was just the fact that Julie from the start had never been demanding that seemed largely to have encouraged her mother to give her so much, as she had done. It was therefore a terrible thing for her when, in her teens, Julie, instead of displaying some gratitude for all that had been done for her and given to her, began to accuse her mother of *never having let her be*. Thus, although it seems to me quite possible that, owing to some genetic factor, this baby was born with its organism so formed that instinctual need and need-gratification did not come easily to it, put in the most general way, added to this was the fact that all the others in its world took this very feature as a token of goodness and stamped with approval the absence of self-action. The combination of almost total failure of the baby to achieve self-instinctual gratification, along with the mother's total failure to realize this, can be noted as one of the recurrent themes in the early beginnings of the relation of mother to schizophrenic child. More research is needed to establish how specific this combination is.

2. *She was weaned without any trouble.* It is in feeding that the baby for the first time is actively alive with another. By the time of weaning the ordinary infant can be expected to have developed some sense of itself as a being in its own right, it has a 'way of its own', and some sense of the permanence of the mother as prototypical other. On the basis of these achievements, weaning occurs without much difficulty. The baby at this stage is given to playing 'weaning games' in which he drops, say, a rattle, to have it returned to him; drops it again, to have it returned; drops it, and so on, interminably. The baby seems here to be playing at an object going away, returning, going away, returning, the central issue of weaning in fact. Moreover, the game has usually to be played *his* way so that we find it 'natural' to collude with him in maintaining the impression that he is in control. In Freud's case, the little boy kept his reel of string attached to him when he threw it away, in contrast to the fact that he could not keep his mother thus under control by an attachment to her 'apron strings'. Now, if, as we have inferred, this girl was, in early months, not achieving the autonomy that is the prerequisite for the ability to go one's own way, to have a mind of her own, then it is not surprising that she should appear to be weaned without difficulty, although it could hardly be called weaning when the infant is giving up something it has never had. In fact, one could hardly speak of weaning having occurred at all in Julie's case. Things went so smoothly at this time that her mother could recall very few actual incidents. However, she did remember that she played a 'throwing away' game with the patient. Julie's elder sister had played the usual version of this game and had exasperated Mrs X by it. 'I made sure that *she* (Julie) was not going to play that game with me. *I* threw things away and she brought them back to *me*,' as soon as she could crawl.

It is hardly necessary to comment on the implications of this inversion of roles for Julie's failure to develop any real ways of her own.

She was said to have been precocious in walking (just over one year), and would scream if she could not get to her mother across the room quickly enough. The furniture had to be rearranged because 'Julie was terrified of any chairs that came between her and me'. Her mother interpreted this as a token of how much her daughter had always loved her. Until she was three or four, she 'nearly went crazy' if her mother was out of her sight for a moment.

This seems to lend confirmation to the suggestion that she was never really weaned because she had never reached a stage when weaning, in any more than a physical sense, could take place. Since she had never established an autonomous self-being, she could not begin to work through the issues of presence and absence to the achievement of the ability to be alone by herself, to the discovery that the physical presence of another person was not necessary for her own existence, however much her needs or desires may have been frustrated. If an individual needs another in order to be himself, it presupposes a failure fully to achieve autonomy, i.e. he engages in life from a basically insecure ontological position. Julie could be herself neither in her mother's presence nor in her absence. As far as her mother remembers, she was never actually physically out of earshot of Julie until she was almost three.

3. *She was clean from the moment that nappies were taken off at fifteen months.* One may note at this point that it is not unusual to find in schizophrenics a precocious development of bodily control although it is not known how they compare with others in this respect. One is certainly often told by parents of schizophrenics of how proud they were of their children because of their precocious crawling, walking, bowel and bladder functioning, talking, giving up crying, and so on. One has to ask, however, in considering the conjunction between what the parent is proud to tell about and what the child has achieved, how much of the infant's behaviour is an expression of its own will. The question is not how good or how naughty a child is, but whether the child develops a sense of being the origin of his own actions, of being the source from which his actions arise: or whether the child feels that his own actions are generated not from within himself, but from within the mother, despite possibly giving every appearance of being the agent of his acts (cf. the person in hypnosis who is under orders to *pretend* to be autonomous). It can happen that the body

may perfect its skills and thus do all that is expected of it; yet genuine self-action seems never to have become established to any extent, but instead all action is in almost total compliance and conformity with outside directives. In Julie's case, her actions appear to have been trained by her mother, but 'she' was not 'in' them. This must have been what she meant by saying that she had never become a person and in her constant reiteration as a chronic schizophrenic that she was a 'tolled bell' (or 'told belle'). In other words, she was only what she was told to do.

4. *She always did what she was told.* As we remarked earlier about telling the truth and lying, there are good reasons for being obedient, but being unable to be disobedient is not one of the best reasons. So far, in Mrs X's account one is unable to see that the mother recognized in Julie any possibilities other than her being what Julie herself called 'the told belle'. She 'gave her life' to the tolled bell, but she totally denied, and still did twenty-five years later, the possibility that this good, obedient, clean little girl, who so loved her that she nearly went crazy when separated from her if only by a chair, was petrified into a 'thing', too terror-stricken to become a person.

5. *She was never a 'trouble'.* It was now clear that from the time that this patient emerged beyond the early months of life she was without autonomy. She had never, as far as can be judged from what her mother remembers, developed ways of her own. Instinctual needs and gratifications had never found any expression through channels of bodily activity.

Real satisfaction arising from real desire for ... real breast had not occurred in the first instance. Her oval as she did its first regarded the con- sequences of this with the sa~ much cake. You just had to say, manifestations. and she wouldn't object.'

'She would now it may come about that hatred is expressed "That's ... ough the very compliance of the false-self system. ... er commended her obedience, but Julie began to carry obedience to such lengths that it became 'impossible'. Thus, she had a spell, at about the age of ten, when she had to be told everything that was going to happen in the course of the day and what she was to do. Every day had to begin with such a catalogue. If her mother refused to comply with this ritual she would start to whimper. Nothing would stop this whimpering, according to her mother, but a sound thrashing. As she grew older, she would not use any money she was given herself. Even when encouraged to say what she wanted or to buy a dress herself or to have friends like other girls, she would not express her own wishes; she had to have her mother to buy her clothes, and she showed no initiative in making friends. She would never take a decision of any kind.

Besides the whimpering mentioned above, there were a few other occasions in childhood when Julie upset her. She had a spell during the years from five to seven when she bit and tore at her nails; from the first beginnings of speech she had a tendency to turn words round back to front. Suddenly, at the age of eight, she started to over-eat, and continued in this for some months before reverting to her usual half-hearted way of eating.

Her mother, however, discounted such things as transitory phases. One has in them, nevertheless, sudden glimpses of an inner world of violent destructiveness with a short-lived desperate access of manifest greed which, however, soon became curbed and submerged again.

II: The 'Bad' Phase.

From about fifteen, her behaviour changed, and from being such a 'good' girl, she became 'bad'. At this time also, her mother's attitude had begun to change towards her. Whereas, previously, she had thought it right and proper that Julie should be with her as much possible, now she began to urge her to get out more, have friends and have boy friends. All the pictures and even to dances, ately' refused to do. Instead, she things the patient 'obstinor wander the streets, never telling her and do nothing, be back. She kept her room extravagantly and she would to cherish a doll which her mother felt she should continued out of'. We shall have occasion to return to th she had a spell, at about the age of ten, when she had to be told everything that was going to happen in the course of the day and what she was to do. Every day had to begin with such a catalogue. If her mother refused to comply with this ritual she would start to whimper. Nothing would stop this whimpering, according to her mother, but a sound thrashing. As she grew older, she would not use any money she was given herself. Even when encouraged to say what she wanted or to buy a dress herself or to have friends like other girls, she would not express her own wishes; she had to have her mother to buy her clothes, and she showed no initiative in making friends. She would never take a decision of any kind.

Besides the whimpering mentioned above, there were a few other occasions in childhood when Julie upset her. She had a spell during the years from five to seven when she bit and tore at her nails; from the first beginnings of speech she had a tendency to turn words round back to front. Suddenly, at the age of eight, she started to over-eat, and continued in this for some months before reverting to her usual half-hearted way of eating.

Her mother, however, discounted such things as transitory phases. One has in them, nevertheless, sudden glimpses of an inner world of violent destructiveness with a short-lived desperate access of manifest greed which, however, soon became curbed and submerged again.

II: The 'Bad' Phase.

From about fifteen, her behaviour changed, and from being such a 'good' girl, she became 'bad'. At this time also, her mother's attitude had begun to change towards her. Whereas, previously, she had thought it right and proper that Julie should be with her as much as possible, now she began to urge her to get out more, have friends, go to the pictures and even to dances, and have boy friends. All these things the patient 'obstinately' refused to do. Instead, she would sit and do nothing, or wander the streets, never telling her mother when she would be back. She kept her room extravagantly untidy. She continued to cherish a doll which her mother felt she should now have 'grown out of'. We shall have occasion to return to this doll later.

may perfect its skills and thus do all that is expected of it; yet genuine self-action seems never to have become established to any extent, but instead all action is in almost total compliance and conformity with outside directives. In Julie's case, her actions appear to have been trained by her mother, but 'she' was not 'in' them. This must have been what she meant by saying that she had never become a person and in her constant reiteration as a chronic schizophrenic that she was a 'tolled bell' (or 'told belle'). In other words, she was only what she was told to do.

4. *She always did what she was told.* As we remarked earlier about telling the truth and lying, there are good reasons for being obedient, but being unable to be disobedient is not one of the best reasons. So far, in Mrs X's account one is unable to see that the mother recognized in Julie any possibilities other than her being what Julie herself called 'the told belle'. She 'gave her life' to the tolled bell, but she totally denied, and still did twenty-five years later, the possibility that this good, obedient, clean little girl, who so loved her that she nearly went crazy when separated from her if only by a chair, was petrified into a 'thing', too terror-stricken to become a person.

5. *She was never a 'trouble'.* It was now clear that from the time that this patient emerged beyond the early months of life she was without autonomy. She had never, as far as can be judged from what her mother remembers, developed ways of her own. Instinctual needs and gratifications had never found any expression through channels of bodily activity.

Real satisfaction arising from real desire for the real breast had not occurred in the first instance. Her mother regarded the consequences of this with the same approval as she did its first manifestations.

'She would never take too much cake. You just had to say, "That's enough, Julie", and she wouldn't object.'

We noted earlier how it may come about that hatred is expressed only in and through the very compliance of the false-self system. Her mother commended her obedience, but Julie began to carry her obedience to such lengths that it became 'impossible'. Thus,

Julie's diatribes against her mother were endless and were always on the same theme: she would accuse her mother of not having wanted her, of not letting her be a person, of never having let her breathe, of having smothered her. She swore like a trooper. Yet to other people she could be charming, when she wanted.

So far we have considered only the relationship of Julie with her mother. But now, before we can go further, we must say a word about the total family constellation.

In recent years, the concept of a 'schizophrenogenic' mother has been introduced. Fortunately an early 'witch-hunt' quality about the concept has begun to fade. This concept can be worked out in various rather different ways, but it can be stated in the following terms: there may be some ways of being a mother that impede rather than facilitate or 'reinforce' any genetically deter- mined inborn tendency there may be in the child towards achieving the primary developmental stages of ontological security. Not only the mother but also the total family situation may impede rather than facilitate the child's capacity to participate in a real shared world, as self-with-other.

It is the thesis of this study that schizophrenia is a possible outcome of a more than usual difficulty in being a whole person with the other, and with not sharing the common-sense (i.e. the community sense) way of experiencing oneself in the world. The world of the child, as of the adult, is '*a unity of* the given and the constructed' (Hegel), a unity for the child of what is mediated to it by the parents, the mother in the first instance, and of what he makes of this. The mother and father greatly simplify the world for the young child, and as his capacity grows to make sense, to inform chaos with pattern, to grasp distinctions and connexions of greater and greater complexity, so, as Buber puts it, he is led out into 'a feasible world'.

But what can happen if the mother's or the family's scheme of things does not match what the child can live and breathe in? The child then has to develop its own piercing vision and to be able to live by that – as William Blake succeeded in doing, as Rimbaud succeeded in stating, but not in living – or else become mad. It is out of the earliest loving bonds with the mother that the infant develops the beginnings of a being-for-itself. It is in and through these bonds that the mother 'mediates' the world to the infant in the first place. The world he is given may be one he can manage to *be* in; it is possible, on the contrary, that what he is given is just not feasible for him at the time. Yet, despite the importance of the first year of life, the nature of the milieu in which the child has to exist throughout its infancy, childhood, and adolescence may still have great effect one way or the other. It is at these subsequent stages that the father or other significant adults may play a decisive role in the child's life, either in direct relation with the child or, indirectly, through effects on the mother.

These considerations suggest that one might do better to think of schizophrenogenic families, rather than too exclusively of schizophrenogenic mothers. At least, doing so might encourage more reports of the dynamics of the family constellation as a whole, instead of studies of mothers, or fathers, or siblings, without sufficient reference to the whole family dynamics.*

Julie's sister, three years older, was a rather forthright assertive married woman, not, however, without femininity and charm. According to her mother, she had been 'difficult' from birth: demanding and always 'a trouble'. In short, she seems to have been a relatively 'normal' child of whom her mother never very much approved. But they appeared to get on well enough together. The sister regarded her mother as a rather dominating person if one did not stand up to her. But 'she's done everything for Julie, and Julie was always her favourite'. It was quite clear that this sister had early on achieved integral autonomous status. If one cared to look closely into her personality, there were many neurotic elements to be found in her, but there seemed little doubt that at least she had achieved the primary ontological status that Julie had never reached. When she was a child, she had friends of her own age, just too old for Julie, and Julie did not appear to have come close to her. Julie, however, had built into her scheme of phantoms a big sister who was one of the few predominantly good figures in her 'world', 'a Sister of Mercy'.

* See particularly Laing and Esterson (1964).

The father had a more obviously significant part to play. In her mother's eyes, he was a 'sexual beast'. In his, her mother was cold and unsympathetic. They spoke to each other no more than was absolutely necessary. He found sexual satisfaction elsewhere. However, although they had many accusations to make against each other, neither built into these accusations any allegations about mistreating their daughter. The father, indeed, as he said, had not much to tell me, because he had 'withdrawn himself emotionally' from the family before Julie was born.

The patient's sister told me two incidents, both of which must have been of very great importance to Julie. The first her mother probably did not know about; the second she could not bring herself to tell me of. We shall return to the second incident later. The first occurred when Julie was fourteen or fifteen. Despite her father's distance from her and his relative inaccessibility, Julie had seemed fond of him. He occasionally took her for a walk. On one occasion Julie came home from such a walk in tears. She never told her mother what had happened. Her mother mentioned this to me to say that she was sure that something awful had taken place between Julie and her husband but she had never discovered what. After this, Julie would have nothing to do with her father. She had, however, confided to her sister at the time that her father had taken her into a call-box and she had overheard a 'horrible' conversation between him and his mistress.

Mrs X did not hesitate to miscall her husband to her daughters, and in piling up innumerable instances of injustices she tried to get them on her side. However, the elder sister took a middle way, and Julie apparently would never openly collude with her mother against her father: after the telephone-box incident, she simply cut herself off from him but would not supply the information for grist to her mother's mill. The father, however, had, as he said, withdrawn himself from the family. He did not make accusations against his wife to his daughters, since he did not need their support against her. Although he regarded her as a useless wife, 'To be fair to her,' as he put it, 'she was a good mother. I have to grant her that.' The elder sister saw faults on both sides but tried as far as possible to be reasonable and balanced, and not to take one side more than another. But if she had to, she took her mother's

side against her father, and her mother's side against Julie. In this
latter respect, it was not unreasonable that she should do so.
Julie's accusations against her mother were, from a matter-of-fact,
common-sense point of view, wild and phantastic from the first.
They must have sounded from the start rather mad. To 'rant and
rave' about being smothered and not being allowed to live and
be a person seemed to this ordinary common-sense family to make
no sense at all. She said her mother had never wanted her, and
yet she was the favourite; her mother had done everything for her
and given her everything. She said her mother was smothering
her, and yet her mother was urging her to grow up. She said her
mother did not want her to become a person, and yet her mother
was urging her to make friends, go to dances, etc.

It is remarkable that, despite the radical disruption of the
relationship between husband and wife, in one respect at least
they maintained a collusion. Both accepted the patient's false self
as good and rejected every other aspect of her as bad. But in the
'bad' phase, a corollary to this was perhaps even more important.
Not only did they reject as bad all of Julie apart from the compliant lifeless shadow which passed in their eyes for a real person,
they completely refused to 'take to heart' any of the reproaches
that Julie had against them.

Julie and her mother were at this time both desperate people.
Julie in her psychosis called herself Mrs Taylor. What does this
mean? It means 'I'm tailor-made'. 'I'm a tailored maid; I was
made, fed, clothed, and tailored.' Such statements are psychotic,
not because they may not be 'true' but because they are cryptic:
they are often quite impossible to fathom without the patient
decoding them for us. Yet even as a psychotic statement this seems
a very cogent point of view and it gives in a nutshell the gist of
the reproaches she was making against her mother when she was
fifteen and sixteen. This 'ranting and raving' was her 'badness'.
What I feel must have been the most schizophrenogenic factor of
this time was not simply Julie's attack on her mother, or even her
mother's counter-attack, but the complete absence of anyone in
her world who could or would see some sense in her point of
view, whether it was right or wrong. For various reasons, neither
her father nor her sister could see that there was any validity in

Julie's side of the argument. Like our group patient (p. 43) she was not fighting to win an argument, but to preserve her existence: in a way, Julie was not simply trying to preserve her existence, she was trying to achieve existence. We can see, I think, that by fifteen or sixteen, Julie could hardly have developed what one might call 'the ability of common sense'. The common family sense accorded 'her' no existence. Her mother had to be right, totally right. When her mother said she was bad, Julie felt this as murder. It was the negation of any autonomous point of view on her part. Her mother was prepared to accept a compliant, false self, to love this shadow, and to give it anything. She even tried to order this shadow to act as though it were a person. But she had never recognized the real disturbing presence in the world of a daughter with her own possibilities. The existential truth in Julie's delusions was that her own true possibilities were being smothered, strangled, murdered. To exist, to be able to breathe, Julie felt that her mother had to admit that she could have been wrong about some things, that she could have made mistakes, that there was a sense in which what her daughter said could be right and have weight. Putting it in one way, one might say that Julie needed to be allowed to project some of her bad-self into her mother, and to be allowed to take some goodness out of her mother, not merely to be given it all the time. But, to the whole family, Julie was trying to prove white was black. Reality did not yield. She began to convert existential truth into physical facts. She became deluded. If she began by accusing her mother of never having let her live, in an existential sense, she ended by talking and acting more than half as though her mother had, in a legal sense, actually murdered an actual child, and it was quite clearly a relief to the family when they could then pity her and no longer have to vindicate themselves by condemning her. Only her father, in a curious way, treated her as a responsible person. He never admitted that she was mad. To him she was wicked.

He was not 'taken in' by her game. It was all an expression of spite and ingratitude. He regarded what we called her catatonic negativism as sheer 'thrawn-ness', her hebephrenic symptoms as vindictive silliness. He was the only one of the family who did not pity her. On some of his occasional visits, he was known to have shaken and pinched her and twisted her arm to get her to 'stop it'.

Phase III: Mad.

Julie's basic accusation was that her mother was trying to kill her. When she was seventeen, an incident occurred that was probably the efficient cause in the transition from being bad to being mad.

This is the second circumstance told me by the sister. Until the age of seventeen, Julie had a doll. She had had this doll from infancy: she dressed and clothed it, played with it in her room, no one knew quite in what way. It was a secret enclave in her life. She called it Julie Doll. Her mother became more and more insistent that she should give up this doll, because she was a big girl now. One day the doll was gone. It was never known whether Julie had thrown it out, or whether her mother had put it away. Julie accused her mother. Her mother denied that she had done anything to the doll and said that Julie must have lost it herself. It was shortly after this that Julie was told by a voice that a child wearing her clothes had been beaten to pulp by her mother, and she proposed to go to the police to report this crime.

I said that either Julie or her mother disposed of the doll because it seems highly probable that at this stage her 'mother' for Julie was already more an archetypal destroyer than her real mother outside. When Julie said that her 'mother' killed the doll, it is quite possible that 'she' did so, that is, that her 'internal' mother had done so. However it happened, in fact the action was catastrophic; for Julie was evidently closely identified with the doll. In her play with the doll, the doll was herself and she was its mother. Now it is possible that in her play she became more and more the bad mother who finally killed the doll. We shall see later that in her psychosis the 'bad' mother acted out and spoke through her a good deal. If the doll had been destroyed by her actual mother, who had admitted it, the event might even have been less catastrophic. Julie's shreds of sanity at this stage depended on the possibility of being able to lodge some bad in her actual mother. The impossibility of doing this, in a sane way, was one of the factors that contributed to a schizophrenic psychosis.

THE GHOST OF THE WEED GARDEN

> *... at some stage a machine which was previously assembled in an allover manner may find its connexions divided into partial assemblies with a higher or lower degree of independence.*
> NORBERT WIENER: *Human Use of Human Beings*

The remarks that follow apply to Julie and to other chronic schizophrenics of the hebephrenic-catatonic type. They are not intended to encompass all forms of chronic psychotic states where splitting in one form or other is very evident. In particular, they are least applicable to paranoid psychoses where there is a much greater integration of the personality, of a kind, than that found in Julie and those like her.

Julie's self-being had become so fragmented that she could best be described as living *a death-in-life existence in a state approaching chaotic nonentity.*

In Julie's case, the chaos and lack of being an identity were not complete. But in being with her one had for long periods that uncanny 'praecox* feeling' described by the German clinicians, i.e. of being in the presence of another human being and yet feeling that there was no one there. Even when one felt that what was being said was an expression of someone, the fragment of a self behind the words or actions was not Julie. There might be someone addressing us, but in listening to a schizophrenic, it is very difficult to know 'who' is talking, and it is just as difficult to know 'whom' one is addressing.

In listening to Julie, it was often as though one were doing group psychotherapy with the one patient. Thus I was confronted with a babble or jumble of quite disparate attitudes, feelings,

---

* From the term dementia praecox formerly used to denote what we now generally call a form of schizophrenia occurring in young people which was thought to go on to a conclusion of chronic psychosis. This 'praecox feeling' should, I believe, be the audience's response to Ophelia when she has become psychotic. Clinically she is latterly undoubtedly a schizophrenic. In her madness, there is no one there. She is not a person. There is no integral selfhood expressed through her actions or utterances. Incomprehensible statements are said by nothing. She has already died. There is now only a vacuum where there was once a person.

expressions of impulse. The patient's intonations, gestures, mannerisms, changed their character from moment to moment. One may begin to recognize patches of speech, or fragments of behaviour cropping up at different times, which seem to belong together by reason of similarities of the intonation, the vocabulary, syntax, the preoccupations in the utterance or to cohere as behaviour by reason of certain stereotyped gestures or mannerisms. It seemed therefore that one was in the presence of various fragments, or incomplete elements, of different 'personalities' in operation at the one time. Her 'word-salad' seemed to be the result of a number of quasi-autonomous partial systems striving to give expression to themselves out of the same mouth at the same time.

This impression is strengthened, though hardly made the less confusing, by the fact that Julie seemed to speak of herself in the first, second, or third person. One requires an intimate knowledge of the individual patient before one can be in a position to say anything about the significance of this (this is true in all other aspects of schizophrenic activity).

Janet has differentiated dissociation or splitting into molar splits and molecular splits. The hysterical split personality is a molar split. Schizophrenia consists of molecular splitting. In Julie's case, there seemed to be both. The overall unity of her being had broken up into several 'partial assemblies' or 'partial systems' (quasi-autonomous 'complexes', 'inner objects'), each of which had its own little stereotyped 'personality' (molar splitting). In addition, any actual sequence of behaviour was fragmented in a much more minute manner (molecular splitting). Even the integrity of words, for instance, would be disrupted.

It is not surprising therefore that we speak of the 'inaccessibility' and 'praecox feeling' in such a case as this. With Julie it was not difficult to carry on a verbal exchange of a kind, but without her seeming to have any overall unity but rather a constellation of quasi-autonomous partial systems, it was difficult to speak to 'her'. However, one must not think primarily in terms of any mechanical analogy since even this state of near-chaotic nonentity was by no means irreversible and fixed in its disintegration. She would sometimes marvellously come together again and display a most pathetic realization of her plight. But she was terrified of these moments of integration, for various reasons. Among others, because she had to sustain in them intense anxiety; and because the process of disintegration appeared to be remembered and dreaded as an experience so awful that there was refuge for her in her unintegration, unrealness, and deadness.

Julie's being as a chronic schizophrenic was thus characterized by lack of unity and by division into what might variously be called partial 'assemblies', complexes, partial systems, or 'internal objects'. Each of these partial systems had recognizable features and distinctive ways of its own. By following through these postulates, many features of her behaviour become explicable.

The fact that her self-being was not assembled in an allover manner, but was split into various partial assemblies or systems, allows us to understand that various functions which presuppose the achievement of personal unity or at least a high degree of personal unity could not be present in her, as indeed they were not.

Personal unity is a prerequisite of reflective awareness, that is, the ability to be aware of one's own self acting relatively unselfconsciously, or with a simple primary non-reflective awareness. In Julie, each partial system could be aware of objects, but a system might not be aware of the processes going on in another system which was split off from it. For example, if, in talking to me, one system was 'speaking', there seemed to be no overall unity within her whereby 'she' as a unified person could be aware of what this system was saying or doing.

In so far as reflective awareness was absent, 'memory', for which reflective awareness would seem to be prerequisite, was very patchy. All her life seemed to be contemporaneous. The absence of a total experience of her being as a whole meant that she lacked the unified experience on which to base a clear idea of the 'boundary' of her being. Such an *overall* 'boundary' was not, however, entirely lacking. Thus Federn's term, *ego* boundary, is unsatisfactory. One needs another term for the total of which the ego is a part. Rather, *each system seemed to have a boundary of its own*. That is to say, to the awareness that characterized one system, another system was liable to appear outside itself. Within an overall unity, a diverse aspect of her being, if sufficiently 'dystonic' to the rest, would set up painful conflict. In her, however, conflict of this kind could not arise. It was only 'from the outside' that one could see that different conflicting systems of her being were active at the same time. Each partial system seemed to have within it its own focus or centre of awareness: it had its own very limited memory schemata and limited ways of structuring percepts; its own quasi-autonomous drives or component drives; its own tendency to preserve its autonomy, and special dangers which threatened its autonomy. She would refer to these diverse aspects as 'he', or 'she', or address them as 'you'. That is, instead of having a reflective awareness of those aspects of herself, 'she' would *perceive* the operation of a partial system as though it was not of 'her', but belonged outside. She would be hallucinated.

Together with the tendency to perceive aspects of her own being as not-her, was the failure to discriminate between what 'objectively' was not-her and what was her. This is simply the other aspect of the lack of an overall ontological boundary. She might for instance feel that rain on her cheek was her tears.

William Blake in his description of split states of being in his Prophetic Books describes a tendency to *become what one perceives*. In Julie all perception seemed to threaten confusion with the object. She spent much of her time exercising herself with this difficulty. 'That's the rain. I could be the rain.' 'That chair . . . that wall. I could be that wall. It's a terrible thing for a girl to be a wall.'

All perception seemed to threaten mergence and all sense of being perceived by the other threatened her similarly. This meant that she was living in a world of constant persecution and felt herself to be doing to others what she dreaded as happening to her. Almost every act of perception appeared to involve a confusion of self with not-self. The ground was prepared for this confusion by the fact that, since large aspects of her person were partially outside her 'self', it was easy to confuse those split-off aspects of her being with other people, e.g. her confusion of her 'conscience' with her mother, and her mother with her 'conscience'.

To love was therefore very dangerous. To like = to be like = to be the same as. If she likes me, she is like me, she is me. Thus she began by saying that she was my sister, my wife, she was a

McBride. I was life. She was the Bride of Life. She developed my mannerisms. She had the Tree of Life inside her. She was the Tree of Life. Or again:

> She is thinking thoughts a, b, c.
> I express closely similar thoughts a^1, b^1, c^1.
> Therefore, I have stolen her thoughts.

The completely psychotic expression of this was to accuse me of having her brains in my head.

Conversely, when she copied or imitated me, she was liable to expect retribution from me for 'coming out' with a bit of me which she felt she had stolen. Of course, the degree of mergence fluctuated from moment to moment. Stealing, for instance, presupposes some boundary between self and not-self.

We shall now illustrate and elaborate the above points by examples.

One of the simplest instances of the operation of a split of her being into two partial 'assemblies' is seen when she issued herself an order and proceeded to obey it. She was doing this continually, either under her breath, out loud, or by hallucinations. Thus 'she' would say, 'Sit down, stand up', and 'she' would sit down and stand up; or an hallucinated voice, the voice of one partial system, would issue the order and 'she', the action of another partial system, would obey it.

Another common simple instance was when 'she' would say something which 'she' would greet with derisive laughter (incongruity of thought and affect). Let us suppose that the statement emanates from system A and the laughter from system B. Then A says to me, 'She's a Royal Queen', while B laughs derisively.

A good deal of what appeared to be something akin to 'jamming' went on. A would say something relatively coherently and then it would become jumbled up and B would start to speak. A would break in again to say: 'She (B) has stolen my tongue.'

These various partial systems could be identified, at least to some extent after getting to know her, by reason of the consistency of the role each played in what one might call the intra-personal 'group' they comprised.

For instance, there was the peremptory bully who was always

ordering her about. The same peremptory voice would make endless complaints to me about 'this child': 'this is a wicked child. This child is wasted time. This child is just a cheap tart. You'll never do anything with this child. . . .' The 'you' here might be referring directly to me, or to one of her systems, or I could be embodying this system.

It was evident that this bullying figure within her was for much of the time 'the boss'. 'She' did not think much of Julie. 'She' did not think Julie would get well, nor that she was worth getting better. She was neither on her side, nor on my side. It would be appropriate to call this quasi-autonomous partial system a 'bad internal mother'. She was basically an internal female persecutor who contained in concentrated form all the bad that Julie ascribed to her mother.

Two other partial systems could be readily identified. One fulfilled the role of an advocate on her behalf to me, and a protector or buffer against persecution. 'She' frequently referred to Julie as her little sister. Phenomenologically, therefore, we may refer to this system as 'her good sister'.

The third partial system that I shall introduce was an entirely good, compliant, propitiating little girl. This seemed to be a derivative of what some years before was probably a system very similar to the false-self system I have described in schizoid cases. When this system spoke, she said, 'I'm a good girl. I go to the lavatory regularly.'

There were derivations also of what seemed to have been an 'inner' self, which had become almost completely volatilized into pure possibility. Finally, as I remarked earlier, there were periods of precarious sanity in which she spoke in a pathetically scared, barely audible tone, but seemed to be more nearly speaking 'in her own person' than at any other time.

Let us now consider these various systems operating together. The examples I give are of her more coherent utterances.

I was born under a black sun. I wasn't born, I was crushed out. It's not one of those things you get over like that. I wasn't mothered, I was smothered. She wasn't a mother. I'm choosey who I have for a mother. Stop it. Stop it. She's killing me. She's cutting out my tongue. I'm rotten, base. I'm wicked. I'm wasted time . . .

Now, in the light of the foregoing discussion, I would offer the following interpretation of what is happening.

She starts by talking to me in her own person to level the same accusations against her mother as she has persisted in for years. But in a particularly clear and lucid way. The 'black sun' (*sol niger*) appears to be a symbol of her destructive mother. It was a frequently recurring image. The first six sentences are spoken sanely. Suddenly she appears to be subject to some terrifying attack, presumably from this bad mother. She breaks off in an intrapersonal crisis. 'Stop it, stop it.' Addressing me briefly again she exclaims, 'She's killing me.' Then follows a defensive denigration of herself, couched in the same terms as her bad mother's condemnations of her, 'I'm rotten, base. I'm wicked. I'm wasted time . . .'

Accusations against her mother were always liable to precipitate some such catastrophic reaction. On a later occasion she made her usual accusations against her mother and the bad mother interrupted with her customary accusations against 'that child': 'That child's bad, that child's wicked. That child's wasted time.' I interrupted these remarks to say, 'Julie's frightened of being killed by herself for saying these things.' The diatribe did not continue, but 'she' said very quietly, 'Yes, that's my conscience killing me. I've been frightened of my mother all my life and always will be. Do you think I can live?' This relatively integrated statement makes clear the remaining *con-fusion* of her 'conscience' and her real mother. Her bad conscience was a bad persecuting mother. As stated above, it may have been one of the schizophrenogenic elements in her life that she could not get her real mother in a real sense to accept her need to project part of her bad conscience into her. That is, for her mother really to admit some validity to Julie's accusations and thus, by allowing her to see some imperfections in her mother, to relieve some of the internal persecution from her 'conscience'.

This child doesn't want to come here, do you realize that? She's my little sister. This child does not know about things she shouldn't know about.

Here her 'big sister' is speaking, making clear to me that Julie is innocent and ignorant and therefore blameless and irresponsible. The 'big sister' system, in contrast to the innocent and ignorant 'little sister' system, was a very knowing and responsible 'person', rather patronizing though kindly and protective. However, 'she' is not on the side of Julie, the little sister, growing up, and is always speaking 'for' the little sister. She wishes to maintain the *status quo*.

This child's mind is cracked. This child's mind is closed. You're trying to open this child's mind. I'll never forgive you for trying to open this child's mind. This child is dead and not dead.

The implication of this last sentence is that, by remaining in a sense dead, she can be not dead in a sense, but if she takes responsibility for being 'really' alive, then she may be 'really' killed.

However, this 'sister' could also speak in this way:

You've got to want this child. You've got to make her welcome ... you've got to take care of this girl. I'm a good girl. She's my little sister. You've got to take her to the lavatory. She's my little sister. She doesn't know about these things. That's not an impossible child.

This big sister contained experience, knowledge, responsibility, reasonableness, in contrast to the little sister's innocence, ignorance, irresponsibility, and waywardness. We see here also that Julie's schizophrenia consisted in the *allover* lack of integration, not simply in the absence of a locus in her of 'sanity'. This 'big sister' component of her being could speak in a reasonable, sane, and balanced way, but it was not *Julie* who was speaking; her sanity was, if you like, split off and encapsulated. Her real sanity depended not on being able to speak sanely in the person of a 'big sister' but in achieving an overall integration of her total being. The schizophrenia is betrayed by her reference to herself as a third party, and in the sudden intrusion of the little sister while the big sister is speaking ('I'm a good girl').

When she did present words or actions to me as her own, this 'self' that was so presented was completely psychotic. Most of the really cryptic condensed statements seemed to belong to the remnants of her self system. When decoded they reveal that this system was probably the derivative of the phantasticized inner self that we described in sane schizoid states.

We have already attempted to give an account of how it comes about that the experience of this self involves such extreme paradoxes of phantastic omnipotence/impotence and so on, at the same time. The phenomenological characteristics of the experience of this self seem in Julie to be in principle similar. However, one must be prepared to paraphrase her schizophrenia into sane speech before one can attempt a phenomenological construct of the experience of this 'self'. I must make it clear once more that in using the term 'self' in this context, I do not mean to imply that this was her 'true' self. This system did, however, seem to comprise a rallying point around which integration could occur. When disintegration occurred this seemed to be 'the centre' which could not hold. It seemed to be a central reference for centripetal or centrifugal tendencies. It appeared as the really mad kernel of her being, that central aspect of her which, so it seemed, had to be maintained chaotic and dead lest she be killed.

We shall attempt to characterize the nature of this 'self' by statements made not only by this 'self' directly but also by statements that appear to originate in other systems. There are not a great many of these statements, at least by the 'self' in person as it were. During her years in hospital, many of them probably had become run together to result in constantly reiterated short telegraphic statements containing a great wealth of implications.

As we saw above, she said she had the Tree of Life inside her. The apples of this tree were her breasts. She had ten nipples (her fingers). She had 'all the bones of a brigade of the Highland Light Infantry'. She had everything she could think of. Anything she wanted, she had and she had not, immediately, at the one time. Reality did not cast its shadow or its light over any wish or fear. Every wish met with instantaneous phantom fulfilment and every dread likewise instantaneously came to pass in a phantom way. Thus she could be anyone, anywhere, anytime. 'I'm Rita Hayworth, I'm Joan Blondell. I'm a Royal Queen. My royal name is Julianne.' 'She's self-sufficient,' she told me. 'She's the self-possessed.' But this self-possession was double-edged. It had also its dark side. She was a girl 'possessed' by the phantom of her own being. Her self had no freedom, autonomy, or power in the real world. Since she was anyone she cared to mention. she was no *one*. 'I'm thousands. I'm an in divide you all. I'm a no un' (i.e. a nun: a noun: no one single person). Being a nun had very many meanings. One of them was contrasted with being a bride. She usually regarded me as her brother and called herself my bride or the bride of 'leally lovely lifely life'. Of course, since life and me were sometimes identical for her, she was terrified of Life, or me. Life (me) would mash her to pulp, burn her heart with a red-hot iron, cut off her legs, hands, tongue, breasts. Life was conceived in the most violent and fiercely destructive terms imaginable. It was not some quality about me, or something I had (e.g. a phallus=a red-hot iron). It was what I was. I was life. Notwithstanding having the Tree of Life inside her, she generally felt that she was the Destroyer of Life. It was understandable, therefore, that she was terrified that life would destroy her. Life was usually depicted by a male or phallic symbol, but what she seemed to wish for was not simply to be a male herself but to have a heavy armamentarium of the sexual equipment of both sexes, all the bones of a brigade of the Highland Light Infantry and ten nipples, etc.

> She was born under a black sun.
> She's the occidental sun.

The ancient and very sinister image of the black sun arose quite independently of any reading. Julie had left school at fourteen, had read very little, and was not particularly clever. It was extremely unlikely that she would have come across any reference to it, but we shall forgo discussion of the origin of the symbol and restrict ourselves to seeing her language as an expression of the way she experienced being-in-her-world.

She always insisted that her mother had never wanted her, and had crushed her out in some monstrous way rather than give birth to her normally. Her mother had 'wanted and not wanted' a son. She was 'an occidental sun', i.e. an accidental son whom her mother out of hate had turned into a girl. The rays of the black sun scorched and shrivelled her. Under the black sun she existed as a dead thing. Thus,

> I'm the prairie.
> She's a ruined city.

The only living things in the prairie were wild beasts. Rats infested the ruined city. Her existence was depicted in images of utterly barren, arid desolation. This existential death, this death-in-life was her prevailing mode of being-in-the-world.

She's the ghost of the weed garden.

In this death there was no hope, no future, no possibility. Everything had happened. There was no pleasure, no source of possible satisfaction or possible gratification, for the world was as empty and dead as she was.

The pitcher is broken, the well is dry.

She was utterly pointless and worthless. She could not believe in the possibility of love anywhere.

She's just one of those girls who live in the world. Everyone pretends to want her and doesn't want her. I'm just leading the life now of a cheap tart.

Yet, as we saw from earlier statements, she did value herself if only in a phantom way. There was a belief (however psychotic a belief it was, it was still a form of faith in something of great value in herself) that there was something of great worth deeply lost or buried inside her, as yet undiscovered by herself or by anyone. If one could go deep into the depth of the dark earth one would discover 'the bright gold', or if one could get fathoms down one would discover 'the pearl at the bottom of the sea'.

References

In addition to the works cited in the text, a few more are included for further reading.

ARIETI, S. (1955). *Interpretation of Schizophrenia*. New York: Brunner.

BATESON, G., JACKSON, D. D., HALEY, J., and WEAKLAND, J. (1956). 'Toward a theory of schizophrenia'. *Behav. Sci.* 1, 251.

BATESON, G. (ed.) (1961). *Percival's Narrative*. Stanford University Press.

BECKETT, S. (1956). *Waiting for Godot*. London: Faber & Faber.

BINSWANGER, L. (1963). *Being-in-the-World*. New York: Basic Books, Inc.

BOSS, M. (1949). *Meaning and Content of Sexual Perversions*. New York: Grune & Stratton.

BOSS, M. (1957). *Analysis of Dreams*. London: Rider.

BRIERLEY, MARJORIE (1951). *Trends in Psycho-Analysis*. London: Hogarth.

BULTMANN, R. (1955). *Essays Philosophical and Theological*. London: SCM Press.

BULTMANN, R. (1956). *Primitive Christianity in its Contemporary Setting*. London: Thames & Hudson.

BULLARD, D. M. (ed.) (1959). *Psychoanalysis and Psychotherapy. Selected Papers of Frieda Fromm-Reichmann*. Chicago: University of Chicago Press.

BYCHOWSKI, G. (1952). *Psychotherapy of Psychosis*. New York: Grune & Stratton.

DEUTSCH, H. (1942). 'Some forms of emotional disturbances and their relationship to schizophrenia'. *Psychoanal. Quart.* II, 301,

DOOLEY, L. (1941). 'The concept of time in defence of ego integrity'. *Psychiatry* 4, 13.

208 *References*

FAIRBAIRN, W. R. D. (1952). *Psychoanalytic Studies of the Personality*. London: Tavistock.

FAIRBAIRN, W. R. D. (1954). 'Observations on the nature of hysterical states'. *Brit. J. Med. Psychol.* 27, 105.

FARBER, L. H. (1958). 'The therapeutic despair'. *Psychiatry* 21, 7.

FEDERN, P. (1955). *Ego Psychology and the Psychoses*. London: Imago.

FREUD, S. (1920). *Beyond the Pleasure Principle*. London: Hogarth, 1950, pp. 12–14.

FROMM-REICHMANN, FRIEDA (1952). 'Some aspects of psychoanalysis and schizophrenics'. In REDLICH, F. C. and BRODY, E. R. (eds.), *Psychotherapy with Schizophrenics*. New York: International Universities Press.

GOFFMAN, E. (1961). *Asylums*. New York: Anchor Books.

GUNTRIP, H. (1952). 'A study of Fairbairn's theory of schizoid reactions'. *Brit. J. Med. Psychol.* 25, 86.

HAYWARD, M. L. and TAYLOR, J. E. (1956). 'A schizophrenic patient describes the action of intensive psychotherapy'. *Psychiat. Quart.* 30, 211.

HEGEL, G. W. F. (1949). *The Phenomenology of Mind*. Trans. Baillie, J. B. London: Allen & Unwin. 2nd ed. rev.

HEIDEGGER, M. (1949). *Existence and Being*. London: Vision Press.

HEIDEGGER, M. (1962). *Being and Time*. London: SCM Press.

HESSE, H. (1964). *Steppenwolf*. London & New York: Holt, Reinhart, & Winston Edition 122 (J. Mileck & H. Frenz, (eds.) Rev. of trans. by B. Creighton).

HILL, L. B. (1955). *Psychotherapeutic Intervention in Schizophrenia*. Chicago: University of Chicago Press.

JACKSON, D. D. (1957). 'The question of family homeostasis'. *Psychiat. Quart.* (suppt.) 31, 79.

JACKSON, D. D. (1957). 'A note on the importance of trauma in the genesis of schizophrenia'. *Psychiatry* 20, 181.

KAPLAN, B. (ed.) (1964). *The Inner World of Mental Illness*. New York: Harper & Row.

KIERKEGAARD, S. (1954). *The Sickness unto Death*. Trans. Lowrie, W. New York: Doubleday.

KLEIN, M. (1946). 'Notes on some schizoid mechanisms'. *Int. J. Psycho-Anal.* 27, 99.

KNIGHT, R. P. (1953). 'Borderline states'. *Bull. Menninger Clinic* 17, 1.

KRAEPELIN, E. (1905). *Lectures on Clinical Psychiatry*. 2nd. rev. ed. London: Baillière, Tindall & Cox.

KUHN, R. (1957). *La Phénoménologie de masque*. Trans. Verdeaux, J. Paris: Desclée de Brouwer.

LAING, R. D. (1961). *The Self and Others*. London: Tavistock.

LAING, R. D. and ESTERSON, A. (1964). *Sanity, Madness and the Family*. *Vol. I. Families of Schizophrenics*. London: Tavistock.

LAING, R. D. and COOPER, D. G. (1964). *Reason and Violence: A Decade of Sartre's Philosophy, 1950–1960*. London: Tavistock.

LIDZ, T. (1958). 'Schizophrenia and the family'. *Psychiatry* 21, 20.

LIDZ, T., CORNELISON, A., TERRY, D., and FLECK, S. (1958). 'The intra-familial environment of the schizophrenic patient: VI The transmission of irrationality'. *A.M.A. Arch. Neur. & Psychiat.* 79, 305.

MACMURRAY, J. (1957). *The Self as Agent*. London: Faber & Faber.

MAY, R., ANGEL, E., and ELLENBERGER, H. F. (eds.) (1958). *Existence – A New Dimension in Psychiatry and Psychology*. New York: Basic Books.

MERLEAU-PONTY, M. (1962). *The Phenomenology of Perception*. London: Routledge & Kegan Paul.

MERLEAU-PONTY, M. (1963). *The Structure of Behaviour*. Boston: Beacon Press.

MINKOWSKI, E. (1927). *La Schizophrénie*. Paris: Desclée de Brouwer, 1953.

MINKOWSKI, E. (1933). *Le Temps vécu*. Paris: Artrey, Coll. de l'évolution psychiatrique.

MINKOWSKI, E. (1948). 'Phénoménologie et analyse existentielle en psychiatrie'. *Evol. Psychiat.* 4, 137.

PERRY, J. W. (1953). *The Self in Psychotic Process – its Symbolization in Schizophrenia*. University of California Press.

REDLICH, F. C., and BRODY, E. R. (eds.) (1952). *Psychotherapy with Schizophrenics*. New York: International Universities Press.

RUMKE, H. C. (1950). 'Signification de la phénoménologie dans l'étude clinique des délirants'. In Congrès Internat. de Psychiatrie, *Psychopathologie des délires*. Paris: Hermann. (French, p. 125; English, p. 174.)

SARTRE, J.-P. (1950). *Psychology of Imagination*. London: Rider.

SARTRE, J.-P. (1956). *Being and Nothingness*. Trans. Barnes, H. London: Methuen.

SCHREBER, D. P. (1955). *Memoirs of my Nervous Illness*. Trans. Macalpine, I., and Hunter, R. A. London: Dawson.

SCOTT, C. (1949). 'The "body-scheme" in psychotherapy'. *Brit. J. Med. Psychol.* 22, 139.

SEARLES, H. F. (1958). 'Positive feelings in the relationships between the schizophrenic and his mother'. *Int. J. Psycho-Anal.* 39, 569.

SÉCHEHAYE, M. A. (1950). *Autobiography of a Schizophrenic Girl.* Trans. Rubin-Rabson, G. New York: Grune & Stratton, 1951.

SÉCHEHAYE, M. A. (1951). *Symbolic Realization – a New Method of Psychotherapy Applied to a Case of Schizophrenia.* New York: International Universities Press.

SÉCHEHAYE, M. A. (1956). *A New Psychotherapy in Schizophrenia.* New York: Grune & Stratton.

SEGAL, H. (1954). 'Schizoid mechanisms underlying phobia formation'. *Int. J. Psycho-Anal.* 35, 238.

SONNEMAN, U. (1954). *Existence and Therapy – an Introduction to Phenomenological Psychology and Existential Analysis.* New York: Grune & Stratton.

SULLIVAN, H. S. (1962). *Schizophrenia as a Human Process.* New York: W. W. Norton & Co.

TILLICH, P. (1944). 'Existential philosophy'. *J. Hist. Ideas* 5, 44.

TILLICH, P. (1952). *The Courage to Be.* London: Nisbet.

TRILLING, L. (1955). *The Opposing Self.* London: Secker & Warburg.

WEIGERT, E. (1949). 'Existentialism and its relations to psychotherapy'. *Psychiatry* 12, 399.

WELLEK, A. (1956). 'The phenomenological and experimental approaches to psychology and characterology'. In David, H. P., and von Bracken, H. (eds.), *Perspectives in Personality Theory.* New York: Basic Books.

WINNICOTT, D. W. (1958). *Collected Papers.* London: Tavistock.

WYNNE, L. C., RYCKOFF, I. M., DAY, J., and HIRSCH, S. (1958). 'Pseudo mutuality in the family relations of schizophrenics'. *Psychiatry* 21, 204.

Index

REFERENCES TO CASES

PENGUIN MODERN CLASSICS

THE UNCANNY
SIGMUND FREUD

Screen Memories / Leonardo da Vinci and a Memory of his Childhood / Family
Romances / Creative Writers and Daydreaming / The Uncanny

Translated by David McLintock

With an Introduction by Hugh Haughton

'Freud … ultimately did more for our understanding of art than any other writer
since Aristotle' Lionel Trilling

Freud was fascinated by the mysteries of creativity and the imagination. The
major pieces collected here explore the vivid but seemingly trivial childhood
memories that often 'screen' far more uncomfortable desires; the links between
literature and daydreaming – and our intensely mixed feelings about things we
experience as 'uncanny'.

His insights into the roots of artistic expression in the triangular 'family
romances' (of father, mother and infant) that so dominate our early lives, and the
parallels between our own memories and desires and the tormented career of a
genius like Leonardo, reveal the artistry of Freud's own writing.

General Editor: Adam Phillips

PENGUIN MODERN CLASSICS

AN OUTLINE OF PSYCHOANALYSIS
SIGMUND FREUD

New Introductory Lectures / An Outline of Psychoanalysis

Translated by Helena Ragg-Kirkby

With an Introduction by Malcolm Bowie

'Freudian psychoanalysis changed the self-image of the western mind' Roy Porter

No discovery has done more to shape modernity than Freud's theory of the unconscious and the part it plays in determining the course of our conscious lives. In psychoanalysis, Freud created a therapeutic tool by which the deepest anguish and desires of the psyche could be revealed.

Yet this vital and rewarding field has remained a mystery to many, and the widespread use of its terminology in everyday life can serve only to confuse matters further. *New Introductory Lectures* (1932) and *An Outline of Psychoanalysis* (1938) take us back to Freud's own account of his theories, and his wish to be the most lucid and inspiring advocate of psychoanalysis.

General Editor: Adam Phillips

PENGUIN MODERN CLASSICS

THE UNCONSCIOUS
SIGMUND FREUD

Formulations on the Two Principles of Psychic Functioning / Drives and their
Fates / Repression / The Unconscious / Negation / Fetishism / The Splitting of the
Ego in Defence Processes

Translated by Graham Frankland

With an Introduction by James Conant

One of Freud's central achievements was to demonstrate how unacceptable
thoughts and feelings are repressed into the unconscious, from where they
continue to exert a decisive influence over our lives.

This volume contains a key statement about evidence for the unconscious, and
how it works, as well as major essays on all the fundamentals of mental
functioning. Freud explores how we are torn between the pleasure principle and
the reality principle, how we often find ways both to express and to deny what we
most fear, and why certain men need fetishes for their sexual satisfaction. His
study of our most basic drives, and how they are transformed, brilliantly
illuminates the nature of sadism, masochism, exhibitionism and voyeurism.

General Editor: Adam Phillips

PENGUIN MODERN CLASSICS

THE CONCEPT OF MIND
GILBERT RYLE

'One of the most original and influential – if still hugely underestimated – works of philosophy of the century' Daniel C. Dennet

If our bodies exist in space and time, subject to the laws of physics, our minds must be somehow hidden within them like strange immaterial 'Ghosts in the Machine'. Introspection may give us direct access to our own mental world, but we can never know much about other people's. Such views have been regarded as common sense since Descartes, argues Gilbert Ryle, but they are based on a disastrous 'category-mistake'. This epoch-making book cuts through confused thinking and forces us to re-examine many cherished ideas about knowledge, emotion, imagination, consciousness and the intellect. The result is a classic example of philosophy in action.

With a new Introduction by Daniel C. Dennet

PENGUIN MODERN CLASSICS

THE AGE OF REASON
JEAN-PAUL SARTRE

'For my money ... the greatest novel of the post-war period' Philip Kerr

Set in the volatile Paris summer of 1938, *The Age of Reason* follows two days in the life of Mathieu Delarue, a philosophy teacher, and his circle in the cafés and bars of Montparnasse. Mathieu Delarue has so far managed to contain sex and personal freedom in conveniently separate compartments. But now he is in trouble, urgently trying to raise 4,000 francs to procure a safe abortion for his mistress, Marcelle. Beyond all this, filtering an uneasy light on his predicament, rises the distant thread of the coming of the Second World War.

The Age of Reason is the first volume in Sartre's *Roads to Freedom* trilogy.

Translated by Eric Sutton

With an Introduction by David Caute

PENGUIN MODERN CLASSICS

MY OEDIPUS COMPLEX AND OTHER STORIES
FRANK O'CONNOR

'O'Connor is an artist, humane, observant, poetic' *Guardian*

W. B. Yeats credited Frank O'Connor with 'doing for Ireland what Chekhov did for Russia', and with these fine, humorous, insightful stories, Ireland comes vividly to life. Childhood, sex, religion, respectability, gossip: these are recurring themes in these short stories, threads running through the lives of the Irish people, woven with tremendous craftsmanship, playfulness and humour.

'An understanding of mood – its changes and subtleties and effects – is part of the Irish make-up, and is certainly part of O'Connor' William Trevor, *Washington Post*

PENGUIN MODERN CLASSICS

THE PROPHET
KAHLIL GIBRAN

'To read it was to transcend ordinary levels of perception, to become aware ... of a more intense level of being' *Independent*

First published in the 1920s, *The Prophet*, Gibran's hugely popular guide to living, has sold millions of copies worldwide and is the most famous work of religious fiction of the twentieth century.

Gibran's Prophet speaks of many things central to daily life: love, marriage, death, beauty, passion, eating, work and play. The spiritual message he imparts, of finding divinity through love, blends eastern mysticism, religious faith and philosophy with simple advice. *The Prophet* became the bible of 1960s culture and was credited with founding the New Age movement, yet it still continues to inspire people around the world today. This edition is illustrated with Gibran's famous visionary paintings.

'His work goes on from generation to generation' *Daily Mail*

With an Introduction by Robin Waterfield

PENGUIN MODERN CLASSICS

THE IMMORALIST
ANDRÉ GIDE

'Few writers in the twentieth century have been as influential as André Gide'
Contemporary Review

Michel knows nothing about love when he marries the gentle Marceline out of duty
to his father. They travel to Tunisia for their honeymoon, where Michel becomes
very ill. During his recovery, he meets a young Arab boy, whose radiant health and
beauty captivate him. This is an awakening for him both sexually and morally and,
in seeking to live according to his own desires, Michel discovers a new freedom.
But, as he also finds, freedom can be a burden.

'*L'Immoraliste* confronts "the fundamental, eternal problem of the moral
conditions of our existence", the gap between what we were and what we have
become' Alan Sheridan

Translated by David Watson
With an Introduction by Alan Sheridan

PENGUIN MODERN CLASSICS

DOWN AND OUT IN PARIS AND LONDON
GEORGE ORWELL

'The white-hot reaction of a sensitive, observant, compassionate young man to poverty' Dervla Murphy

George Orwell's vivid memoir of his time living among the desperately poor and destitute is a moving tour of the underworld of society.

Written when Orwell was a struggling writer in his twenties, it documents his 'first contact with poverty': sleeping in bug-infested hostels and doss-houses of last resort, working as a dishwasher in Paris, surviving on scraps and cigarette butts, living alongside tramps, a star-gazing pavement artist and a starving Russian ex-army captain. Exposing a shocking, previously hidden world to readers, Orwell gave a human face to the statistics of poverty for the first time. In doing so, he found his voice as a writer.

'Orwell was the great moral force of his age' *Spectator*

PENGUIN MODERN CLASSICS

MODERN TIMES: SELECTED NON-FICTION
JEAN-PAUL SARTRE

'One of the most brilliant and versatile writers as well as one of the most original thinkers of the twentieth century' *The Times*

Philosopher, novelist, playwright and polemicist, Jean-Paul Sartre (1905–80) was perhaps the central figure in post-war European culture and political thinking.

Designed for a new generation of readers, this superb anthology includes Sartre's personal responses to New York and Naples, an essay on surrealism and on Brecht, a spoof psychoanalytical dialogue, an extended essay on sexual desire and shorter pieces on maternal love and masturbation. It explores Sartre's celebrated quarrel with Camus, his constant but clear-eyed fascination with communism and, in 'Portraits' of Gide, Genet, Tintoretto and Baudelaire, his revolutionary approach to biography. There could be no better introduction to one of the greatest witnesses to the twentieth century.

Translated by Robin Buss

Edited with an Introduction by Geoffrey Wall

PENGUIN MODERN CLASSICS

STYLES OF RADICAL WILL
SUSAN SONTAG

'One of the most interesting and valuable critics we possess' *New Republic*

Susan Sontag's second collection of groundbreaking essays contains some of
the most important pieces of criticism of the twentieth century, including the
classics 'The Aesthetics of Silence', a brilliant account of language, thought and
consciousness, and 'Trip to Hanoi', written during the Vietnam War. Here too is
an excoriating account of America's identity and future, a robust and surprising
discussion of pornography and other richly rewarding writings on art, film,
literature and politics.

'Sontag emerges from *Styles of Radical Will* as an open and vulnerable intellect, a
consciousness in process of transformation … brilliant and important' *The Nation*

PENGUIN MODERN CLASSICS

AGAINST INTERPRETATION AND OTHER ESSAYS
SUSAN SONTAG

'A dazzling intellectual performance' *Vogue*

Against Interpretation was Susan Sontag's first collection of essays and made her name as one of the most incisive thinkers of our time. Sontag was among the first critics to write about the intersection between 'high' and 'low' art forms, and to give them equal value as valid topics, shown here in her epoch-making pieces 'Notes on Camp' and 'Against Interpretation'. Here too are impassioned discussions of Sartre, Camus, Simone Weil, Godard, Beckett, Lévi-Strauss, science-fiction movies, psychoanalysis and contemporary religious thought. Originally published in 1966, this collection has never gone out of print and has been a major influence on generations of readers, and the field of cultural criticism, ever since.

'Sontag offers enough food for thought to satisfy the most intellectual of appetites' *The Times*

Contemporary ... Provocative ... Outrageous ...
Prophetic ... Groundbreaking ... Funny ... Disturbing ...
Different ... Moving ... Revolutionary ... Inspiring ...
Subversive ... Life-changing ...

What makes a modern classic?

At Penguin Classics our mission has always been to make the best books ever written available to everyone. And that also means constantly redefining and refreshing exactly what makes a 'classic'. That's where Modern Classics come in. Since 1961 they have been an organic, ever-growing and ever-evolving list of books from the last hundred (or so) years that we believe will continue to be read over and over again.

They could be books that have inspired political dissent, such as *Animal Farm*. Some, like *Lolita* or *A Clockwork Orange*, may have caused shock and outrage. Many have led to great films, from *In Cold Blood* to *One Flew Over the Cuckoo's Nest*. They have broken down barriers – whether social, sexual, or, in the case of *Ulysses*, the boundaries of language itself. And they might – like *Goldfinger* or *Scoop* – just be pure classic escapism. Whatever the reason, Penguin Modern Classics continue to inspire, entertain and enlighten millions of readers everywhere.

'No publisher has had more influence on reading habits than Penguin'
Independent

'Penguins provided a crash course in world literature'
Guardian

The best books ever written

PENGUIN 🐧 CLASSICS

SINCE 1946

Find out more at www.penguinclassics.com